EMERGING APPLICATIONS OF CELLULAR AUTOMATA

Edited by **Alejandro Salcido**

Emerging Applications of Cellular Automata

http://dx.doi.org/10.5772/3370
Edited by Alejandro Salcido

Contributors

Jeffrey Zhi Jie Zheng, Christian Zheng, Tosiyasu Kunii, Amir Hosein Fathy Navid, Hugo Fort, Khalid Al-Ahmadi, Sartra Wongthanavasu, Jetsada Ponkaew, Stephen Fong

Published by InTech

Janeza Trdine 9, 51000 Rijeka, Croatia

Publishing Process Manager Sandra Bakic
Typesetting InTech DTP Team
Cover InTech Design Team

Additional hard copies can be obtained from orders@intechopen.com

Emerging Applications of Cellular Automata, Edited by Alejandro Salcido
p. cm.
ISBN 978-953-51-1101-6

For EU product safety concerns:
IN TECH d.o.o., Prolaz Marije Krucifikse Kozulić 3, 51000 Rijeka, Croatia,
info@intechopen.com or visit our website at intechopen.com.

Meet the editor

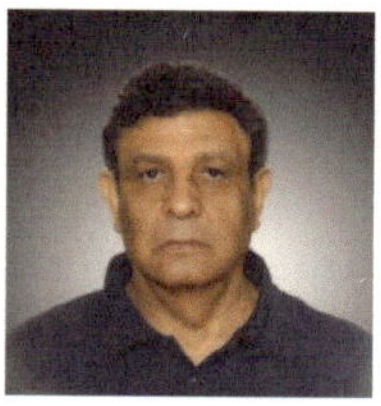

Alejandro Salcido is currently Lead Scientist in the Alternative Energies Division (División de Energías Alternas) at the Institute of Electrical Research (Instituto de Investigaciones Eléctricas) in Cuernavaca, Mexico. Dr. Salcido received his PhD in Physics from the Physics Department of the Faculty of Sciences at the National University of Mexico (Universidad Nacional Autónoma de México, UNAM) in 1992. Up to 1991, Dr. Salcido was Staff Scientist (Statistical Physics and Lattice Gas Models) and Faculty Professor (Thermodynamics, Fluid Mechanics and Electrodynamics) at the Physics Department of UNAM. Dr. Salcido has published close to a hundred scholarly articles in international journals, proceedings of conferences and book chapters, where his main research topics include micrometeorology, air pollution modeling, wind taxonomy, traffic cellular automata, and non-equilibrium thermodynamics. Recently, Dr. Salcido has edited two books on cellular automata published by In Tech.

Contents

Preface

The first investigations on cellular automata were carried out by John von Neumann (with some important contributions from Stanislaw Ulam) in the early 1950's. Von Neumann's primary aim was to devise a simple dynamical system capable of reproducing itself in the manner of a living organism. In 1970, almost twenty years later, the mathematician John Horton Conway invented "the game of life", a cellular automaton he devised as an attempt to drastically simplify the ideas of von Neumann. As the name suggests, the Conway's model also has a biological aspect: cells are born, live or die depending on the local population density. The "game of life" opened up a whole new field of mathematical research, the field of cellular automata. Cellular automata make up a very important class of completely discrete dynamical systems, and nowadays this field of research is a core subject in the sciences of complexity.

The physical environment of cellular automata is constituted of a finite-dimensional lattice, with each site having a finite number of discrete states. The evolution in time of a cellular automaton goes on in discrete steps, and its dynamics is specified by some local transition rule, fixed and definite. In spite of their conceptual simplicity, cellular automata systems are able to exhibit a wide variety of amazingly complex behavior. This feature of cellular automata has attracted the researchers' attention from a wide range of divergent fields of physical sciences and engineering, and also from disciplines as the biological and social ones, and many others.

In this book, six outstanding emerging cellular automata applications have been compiled. These contributions underline the versatility of cellular automata as models for a wide diversity of complex systems.

In Chapter 1, it is considered the application of cellular automata to two different important problems in ecology where the space introduces important information or it simply cannot be neglected. The second problem represents a major challenge in ecology: to understand and predict the organization and spatial distribution of biodiversity using mechanistic models.

Chapter 2 presents the validation process of a fuzzy cellular urban growth model, which has been applied to the city of Riyadh, Saudi Arabia. A number of different validation methods are used on three model simulations during three periods of urban growth: 1987-1997, 1997-2005 and the combined time period of 1987-2005. These methods include: visual inspection, accuracy and spatial statistics, metrics for spatial patterns and district structures as well as spatial multi-resolution validation.

Chapter 3 presents a non-uniform cellular automata-based algorithm with binary classifier, called Two-class Classifier Generalized Multiple Attractor Cellular Automata with artificial point, for pattern recognition. The model is built around the simple structure of evolving non-uniform cellular automata called attractor basin, and classify the patterns on the basis of two-class classifier architecture similar to support vector machines.

Chapter 4 presents cellular automata models are useful tools to simulate biological systems. One of the prominent issues in cellular automata modeling is choosing correct parameter values in the absence of experimental results. This chapter addresses this issue with global sensitivity analysis. By means of "first-order" and "total effect" indices, this Monte Carlo based method explains the influence individual parameters have on the model output.

Chapter 5 proposes routing misbehavior detection in wireless sensor networks using irregular cellular learning automata. The proposed protocol uses the concept of cellular learning automata to detect suspect nodes based on behavior and energy level of each node in packet forwarding in order to achieve an energy aware intrusion detection system. Simulation results show that the system has good detection capabilities in finding malicious nodes in network.

Chapter 6 provides a brief investigation for variant phase spaces construction. Ten propositions and four predictions are established in the chapter as the main results to provide a foundation for further exploration on quantum interpretation, statistical mechanics, complex dynamic systems and cellular automata.

We hope that, after the reading of the outstanding contributions compiled in this book, we will have succeeded in bringing across what engineers and scientists are now doing about the application of cellular automata for solving practical problems in diverse disciplines. We also hope that this book will have been to your interest and liking.

Lastly, we would like to thank all the authors for their excellent contributions in the different topics of the field of cellular automata covered in this book.

Alejandro Salcido
Instituto de Investigaciones Eléctricas
Cuernavaca, Mexico

Chapter 1

Two Cellular Automata Designed for Ecological Problems: Mendota CA and Barro Colorado Island CA

H. Fort

Additional information is available at the end of the chapter

http://dx.doi.org/10.5772/52068

1. Introduction

Our world is changing at an unprecedented rate and we need to understand the nature of the change and to make predictions about the way in which it might affect systems of interest. In order to address questions about the impact of environmental change, and to understand what might be done to mitigate the predicted negative effects, ecologists need to develop the ability to project models into novel, future conditions. This will require the development of models based on understanding the (dynamical) processes that result in a system behaving the way it does. The majority of current ecological models are excellent at describing the way in which a system has behaved, but they are poor at predicting its future state, especially in novel conditions [1].

One fruitful model strategy in ecology has been the "biology-as-physics" way to approach ecosystems, i.e. setting up simple equations from which they could obtain precise answers [2]. This tradition of modelling has a long history that can be traced back to the work of the mathematical physicist Vito Volterra, who used simple differential equations to examine trends in prey and predatory fish populations in the Adriatic [3]. Such models have the advantage of mathematical tractability; often they can be solved analytically to give precise answers and can be easily interrogated to determine the sensitivity of the model to its parameters [1]. On the other hand, it seems obvious that simple models will never accurately reflect any particular system since they lack realism.

A common simplification of these mathematical ecological models is that they rely on the well-mixed assumption or, in the physics parlance, the mean-field (MF) approximation. It is well known that the MF assumption can simplify a complex n-species system by replacing all interactions for any one species with the average or effective interaction strength. While the MF assumption seems reasonable in the case of, for example, plankton dynamics, it seems hardly appropriate for other situations. One of such case is when there is spatial heterogeneity, produced for instance by a gradient in some parameter that controls the dynamics. This is the situation in the first problem that we will analyze here. Another case if in which MF breaks down is for example for sessile species whose individuals by definition may only interact with others in a limited neighborhood provided that their niches overlap. The latter is the case for forest trees (the second system we will analyze here). Relaxing the MF assumption requires us to take into account the extent to which the strength of interactions among many species changes with the relative distances between individuals in space [4]. Many features of ecological dynamics such as the patterns of diversity and spatial distributions of species can be fundamentally changed when abandoning the MF assumption [4, 5]. A common way of relaxing the MF assumption is by formulating a spatially explicit individual-based model (IBM), or multi-agent system, whose straightforward implementation is by means of a cellular automaton.

Therefore, in order to go beyond MF and taking into account spatial heterogeneity, we will consider the application of cellular automata (CA) to two different important problems in Ecology where the space introduces important information or it simply cannot be neglected.

The first problem is about getting spatio-temporal early warnings of *catastrophic regime shifts* in ecosystems [6]. There is increasing evidence that ecosystems can pass thresholds and go through regime shifts where sudden and large changes in their functions take place. An example of such a regime shift is lakes that suddenly switch from clear to turbid water due to algae blooms. These blooms are connected to *eutrophication* i.e. the overenrichment of aquatic ecosystems with nutrients, principally phosphorous [7]. This is a widespread environmental problem because when it occurs, many of the ecosystem services which humans derive from these systems, such as fisheries and places for recreation, can be lost. Furthermore, it is often difficult, costly and impossible to reverse these changes once a certain threshold has been crossed. This is why early warnings of these shifts are so important to ecosystem management. In the case of MF models the rising of the temporal variance for the nutrient concentration was shown that it works as an early warning signal [8]. Later on it was shown that in many cases if one takes into accounts explicitly the space the spatial variance provides an even earlier early warning [9,10]. Thus, in section 2, I will present a cellular automaton that models a lake as a square lattice with the phosphorous concentration as the dynamical variable defined on lattice cells.

The second problem represents a major challenge in ecology: to understand and predict the organization and spatial distribution of biodiversity using mechanistic models. Ecologists have long strived to understand the distribution of relative species abundance (RSA) as well as the species–area relationships (SAR) in different communities [11, 12]. These metrics provide critical information that together can help uncover the forces that structure and maintain ecological diversity [13, 14]. Competition between species is one of the main mechanisms proposed to explain the observed RSA and SAR in different communities. In its basic form, the dynamics of competition-driven communities result from the degree to which species have overlapping niches because of their sharing of similar resource needs [15]. Hence in section 3 I will introduce a simple microscopic spatially explicit model to ad-

http://dx.doi.org/10.5772/52068

dress the biodiversity distribution and spatial patterns observed in natural communities. This model, in terms of local competitive interactions between sessile species (for example trees), requires both niche overlap and spatial proximity.

2. *Mendota* cellular automaton: catastrophic shift in lakes and its spatial early warnings

2.1. The Cellular Automaton

The *Mendota* cellular automaton (MCA) described in this section is proposed to analyze the catastrophic transition from clear to turbid water and discuss possible early warning signals to this shift. The model will be a spatial version of a mean field model introduced by Carpenter [16] consisting of the three differential equations for phosphorus densities in soil (U), in surface sediment (M) and in water (P). In fact P and M, who are attached to the lake, are local spatial variables, while U, which describes the surroundings of the lake is taken as a global (non-spatial) variable. The evolution equations for $U(t)$, $P(x,y;t)$ and $M(x,y;t)$ are:

$$dU(t)/dt = W + F - H - cU(t) \quad (1)$$

$$dP(x,\ y;t)/dt = cU(t) - (s+h)P(x,\ y;t) + rM(x,\ y;t)f(P) + D\tilde{N}^2 P(x,\ y;t) \quad (2)$$

$$dP(x,\ y;t)/dt = cU(t) - (s+h)P(x,\ y;t) + rM(x,\ y;t)f(P) + D\tilde{N}^2 P(x,\ y;t) \quad (3)$$

where

$$f(P) = P^q / (P^q + m^q) \quad (4)$$

Parameters of the model are defined in Table 1. We have also included diffusion with a diffusion coefficient $D = 0.1$. Another modification, in order to incorporate the effect of mechanical stirring of the lake waters (wind, currents, animals) is that we consider that at each time t, $a(t) \equiv cU(t)$ $a(x,y;t)$ fluctuates locally, from point to point, around its average global value $a(t)$ in the interval $[a(t) - \Delta, a(t) + \Delta\ ]$ where we have taken $\Delta = 0.125$ and have verified that the results do not depend much on this value.

The lake is represented by a square lattice of $L \times L$ cells each one identified by its integer coordinates (i,j). Of course lakes of arbitrary shape could be studied by embedding them into a square lattice like the one above, with appropriate boundary conditions. Another approximation is that the system is two-dimensional, there is no depth. That is, on each cell there are two local variables assigned: $P(i,j)$ and $M(i,j)$. Therefore, equations (1) to (3) lead to the following CA synchronous update rules in discrete time, where now t represent the time measured in years:

$$U(t+1)=U(t)+W(t)+F(t)-H(t)-cU(t) \quad (5)$$

$$P(i,j;t+1)=P(i,j;t)+a(i,j)-(s+h)P(i,j;t)+rM(i,j;t)P(i,j;t)^q/\left(P(i,j;t)^q+h^q\right)+$$
$$0.25D(P(i-1,j;t)+P(i+1,j;t)+P(i,j-1;t)+P(i,j+1;t)-4P(i,j;t)) \quad (6)$$

$$M(i,j;t+1)=M(i,j;t)+sP(i,j;t)-bM(i,j;t)+rM(i,j;t)P(i,j;t)^q/\left(P(i,j;t)^q+h^q\right) \quad (7)$$

Symbol	Definition	Units	value
b	Permanent burial rate of sediment P	y_1	0.001
c	P runoff coefficient	y_1	0.00115
F-H	Annual agricultural import minus export of P per unit lake area to the watershed	g_m_2y_1	0 or 13
h	Outflow rate of P	y_1	0.15
m	P density in the lake when recycling is 0.5 *r*	g_m_2	2.4
r	Maximum recycling rate of P	g_m_2y_1	0.019
q	Parameter for steepness of *f*(P) near *m*	Unitless	8
s	Sedimentation rate of P	y_1	0.7
W0	Nonagricultural inputs of P to the watershed before disturbance, per unit lake area	g_m_2_y_1	0.147
WD	Nonagricultural inputs of P to the watershed after disturbance, per unit lake area	g_m_2_y_1	1.55

Table 1. Model parameters

2.2. Observables

Catastrophic shifts have characteristic fingerprints or 'wave flags'. Some of the standard

catastrophe flags are: modality (at least two well defined attractors), sudden jumps and a large or anomalous variance [17]. Therefore we will calculate the following corresponding observable quantities for the phosphorous density in water *P*, which is the relevant variable in our case.

1. The *spatial variance* of *P(x,y;t)*, σ_s^2, defined as

$$\sigma_s^2 \equiv <P^2> - <P>^2 = \frac{\sum_{x,y=1}^{L} P(x,y;t)^2 - \left(\sum_{x,y=1}^{L} P(x,y;t)\right)^2}{L^2} \quad (8)$$

2. The *patchiness or cluster structure.*

The reason leading to the rise in σ_s is the onset of fluctuations in the spatial dependence of $P(x,y;t)$ at a given time.

3. Similarly to the mean free model, the *temporal variance* σ_t^2, which has been suggested by Brock and Carpenter [8] as an early warning signal. At an arbitrary point, say $(x,y) = (0,0)$, is defined as for temporal bins of size τ.

$$\sigma_t^2 = \frac{\sum_{t'=t-\tau+1}^{t} P(0,0;t')^2 - \left(\sum_{t'=t-\tau+1}^{t} P(0,0;t') \right)^2}{\tau} \tag{9}$$

2.3. Simulations and Results

Different simulations were run for 1500 years to illustrate changes of the system over time. The first 250 years of each simulation are a highly simplified representation of the history of Lake Mendota. The remaining years of each simulation illustrate contrasting management policies for soil phosphorus.

Following [16], simulations were initiated at stable equilibrium values calculated with $F = H = 0$ and W for undisturbed conditions. These represent presettlement conditions, and were maintained for years 0–100. For years 100–200, W was changed to the value for disturbed conditions (*WD*, Table 1), representing the advent of agriculture in the region. For years 200–250, F and H were increased to the values estimated for a period of intensive industrialized agriculture in the Lake Mendota watershed, and W was maintained at W_D (Table 1). That is, four different stages are considered:

1. years 0-100 $W=W_0=0.147$, $F\text{-}H = 0$.
2. years 101-200 $W=1.55$, $F\text{-}H = 0$.
3. years 201-250 $W=1.55$, $F\text{-}H = 31.6\text{-}18.6=13$.
4. after year 250 $W=1.55$, $F\text{-}H = 0$.

After year 250, the simulations were different. Simulation 1 represents management to balance the phosphorus budget of agriculture. In this simulation, after year 250 $F = H$ and W is maintained at W_D.

As one can see from Figure 1, the 1500 years history of lake Mendota produced by the Mendota CA is similar to the Carpenter's 2005 non spatial model [16]: a gradual first shift for P that start at year 250 and a second more drastic shift between years 440 and 485. Notice that the σ_s produced by the BCI CA reaches at year 425 three times the constant value it had along the first 400 years while it reaches its maximum value at year 467. The anticipation of the early warning depends on the convention chosen to establish when the shift actually happens. If we adopt the *Maxwell convention* [17] i.e. the shift coincides with the time when the variance reaches its maximum value [9]. If, on the other hand, we chose the Delay Convention the shift occurs when the system stabilizes in its final attractor i.e. at year 485 (see

Figure 1). Therefore σ_s provides an early warning of the coming shift that varies between 40 and 60 years.

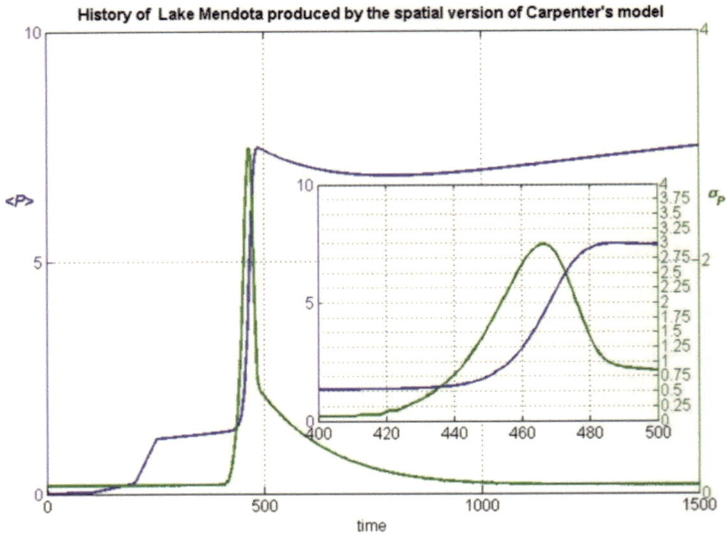

Figure 1. blue) and σ_s (green) vs. time (in years). The inset is a zoom showing in detail the time region around the catastrophic transition, which shows clearly the delay between both quantities.

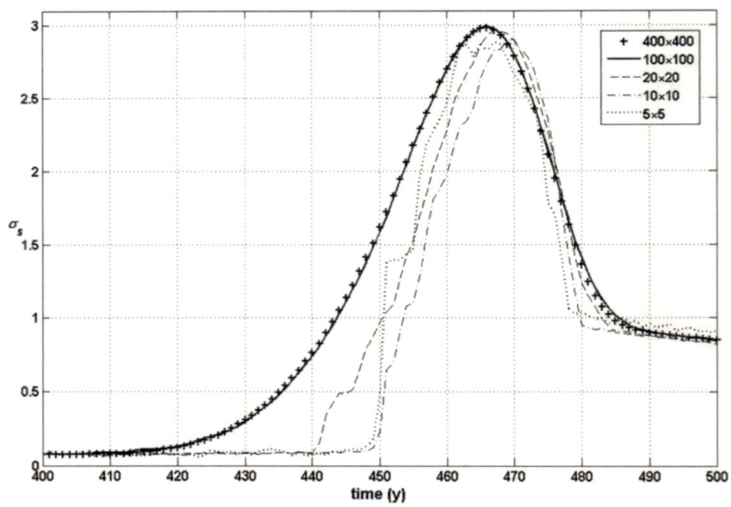

Figure 2. σ_s computed for different lattice sizes: L=5, 10, 20, 100 & 400. The larger the lattice the earliest the signal.

Concerning the practical use of σ_s as an early warning, Figure 2 shows that the time at which the signal becomes appreciable depends on the number of points of the grid (or lattice size *L*). As expected, there is a trade-off between anticipation and cost: the larger the number of points involved in the statistics, the sooner will be this early signal, until, for grids above 100×100 = 10,000 points, the curve doesn't change very much. For instance, for a 20×20 grid the early warning becomes noticeable 20 years later than when computed for the entire lattice.

Figure 3 shows color maps representing different configurations when the lake moves towards a catastrophic shift from clear to turbid water. Figure 3(A) to (C)correspond, respectively, to pictures of the lake at t = 250 yrs (when still *F=H*), at t = 437 yrs (30 years before the peak in σ_s) and at t = 467 yrs (just at this peak of σ_s). For t = 467 typically there occur patches covering a wide scale of sizes (Figure 3(C)).

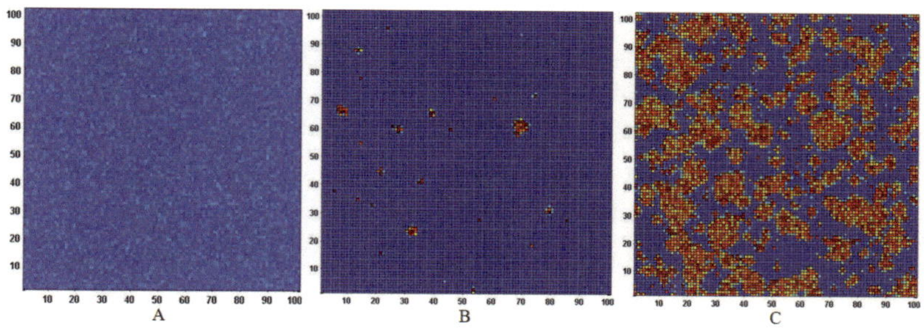

Figure 3. Maps of P density (values of *P(x,y;t)* at each lattice cell) for a 100x100 grid. (A) *t*=250, well before the transition,. (B) *t*=437. (C): *t*=467, where σ_s has it maximum value.

Finally let us have a look to σ_t and compare it versus σ_s. Figure 4 shows both variances. The temporal variance exhibits a temporal delay of around 40 years leaving much less margin for eventual remedial management actions. This delay can be easily understood since σ_t employs data in times where the fluctuations are still small.

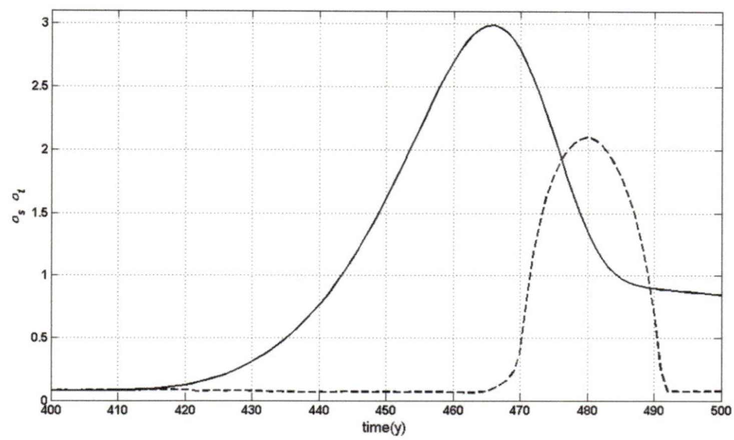

Figure 4. σ_s (solid line) vs. σ_t (dashed line).

2.4. Discussion and some Remarks

We have proposed a CA that describes the evolution of the P concentration, which dominates the eutrophication process in lakes, with its parameters calibrated for Lake Mendota. We have considered different possible early warnings for eutrophication shifts in lakes. In the case of σ_s, by measuring samples of P on a grid of points on the lake surface, it was found that a grid containing few points might be sufficient for the purpose of extracting an appropriate signal, and that a significant growth in σ_s could serve as an early warning of an imminent transition. The spatial variance appears to have an advantage over the temporal one, as σ_t is delayed with respect to σ_s.

When studying the origin of the rise in σ_s, we found that it is connected to the appearance of spatial patterns, in the form of clusters of clear and turbid water. The spatial patchiness under routine conditions is quite different from spatial patchiness near a regime shift. This is because in the last case in some places the clear water state is realized while in others the turbid water state occurs. In mathematical terms, close to the regime shift there are two competing attractors or alternative states (clear and turbid water) one occurs in a given set of cells and the other in the set of remaining cells. This explains the spatial fluctuations in the concentration of P. Under routine conditions, either before or after the catastrophic shift, only one attractor remains.

We then conclude that the visualization of the onset of those patches, for example by aerial or satellite imaging of the lake surface, may be an effective way of anticipating an eutrophication transition.

However a note of caution is required, in thermally stratified real lakes two main layers can be distinguished. The hypolimnion is the dense, bottom layer of water in thermally-stratified lakes, which is isolated from surface wind-mixing. The epilimnion is top-most layer, occurring above the deeper hypolimnion and being exposed at the surface, it typically becomes turbulently mixed as a result of surface wind-mixing. On the one hand, the flow of phosphorus in recycling occurs first from sediment to and also from decomposition in the hypolimnion. Dissolved P in the hypolimnion tends to be rather well-mixed and homogeneous. Then vertical mixing of hypolimnetic and epilimnetic water occurs from time to time (roughly 10-15 day return time [18]. Horizontal dispersion of dissolved P is fast after a vertical mixing event, within a day or so, smoothing over the patchiness structure in the epilimnion. As a consequence patches could never survive during a year, which is the unit of time in our model. On the other hand, some lakes show important spatial differences in terms of total phosphorus related to the spatial distribution of submerged plants or cyanobacteria blooms. The biomass tends to accumulate in several zones, by the hydrodynamic and wind actions, and determine strong differences of algal biomass as well as total phosphorous [19]. In any case, since the spatial model we are analyzing is two-dimensional and there is no depth (the hypolimnion and the epilimnion are collapsed to a single layer), the above processes are not included. Indeed it seems that the patches produced by the spatial model, instead of long lasting structures, should be interpreted as frequent popping in and out clusters. This dynamic patchy pattern changes many times during the course of one year.

It is worth to remark that the quantitative details of our conclusions depend on the choice of parameter values employed in our model. We have verified that the qualitative behavior of our results do not depend strongly on those values. Furthermore our model as presented in this work is schematic in the sense that the quality of the lake's water is dependent of a single parameter, the amount of Phosphorous in solution. In real cases other environmental factors might be playing an important role in the evolution, and the model and its predictions could be much more complicated. Nevertheless it appears that our main conclusions should hold in the more realistic case: spatial variance of critical quantities is an earlier signal than the temporal variance, and its associated cluster structure of the patterns formed in the eutrophication process could be the fastest detectable warning that a catastrophic change is about to occur.

3. *Barro colorado island* cellular automaton: species competition in physical and niche spaces

3.1. Niche Lotka-Volterra Competition Cellular Automaton

The model combines features from both niche-based models of interspecific competition [20] and from the neutral theory of biodiversity [21].

The CA considered in this section is based on the Lotka–Volterra competition equations for N_{sp} species [20]: $dns/dt = g_s n_s(1 - {}_r \alpha_{sr} n_r)$, where s and r run from 1 to Nsp, n_s is the density of species s; g_s its maximum per capita growth rate, and the coefficients α_{sr} represent the competitive interaction of species r over species s. Estimating the interaction strengths among species is, however, far from trivial because of the large number of potential interactions in diverse natural communities, feedback effects and non-linearities in interaction-strength functions [22]. In fact the Lotka-*Volterra Competition Model* (LVCM) include $N_{sp}\times(N_{sp}-1)$ competition coefficients α_{sr}. In the case of a tropical forest, where there are typically some hundreds of different coexisting species, estimating the corresponding several thousand coefficients becomes definitely an impossible task. Thus community ecologists have resorted to different approaches to include these diverse interaction strengths into their dynamics. Following the commonly used MacArthur and Levins' approach [23,20], we consider the simplest one-dimensional finite niche wherein the resource utilization function of each species s can be represented by a normal distribution $P_s(x) = \exp[-(x - \mu_s)^2 / 2\sigma_s{}^2]$, with mean μ_s and a standard deviation σ_s that measures the niche width. Then for each pair of species s and r, the strength of its competition is determined by their niche overlap, i.e. the overlapping between $P_s(x)$ and $P_r(x)$ (see Figure 5). We call this model the *Niche Lotka-Volterra Competition Model* (NLVCM). Assuming a finite normalized niche ($x \in [0, 1]$), the competition coefficients α_{sr} can thus be computed as:

$$\alpha sr = \frac{\int_0^1 P_s(x)P_r(x)dx}{(1/2)\left(\int_0^1 P_s^2(x)dx + \int_0^1 P_r^2(x)dx\right)} \tag{10}$$

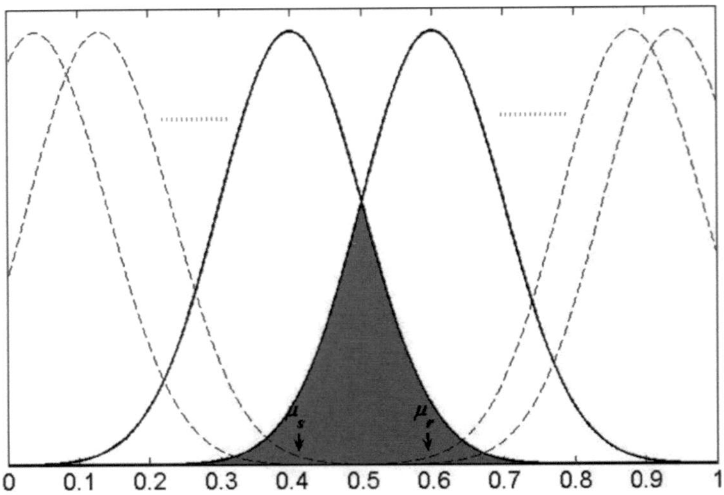

Figure 5. Competition and niche overlap: the gray area common to the normal distributions for species *s* and *r*, centered respectively at $\mu_s = 0.4$ and $\mu_r = 0.6$, is equal to the value of the competition coefficient between them α_{sr}.

On the other hand, inspired by neutral theory and to keep things as simple as possible, we assume two important simplifications. Firstly, that all species have the same maximum growth rate i.e. $g_s = 1$ and the same niche width i.e. $\sigma_s = \sigma$. The robustness of this simplification was recently analyzed for the NLVCM [24]. Therefore, each species' growth rate depends both on its position in the niche axis and on the niche positions of the individuals of other species that make its competitive neighborhood at each time step. The (intrinsic) functional equivalence between species is consistent with the chosen normalization for the α_{rs} in (Fig. 5) that ensures that the matrix α is symmetric and allows it to be expressed as:

$$\alpha_{rs} = e^{-((\mu_r-\mu_s)72\sigma)^2} \frac{\mathrm{erf}((2-\mu_r-\mu_s)/2\sigma) + \mathrm{erf}((\mu_r+\mu_s)/2\sigma)}{\mathrm{erf}((1-\mu_r)/\sigma) + \mathrm{erf}((\mu_r)/\sigma) + \mathrm{erf}((1-\mu_s)/\sigma)\mathrm{erf}((\mu_s)/\sigma)} \tag{11}$$

where 'erf' denotes the standard error rate function. Secondly, we consider that the community has a constant, finite size N [21] such that local reproductive and mortality events are tightly synchronized (see the used update rule below); this is equivalent to the 'zero-sum assumption' of Hubbell's neutral model of biodiversity [21].

The model is defined as follows:

* Landscape. We work on a $L\times L = N$ square lattice with periodic boundary conditions to avoid border effects. Each lattice cell (i,j) is always occupied by one individual belonging to a certain species specified by its niche position $\mu_s(i,j)$, s =1,2,...,N_{sp}, where N_{sp} is the number of initially coexisting species.

* Initial conditions. Because the initial spatial distribution of individuals at BCI is of course unknowable, we run the model from 100 different initial spatial configurations of completely random assignation of species (i.e. corresponding to the maximum entropy).

* Dynamics and update rule. The dynamics is asynchronous. At each time step t a focal cell is chosen at random. The LVC dynamics is implemented by using the "copy the fittest" rule i.e. by replacing each focal individual by the individual having the maximum fitness in the Moore neighborhood (the focal individual and its eight surrounding neighbors), which eventually can be itself and thus no change occurs at the focal node.

We will compute in addition of RSA and SAR, aggregation properties.

3.2. Comparison with empirical data from tropical forests

In this subsection we will contrast the model against field data from a well-studied ecological community, the tropical forest at Barro Colorado Island (BCI), Panama [25,26,27]. Population structure and spatial patterns have been particularly important themes in the ecology of tropical trees [21]. The long-term research program coordinated by the Smithsonian Center for Tropical Forest Science [28] includes inventory data collected for the first time in 1982 and then every 5 years from 1985 to 2005, with measurements of all trees with diameter at breast height (dbh) > 1 cm for a plot of 50 ha in BCI [29].

3.3. *Fitting parameters and biodiversity indices*

We set the initial number of species Nsp = 320. This is the maximum number of species found for BCI in the six censuses for 1982 and 1985, although this number steadily declined afterward from census to census until in 2005 the number of species recorded was 283 [29]. The number of individuals was kept fixed as N = 250,000 (L = 500) that is close to the maximum number of individuals observed in the set of BCI censuses. Therefore, the only free model parameters to be fitted are σ, controlling the intensity of interspecies competition, and the number of steps of simulation t.

This second parameter is needed because we are interested in transient states rather than in the steady state. The reason for this is simple: the set of censuses for tropical forests collected by the Center for Tropical Forest Science reveal that they are non-stationary systems: species richness decreases from one census to the next in *all* tropical forests and in many cases at a considerable pace [28]. Just to cite some examples: at BCI (Panama), roughly 3% of the number of species have been disappearing every 5 years; for Bukit Timah (Singapore), this percentage varies between 3% and 8% between consecutive censuses; for Edoro (Congo) 12% of the species disappeared between the 1994 census and the 2000 census, etc. The dynamics of the RSA between censuses in each forest are also far from being steady. It is noteworthy that most analyses of the BCI (and of other tropical forests) largely involve fitting separately several metrics of community structure and organization (e.g. SAR, RSA, indices of diversity) for each census rather than considering them as a dynamic sequence whose attributes needs be fitted together [25], [30],[31].

Moreover, the BCI CA reaches a steady state with four species after a long transient of the order of 3 billion time steps (data not shown). This a known result for MF [32] that was analyzed in detail in [24][33]. It is of course impossible to decide whether this steady state could be a reasonable result in a more or less distant future, and it is indeed absurd to run any ecological model for such a long time horizon without including the effect of speciation at this very long temporal scale. Rather the BCI CA aims to describe the transient corresponding to an entire set of censuses (rather than viewing them as separate snapshots as is generally done), which requires specifying the simulation time t as a parameter.

The decrease (although moderate) of Shannon entropy provides another way to verify the non-equilibrium nature of the BCI forest and this negative entropy production corresponds to the loss of species and the changes in community structure over time (see below).

We searched for the combination of σ and the number of time steps that produce the best agreement between the theoretical and the empirically observed biodiversity for the entire set of six BCI censuses. In addition to RSA we used two well known and often used indices of diversity, the Shannon entropy S and the Simpson index 1- D [34], to describe community structure for each census. Normalized versions of these indices are given by

$$S = -\frac{1}{\ln N_{sp}} \sum_{s=1}^{N_{sp}} (f_s \ln f_s), \tag{12}$$

and

$$1 - D = 1 - \sum_{s=1}^{N_{sp}} f_s{}'^2, \tag{13}$$

where fs is the relative abundance of species s. For both indices, the greater the value, the larger the sample diversity.

The procedure to find the optimal σ and t is as follows:

First, for a given value of σ, each simulation is run until the entropy S becomes equal to the entropy corresponding to the BCI population distribution for the first census (1982), i.e. $S1$ = 0.694. It turns out that for most values of σ except for a narrow set of values centered around σ = 0.09, the RSA are clearly different from those of BCI in 1982. A useful representation in ecology to perform such comparison between theoretical and empirical RSA is provided by the commonly used *dominance–diversity curves*. These curves are obtained by ranking the species according to their population abundance and plotting the RSA (%) versus species rank. Specifically, we found that the theoretical dominance–diversity curve converges to the empirical one as σ approaches 0.09. The Simpson diversity index $1 - D1 = 0.949$ observed for the first census served to narrow even further the range of values of σ around 0.09.

Second, for $\sigma = 0.09$, we look for the best fit to the entire sequence of six BCI censuses. We found that the optimal fit occurs for $t_1 = 37$ million of time steps (Mts) for the first 1982 census and then there is a correspondence of 1 year ←→ 250 000 time steps. Therefore, the census years 1982, 1985, 1990, 1995, 2000 and 2005 correspond, respectively, to $t = 37$, 37.75, 39, 40.25, 41.5 and 42.75 Mts. The Barro Colorado cellular automaton (BCI CA) is then defined by $L = 500$, $Nsp = 320$, $\sigma = 0.09$ and $t_1 = 37$ Mts.

Figure 6 shows the close agreement between the S and $1 - D$ calculated for BCI and the predicted average values obtained for 100 simulations each starting from different initial conditions, for the sequence of six censuses. This figure also shows the MF results, i.e. numerical integration of LVC equations, indicating that this MF cannot simultaneously and accurately predict the values of both biodiversity indices.

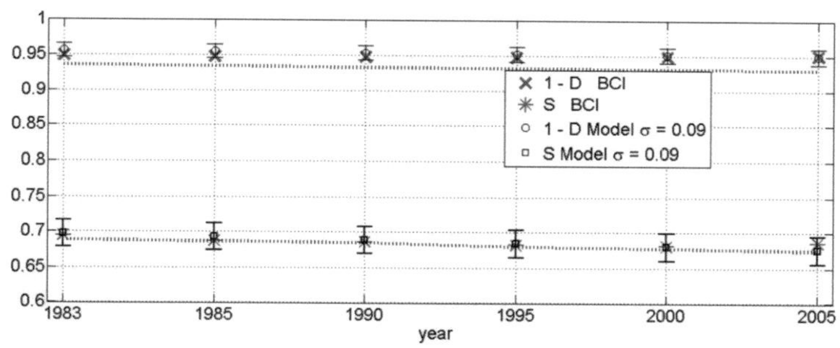

Figure 6. S and $1 - D$: the six BCI censuses and averages produced by BCI CA with error bars corresponding to 1 standard deviation (SD) and those of MF (dashed lines) for $\sigma = 0.09$ (see text).

In addition, the RSA curves for the MF approximation showed a poorer agreement with the empirical ones for each census (not shown).

3.4. *Dominance–diversity curves*

As in most biological communities, most trees species on BCI have few individuals: only five species *Hybanthus prunifolius, Faramea occidentalis, Trichilia tuberculata, Desmopsis panamensis* and *Alseis blackiana* individually had more than 5% of the total community size.

Figure 7 compares the predicted and observed dominance–diversity curves for the BCI 1995 and 2005 censuses. In both cases the predicted curve slightly underestimates the abundance (notice the logarithmic vertical scale) of rare species, i.e. those representing a RSA smaller than 0.05% which is a percentage well below 0.35% and 0.31%, the average values of RSA at BCI for 1995 and 2005, respectively (horizontal lines in figure 7). It turns out that for values of σ departing from 0.09 this agreement found for common species becomes worse.

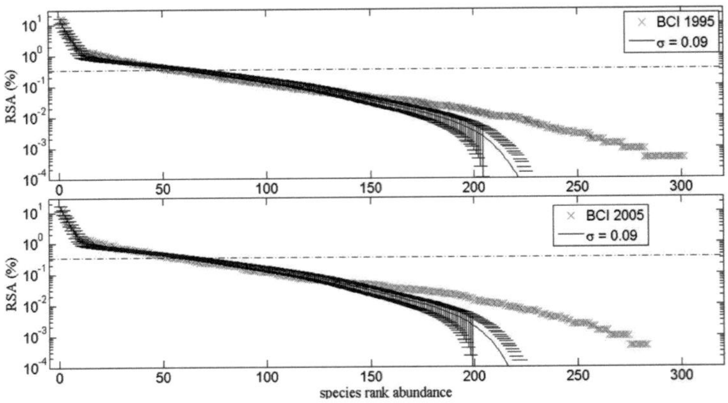

Figure 7. Dominance–diversity curves: BCI 1995 and 2005 censuses (x) and BCI CA predictions with error bars corresponding to 1 SD (black).The dot-dashed horizontal line corresponds to the average BCI RSA (%).

The most abundant species that yield the BCI CA are those at both ends of the niche axis, i.e. μ_s 0 or 1. The explanation is quite simple: species at the ends of the niche axis are exposed to less competition than those which depart from the ends and experiment competition from the two sides instead of from only one.

3.5. *Spatial patterns*

A prediction of BCI CA model is that local interactions in physical space introduce an interesting fact: individuals of different species close in niche space become spatially segregated. This is shown in Figure 8-A which corresponds to a 100 × 100 patch of the entire lattice depicting the spatial distribution of the three most abundant species at the right end of the niche axis (i.e. all with μ_s close to one) after 40 Mts. In order to contrast this against empirical data, Figure 8-B reproduces the spatial distribution found in 1982 for three species of quite similar trees with comparable population sizes, *Faramea occidentalis, Trichilia tuberculata* and *Alseis blackiana,* in a 141 m × 141 m [1] patch of the BCI 50 ha plot [25,26,27]. Notice that these three species also show spatial segregation, although the empirical segregation seems to be lower than the theoretical one. A simple explanation for this is that the BCI CA is little too simplistic, only local replacement of species is taking into account. Indeed we have checked that by introducing a global migration parameter *m,* modeling dispersal of seeds by winds or birds, the agreement between theoretical and empirical segregation patterns considerably improves.

The message is then that, while individuals of these three species could potentially have strong competitive interactions because of similarities of their niches, their spatial segregation attenuates the strength of their interspecific competitive interactions whenever these are local. Spatial segregation is known to be a mechanism that allows the coexistence of compet-

1 Since we use a sqaure 500 (500 lattice CA to represent the rectangular 500 m (1000m BCI plot, it turns that the lattice spacing corresponds to (2 (1.41 m.

ing species with similar niches even when space is introduced only implicitly in a MF model [35]. Furthermore, space is known to be important in the formation and maintenance of stable vegetation patterns [36,37]. Thus, the local competitive interactions might actually reinforce the *emergent neutrality* found in non-spatial competition models [38].

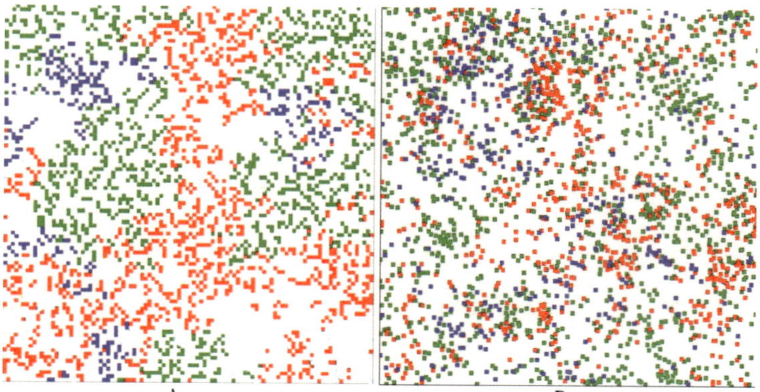

Figure 8. Theoretical and empirical distributions of abundant species: A) A patch 100×100 produced by the BCI CA showing the spatial distribution for three species with larger values of μ_s (i.e. located at the right end of the niche axis).B) A comparable patch, extracted from the entire 500m×1000m BCI plot as recorded in the 1982 census, showing the locations of three species: *Faramea occidentalis* (green), *Trichilia tuberculata* (red) and *Alseis blackiana* (blue).

There are many options to quantify whether there is spatial segregation among these dominant species. One of them is to partition a square patch L_P of side multiple of 3 (e.g. $L_P = 99$) into 3×3 Moore neighborhoods and measure the fraction f_c of these $(L_P/3)^2$ in which there is coexistence of species (at least two of the three species are present). Then by repeating the same procedure for exactly the same number of individuals belonging to each of these three species but *randomly* distributed, and calculating the fraction fr_c, the segregation index γ can be constructed as:

$$\gamma \equiv f_c / fr_c \tag{14}$$

When $\gamma < 1$ (>1) there is (there is not) spatial segregation among the species. We found $\gamma = 0.41$, confirming then that these three dominant species, whose niches are tightly packed at the right end of the niche axis, are actually spatially segregated.

The SAR (average number of species in a sampled area) constitute one of the main metrics in spatial community ecology [14], [21]. To generate SAR, we proceed as in [34] by dividing the entire area into non-overlapping squares and rectangles and counting the number of species present in quadrats of 20 × 20, 25 × 20, 25 × 25, 50 × 25, 50 × 50, 100×50, 100×100, 250×100, 250×250 and 500×500. This procedure yields the mean number of species in each size quadrat that make up the SAR for each year. Figure 9 shows that after 39 Mts, the model produces a SAR that fits quite well to the one obtained from the 1990 BCI census [34] for large area plots (above 1 ha). However, as the area of plots decreases, the agreement with data worsens. This is expected, because we know that our model underestimates the abundance of the scarcest species as shown in the dominance-diversity curves (figure 7) whose presence becomes more and more significant as the plot sizes become smaller than in larger plots that typically contain more individuals of many different species. Another useful spatial metric is provided by species–individuals curves, which are obtained exactly as the SAR but using the mean number of individuals in quadrats of each area instead of sampled area in the horizontal axis. Again, there is a qualitatively good agreement between model predictions and field data (not shown here).

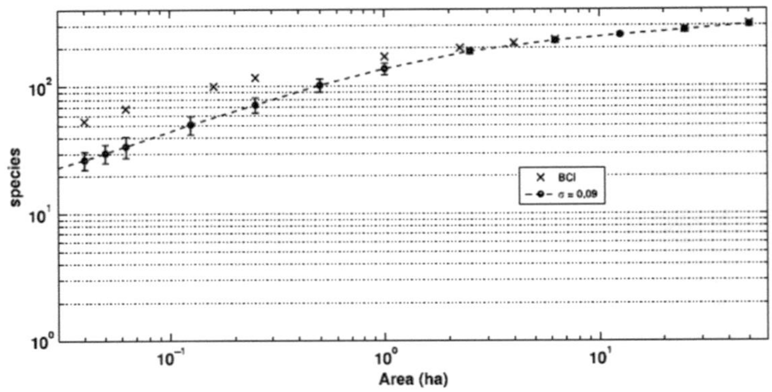

Figure 9. SAR: model for $\sigma = 0.09$ with error bars corresponding to 2 SD and data from BCI 1990 census (×).

3.6. On the importance of the locality of the competition and possible extensions to other realms.

The BCI CA is a model of local competition that jointly considers organisms in both physical and niche space. It must be viewed as a minimalistic model of local competition, with basically only two parameters: σ, the species' niche width controlling the intensity of the interspecific competition that drives the spatiotemporal dynamics, and the simulation time t (since it is focused on transients rather than in the equilibrium state). This 'microscopic' model of local competition can predict with reasonable accuracy the dynamic sequence of patterns of community structure, species-packing and the spatial distribution of forest species. Interestingly, the model shows that when the well-mixing assumption underlying the MF approximation breaks down, species that are clumped in niche space appear spatially segregated. Including space is well known to allow the long-term coexistence of strongly competing species and to permit the formation of stable patterns [5],[35],[37].

4. Conclusions

Each one of the two CA presented here address an open problem in ecology, namely how to anticipate catastrophic shifts in ecosystems and understanding the forces that shape community biodiversity, respectively. Both are fundamental scientific questions that go beyond ecology and require a major interdisciplinary effort and would have a significant impact on ecosystem management and conservation. The two CA represent minimal spatially explicit ecological models, that could be called "physicist's models" since they include the minimal number of adjustable parameters.

First, let us consider some guidelines for future work concerning the problem of eutrophication of lakes and the more general problem of the development of early warning signals of catastrophic shifts. The eutrophication is a result of a combination of natural processes and human impacts [39]. CA like Mendota could serve to disentangle the effect of these natural processes, like climate change [40], from anthropic effects. This could be done using paleolimnological analysis to estimate and connect historic input and run-off rates with temperature and humidity indices [41]. Another interesting extension of this CA could be from 2D to 3D, to take into account the depth, in order to describe the flow of phosphorus in recycling from sediment and also from decomposition in the hypolimnion. Going beyond lakes, the analysis of spatially explicit models is relevant, for example, to understand phenomena like clumping and spatial segregation in plant communities [42]. It was shown that vegetation patches, which have been extensively studied for arid lands, can be approached as a pattern formation phenomenon [43]-[44]. It has been hypothesized that this vegetation patchiness could be used as a signature of imminent catastrophic shifts between alternative states [36]. Evidences that the patch-size distribution of vegetation follows a power law were later found in arid Mediterranean ecosystems [37]. This implies that vegetation patches were present over a wide range of size scales, thus displaying scale invariance. It was also found that with increasing grazing pressure, the field data revealed deviations from power laws. Hence, the authors proposed that this power law behavior may be a warning signal for the onset of desertification. These spatial early warnings complement temporal ones like the variance of time series.

Second, in the case of tropical forests, these are extremely diverse ecosystems -many of which contain in 50 ha sample plots more tree species as occur in all of US and Canada combined- for which a huge volumes of data (covering 47 permanent plots in 21 Countries with 4.5 million trees of 8,500 species [28]) has been accumulated throughout the last thirty years. This mega diversity, together with the abundance of available data, makes tropical forests a paradigm for research on the interdisciplinary field of complex systems dynamics. The BCI CA parameters could be easily calibrated for modelling other tropical forests different from BCI and contrast with empiric data. Future natural extensions of this CA that are worth considering are the inclusion of a migration rate, due to animals or wind propagating seeds beyond local neighborhoods, and noise. These two factors would add a dose of stochasticity, making the model more realistic. Considering to other realms, beyond ecology, the type of competition of BCI CA could be applied to understand other natural as well as non-natural communities. For example in the case of social and economic systems [45], communities formed by different kinds of interacting firms [46] -for example stores, banks, restaurants, etc- wherein territorial competition between heterogeneous individuals (i.e. occupying different niche positions) occurring in distinct local neighborhoods is a key factor controlling their dynamics. Of particular interest would be study the role of space in the winner-takes-all markets [47], in which in principle slight differences in performance of the firms can lead to enormous differences in reward. Long familiar in sports and entertainment, this payoff pattern has increasingly permeated law, finance, fashion, publishing, and other fields [48].

Acknowledgements

I thank financial support from ANII (SNI), Uruguay. I am indebted to Steven Carpenter and Néstor Mazzeo for discussion on the material presented in section 2 and to Pablo Inchausti since the material of section 3 is based on a recent paper we wrote [49].

Author details

H. Fort*

Complex Systems and Statistical Physics Group Instituto de Física, Facultad de Ciencias, Universidad de la República, Iguá 4225, 11400 Montevideo, Uruguay

References

[1] Evans, M. R. (2012). Modelling ecological systems in a changing world. *Philos. Trans. of the Royal Society B*, 367-181.

[2] Levins, R. (1966). The strategy of model building in population ecology. *Am. Sci.*, 54-421.

[3] Volterra, V. (1926). Fluctuations in the abundance of a species considered mathematically. *Nature*, 118-558.

[4] Dieckmann, U., Law, R., & Metz, J. A. (2000). *The Geometry of Ecological Interactions*, Cambridge, Cambridge Univiversity Press.

[5] Tilman, D., & Kareiva, P. (1997). *Spatial Ecology*, Princeton, NJ, Princeton University Press.

[6] Scheffer, M., & Carpenter, S. R. (2003). Catastrophic regime shifts in ecosystems: linking theory to observation. *Trends Ecol. Evol.*, 12-648.

[7] Carpenter, S. R. (2008). Phosphorus control is critical to mitigating eutrophication. *Proc. Nat. Acad. Sci.*, 105(32), 11039-11040.

[8] Carpenter, S.R., & Brock, W.A. (2006). Rising variance: A leading indicator of ecological transition. *Ecol. Lett.*, 9(3), 311-318.

[9] Fernández, A., & Fort, H. (2009). Catastrophic phase transitions and early warnings in a spatial ecological model. *Jour. Stat. Mech.*, 09014, http://iopscience.iop.org/1742P09014.

[10] Donangelo, R., Fort, H., Dakos, V., Scheffer, M. E. H., & van Nes, E. (2010). Early warnings of catastrophic shifts in ecosystems: Comparison between spatial and temporal indicators. *Int. Jour. Bif. and Chaos*, 20(2), 315-321.

[11] Preston, F.W. (1948). The Commonness, And Rarity, of Species. *Ecology*, 29, 254-283.

[12] Gaston, K. J., & Blackburn, T. M. (2000). *Pattern and Process in Macroecology.*, Oxford, Oxford University Press.

[13] Brown, J.H. (1995). *Macroecology.*, Chicago, IL, University of Chicago Press.

[14] Harte, J., et al. (2005). A theory of Spatial-Abundance and Species-Abundance Distributions in Ecological Communities at Multiple Spatial Scales. *Ecol. Monogr.*, 75-179.

[15] Begon, M., Townsend, C., & Harper, J. (2006). *Ecology: From Individuals to Ecosystems*, 4th edn, New York, Blackwell.

[16] Carpenter, S. (2005). Eutrophication of aquatic ecosystems: Bistability and soil phosphorus. *Proc. Nat. Acad. Sci.*, 102(29), 10002-10005.

[17] Gilmore, R. (1981). *Catastrophe Theory for Scientists and Engineers.*, New York, Dover.

[18] Carpenter, S. *Personal communication.*

[19] Mazzeo, N. *Personal communication.*

[20] May, R.M. (1974). *Stability and Complexity in Model Ecosystems.*, Princeton, NJ, Princeton University Press.

[21] Hubbell, S.P. (2001). *The Unified Neutral Theory of Biodiversity and Biogeography.*, Princeton, NJ, Princeton University Press.

[22] Wootton, J. T., & Emmerson, M. (2005). Measurement of interaction strength in nature. *Annu. Rev. Ecol. Evol. Syst.*, 36-419.

[23] MacArthur, R. H., & Levins, R. (1967). The limiting similarity, convergence and divergence of coexisting species. Am. Nat. , 101-377.

[24] Fort, H., Scheffer, M., & van Nes, E. (2010). Biodiversity patterns from an individual-based competition model on niche and physical spaces. *Jour. Stat. Mech.*, 05005, http://iopscience.iop.org/1742-5468/2012/02/P02013.

[25] Hubbell, S. P., Foster, R. B., O'Brien, S. T., Harms, K. E., Condit, R., Wechsler, B., Wright, S. J., & de Lao, Loo S. (1999). Light gap disturbances, recruitment limitation, and tree diversity in a neotropical forest. *Science*, 283-554.

[26] Hubbell, S. P., Condit, R., & Foster, R. B. (2005). Barro Colorado Forest Census Plot Data. http://ctfs.arnarb.harvard.edu/webatlas/datasets/bci

[27] Condit, R. (1998). *Tropical Forest Census Plots*, Springer-Verlag and R. G. Landes Company, Berlin, Germany, and Georgetown, Texas.

[28] Center for Tropical Forest Science. www.ctfs.si.edu.

[29] www.ctfs.si.edu/site/Barro+Colorado+Island.

[30] Volkov, I., et al. (2003). Neutral theory and relative species abundance in ecology. *Nature*, 424-1035.

[31] Mc Gill, B.J. (2010). Towards a unification of unified theories of biodiversity. *Ecol. Lett.*, 13-627.

[32] Scheffer, M., & van Nes, E. (2006). Self-organized similarity, the evolutionary emergence of groups of similar species. *Proc. Nat. Acad. Sci.*, 103-6230.

[33] Fort, H., Scheffer, M., & van Nes, E. (2009). The paradox of the clumps mathematically explained. *Theor. Ecol.*, 2-171.

[34] Condit, R., et al. (1996). Species-area and species-individual relationships for tropical trees: a comparison of three 50ha plots. *.J. Ecol.*, 84, 549-562.

[35] Tilman, D. (1994). Competition and Biodiversity in Spatially Structured Habitats. *Ecology*, 75, 2-16.

[36] Rietkerk, M., et al. (2002). Self-organization of vegetation in arid ecosystems. *Am. Nat.*, 160-524.

[37] Kéfi, S., et al. (2007). Spatial vegetation patterns and imminent desertification in Mediterranean arid ecosystems. *Nature*, 449-213.

[38] Vergnon, R., van Nes, E. H., & Scheffer, M. (2012). Emergent neutrality leads to multimodal species abundance distributions. *Nature Communications*, 3(663).

[39] Smol, J. (2008). *Pollution of Lakes and Rivers: A Paleoenvironmental Perspective*, Blackwell, Oxford 2nd Ed.

[40] Sayer, C. D., Davidson, T. A., Jones, J. I., & Langdon, P. G. (2010). Combining contemporary ecology and palaeolimnologyto understand shallow lake ecosystem change. *Freshwater Biology*, 55-487.

[41] García-Rodriguez, F., et al. (2004). Holocene trophic state changes in relation to the sea level variation in Lake Blanca, SE Uruguay. *Jour. of Paleolimnology*, 31-99.

[42] Levin, S. A., & Pacala, S. W. (1997). Theories of simplification and scaling of spatially distributed processes. D. Tilman and P. Kareiva, editors, Ecology: achievement and challenge, 271296Princeton University: NY.

[43] Klausmeier, C.A. (1999). Regular and irregular patterns in semiarid vegetation. *Science*, 284, 1826-1828.

[44] von Hardenberg, J., et al. (2001). Diversity of vegetation patterns and desertification. *Phys. Rev. Lett.*, 87(1981011).

[45] Farmer, D., & Foley, D. (2009). The economy needs agent-based modelling. *Nature,* 460-685.

[46] Westerhoff, F. (2010). An agent-based macroeconomic model with interacting firms, socio-economic opinion formation and optimistic/pessimistic sales expectations. *New J. Phys.,* 12(075035).

[47] Frank, R.H., & Cook, P.J. (1996). *The Winner-Take-All Society: Why the Few at the Top Get So Much More Than the Rest of Us.*, Penguin Books , USA NY.

[48] Frank, R.H. (2009). *The Economic Naturalist's Field Guide: Common Sense Principles for Troubled Times,* Basic Books, NY.

[49] Fort, H., & Inchausti, P. (2012). Biodiversity patterns from an individual-based competition model on niche and physical spaces. *J. Stat. Mech.,* 02013, http://iopscience.iop.org/1742-5468/2012/02/P02013.

[50] Carpenter, S.R. (2003). Regime Shifts in Lake Ecosystems: Pattern & Variation. *Ecology Institute, Oldendorf/Luhe: Germany.*

Chapter 2

Validating Spatial Patterns of Urban Growth from a Cellular Automata Model

Khalid Al-Ahmadi, Linda See and Alison Heppenstall

Additional information is available at the end of the chapter

http://dx.doi.org/10.5772/51708

1. Introduction

The dynamics of urban growth are the direct consequence of the actions of individuals, and public and private organisations, which act to change the urban landscape simultaneously over space and time. Since previous urban form has a strong influence on the present, a prime concern of urban planners, spatial scientists and government authorities is to understand how a city has grown in the past in order to predict the growth of the city in the future. This requires flexible tools that allow planners to examine the impacts and potential consequences of applying different development policies, strategies and future plans [1]. However, traditional linear, static and top-down models are unable to adequately capture the processes underlying urban change. The non-linearity of spatial and temporal relationships and irregular, uncoordinated and uncontrolled local decision-making gives rise to seemingly coordinated global patterns that define the size and shape of cities in familiar ways [2-7]. Cities are now increasingly recognized as complex systems and display many of the characteristic traits of complexity, i.e. non-linearity, self-organization and emergence. Cellular Automata (CA) offer a modeling framework and a set of techniques for modelling the dynamic processes and outcomes of self-organizing systems [8-13]. Since the late 1980s they have demonstrated significant potential benefits for urban modelling through their simplicity, flexibility and transparency [8, 14-17]. CA are capable of generating complex patterns in aggregate form by using relatively simple local transition rules, i.e. by recursive development decisions being made at individual cells or sites [2, 15, 18]. However, cities are also influenced by global factors representing government polices (such as broader social, economic and technological factors). This has led to a number of hybrid-type urban growth models, which take into consideration local, regional and global factors [19-22]. When integrated with other technologies such as GIS and remote sensing, the potential of CA for geospatial, temporal and sectoral studies increases significantly through the ability of CA to utilise physical, environmental, social and economic data in their simulations [23]. For example, remote sensing and GIS can be integrated with CA for providing detailed land use information as well as information on other characteristics of cities to produce realistic simulations of urban change [24].

A current challenge facing CA urban growth models is the lack of rigorous calibration procedures [21, 25-27]. Progress in the evolution of algorithms, particularly from artificial intelligence (AI), has, however, created many new options for calibrating these complex models. For example, [28] suggested that heuristic-based searches using AI would be an effective approach for optimising spatial problems, since they offer many advantages for model calibration compared to traditional methods. An example of an urban growth CA model calibrated using AI was developed in [29-31]. They presented an urban planning tool for the city of Riyadh, Saudi Arabia, which is one of the world's major cities undergoing rapid development. At the core of the system is a Fuzzy Cellular Urban Growth Model (FCUGM), which is capable of simulating and predicting the complexities of urban growth. This model was shown to be capable of replicating the trends and characteristics of an urban environment during three periods: 1987-1997, 1997-2005 and 1987-2005.

Along with calibration, one of the most significant aspects of any model is to verify, validate and assess its performance. This is normally undertaken by verifying the model's output against the real-world system through evaluation of goodness-of-fit tests. Validation can be defined as 'a demonstration that a model within its domain of applicability possesses a satisfactory range of accuracy consistent with the intended application of the model' [32]. In terms of urban CA models, the validation process refers to the approach by which the performance of the model is assessed by comparing the simulated map (one generated by the model) with the observed map (based on ground truth). The observed map should be accurate and shape the benchmark for comparison. A good performing urban CA model generates outcomes that capture the basic features of urban forms between simulated and observed spatial patterns [1]. Researchers have utilised a combination of different methods for validating CA models. For example, in [33], thirty-three urban CA models were reviewed and compared using a number of different criteria including the types of validation method employed. In some cases no validation method was used since the models were largely hypothetical or idealized, while in other models, a range of different methods were employed including one or a combination of the following approaches: visual comparison, confusion matrices [21], statistical measures [18], a fractal index and analysis [8, 21, 34], landscape metrics [35], spatial statistics, for example, Moran's I index [8, 25] and structural measurements such as the Lee-Sallee index [25]. It it clear from the review [33], however, that there is no consensus on how CA models of urban growth should be validated and research in this area has not progressed that much [26-27].

The focus of this chapter is on the techniques used to validate the performance of the FCUGM model; however these approaches are applicable to urban CA models more generally. A brief overview of the fuzzy cellular urban growth model (FCUGM) for the city of Riyadh is first provided. We then present seven different validation metrics including visual

http://dx.doi.org/10.5772/51708

inspection, accuracy and spatial statistics, metrics for spatial pattern and district structure detection as well as spatial multi-resolution validation. Results of these methods are given followed by a discussion of the usefulness of the different validation approaches in relation to the assessment of the FCUGM.

2. The Fuzzy Cellular Urban Growth Model (FCUGM) for the City of Riyadh

The Fuzzy Cellular Automata Urban Growth Model (FCUGM) is driven by the following simple rule of development:

$$\text{If } DP_{ij}^{t} \geq \lambda \text{ Then } S_{ij}^{t+1} = \text{Urban, Otherwise} = \text{Non-Urban} \tag{1}$$

where a new urban cell, S_{ij}^{t+1}, is created at time t+1 if the cell's development possibility (DP) is greater than or equal to a transition threshold parameter, λ, which is determined through the calibration process. The DP is a function of the development suitability (DS_{ij}^{t}) of a cell and a stochastic disturbance factor. The development suitability is, in turn, a function of four driving forces, i.e. transportation (TSF_{ij}^{t}) , urban agglomeration and attractiveness ($UAAF_{ij}^{t}$) , topographical constraints (TSF_{ij}^{t}) and a factor that encompasses planning policies and regulations ($PPRF_{ij}^{t}$) :

$$DS_{ij}^{t} = f\left(TSF_{ij}^{t},\ UAAF_{ij}^{t},\ TCF_{ij}^{t},\ PPRF_{ij}^{t}\right) \tag{2}$$

The four driving forces of urban growth (TSF, UAAF, TCF and PRF) are themselves functions of a series of fuzzy input variables expressed as follows:

$$TSF_{ij}^{t} = f\left(ALR_{ij}^{t},\ AMR_{ij}^{t},\ AMJR_{ij}^{t}\right) \tag{3}$$

$$UAAF_{ij}^{t} = f\left(UD_{ij}^{t},\ AECSES_{ij}^{t},\ ATC_{ij}^{t}\right) \tag{4}$$

$$TCF_{ij}^{t} = f\left(G_{ij}^{t},\ A_{ij}^{t}\right) \tag{5}$$

$$PPRF_{ij}^{t} = f\left(PA_{ij}^{t},\ EA_{ij}^{t}\right) \tag{6}$$

where the TSF is a function of Accessibility to Local Roads (ALR), Accessibility to Main Roads (AMR) and Accessibility to Major Roads (AMJR); the UAAF is determined by a combination of Urban Density (UD), Accessibility to Town Centres (ATC) and Accessibility to Employment Centres and Socio-Economic Services (AECSES); the TCF is a function of

Gradient (G) and Altitude (A); and the PPRF takes Planned Areas (PA) and Excluded Areas (EA) into account. These drivers of urban growth are integrated via a fuzzy rule base, where the membership functions and the rules are determined through calibration. A fuzzy inference engine is used to process the fuzzy rules and produce a fuzzy development suitability score at each cell. These fuzzy values are then defuzzified and used in combination with the stochastic disturbance factor and the transition threshold to determine whether a given cell becomes an area of further urban development. The full details of the model are provided in [29, 31].

To calibrate the model, a stratified random sample consisting of 60% urban and 40% non-urban cells was utilised in combination with a genetic algorithm (GA) where a single objective function consisting of the mean squared error and the root mean squared error was employed. The use of these two measures together was designed to penalise model instances in which the parameters fell outside of an acceptable range. Nine different model instances were developed, which are listed in Table 1. These nine instances were based on different complexities of fuzzy rule (the modes) and different drivers (the scenarios). Mode 1 included fuzzy rules with only a single driver, e.g. transportation or topography while modes 2 and 3 had multiple drivers connected by the AND operator in the fuzzy rules. Scenarios considered different combinations of drivers in order to determine how well the different drivers were able to explain the observed urban development on their own and in combination. Thus M3-S1 is the most complex of the FCUGM instances. The top three performing models were M1-S4, M2-S4 and M3-S1, which clearly indicates that all the drivers are important in explaining urban growth in the city of Riyadh. These three simulations will be the focus of the validation process in this chapter.

Mode/Scenario	Acronym	Name of Simulation
Mode 1 – Scenario 1	M1-S1	Transportation
Mode 1 – Scenario 2	M1-S2	Urban density-attractiveness
Mode 1 – Scenario 3	M1-S3	Topography
Mode 1 – Scenario 4	M1-S4	Transportation, urban density-attractiveness and topography
Mode 2 – Scenario 1	M1-S1	Transportation and topography
Mode 2 – Scenario 2	M2-S2	Transportation and urban density-attractiveness
Mode 2 – Scenario 3	M2-S3	Topography and urban density-attractiveness
Mode 2 – Scenario 4	M2-S4	Transportation, urban density-attractiveness and topography
Mode 3 – Scenario 1	M3-S1	Transportation, urban density-attractiveness and topography

Table 1. Modes and scenarios of the FCUGM.

Once calibrated, the FCUGM was used to simulate the Urban Growth Boundary (UGB) in the city of Riyadh for the following three periods: UGB I (1987–1997), UGB II (1997–2005)

http://dx.doi.org/10.5772/51708

and UGB I+II (1987–2005) using the calibrated weights and parameters derived from the GA. Figures 1 to 3 show the simulations for the three time periods respectively for the three top performing simulations, i.e. M1-S4, M2-S4 and M3-S1. The new urban developments that are simulated by the model are shown in red while blue cells indicate those areas that have already been developed. For UGB I (1987-1997), simulation M1-S4 shows more compact urban patterns compared with the other two simulations (M2-S4 and M3-S1), where the latter show more urban development across the peripheral areas, in particular for M3-S1. This might be attributed to the high weight assigned to the urban density variable for M1-S4 and to the form of the distance decay effect captured through the membership functions. However, the morphology of the simulated urban spatial structure that is located to the north and north east shows quite some dispersed and scattered development. Generally, development sites are more linked in order to provide necessary infrastructure and service facilities. However, dispersed development is one of the characteristics of Riyadh's urban pattern. Typically, urban sprawl is produced by the three simulations regardless of the overall macroscopic pattern. This sprawl might be attributed to a lack of implementation of a policy to limit urban growth, which the government introduced to prevent chaotic development. In addition, this sprawl mimics the non-continuous or leap-frog pattern of urban growth characteristic of this period.

Figures 1 to 3 also show that the direction of growth is generally radial, where urban growth takes place around most of the already developed lands. In particular, most of the growth is to the south west and to the east of the city, while only moderate growth is simulated in the top south eastern part. Growth also rarely occurs to the west of the city. The pattern of growth might be a result of the government's free grant program. Most of the lands in these two areas were granted by the government to households with low incomes. Another reason may be the lower price of this land compared with the high price of land located to the north of the city. Moreover, moderate growth in the south east of the city could be due to the concentration of heavy industry in this part of the city and to the low urban environmental quality due to proximity to industrial zones and the oil refinery. It can also be seen that there is almost no urban growth simulated to the west of the city, where areas are either steep or located at higher altitudes, indicating that topographical constraint factors have confined growth in such areas. Topographical characteristics have also constrained growth in the south western part of the city, where the steep areas located between the two big urban clusters are simulated as non-urban.

In UGB II (1997-2005), the simulated urban pattern contrasts with that shown in UGB I (1987-1997) where the pattern showed compact development around those areas already developed, and dispersed in the outskirts of the city and peripheral areas. During this second period (UGB II), the simulated pattern followed an in-filling strategy, where most of the development took place within already developed lands and no development occurred beyond the boundary of the developed areas. This can be seen where small simulated clusters (shown in red) are located within the existing urban areas (shown in blue). This is also an expected finding, since during this historical period, the planning authority in Riyadh strictly applied a policy to limit urban growth to avoid further urban sprawl that characterised the period UGB I. As a result of this policy, most of the development occurred on vacant land with the greatest development possibility occurring within existing developed areas. This particular pattern was simulated by all three model instances.

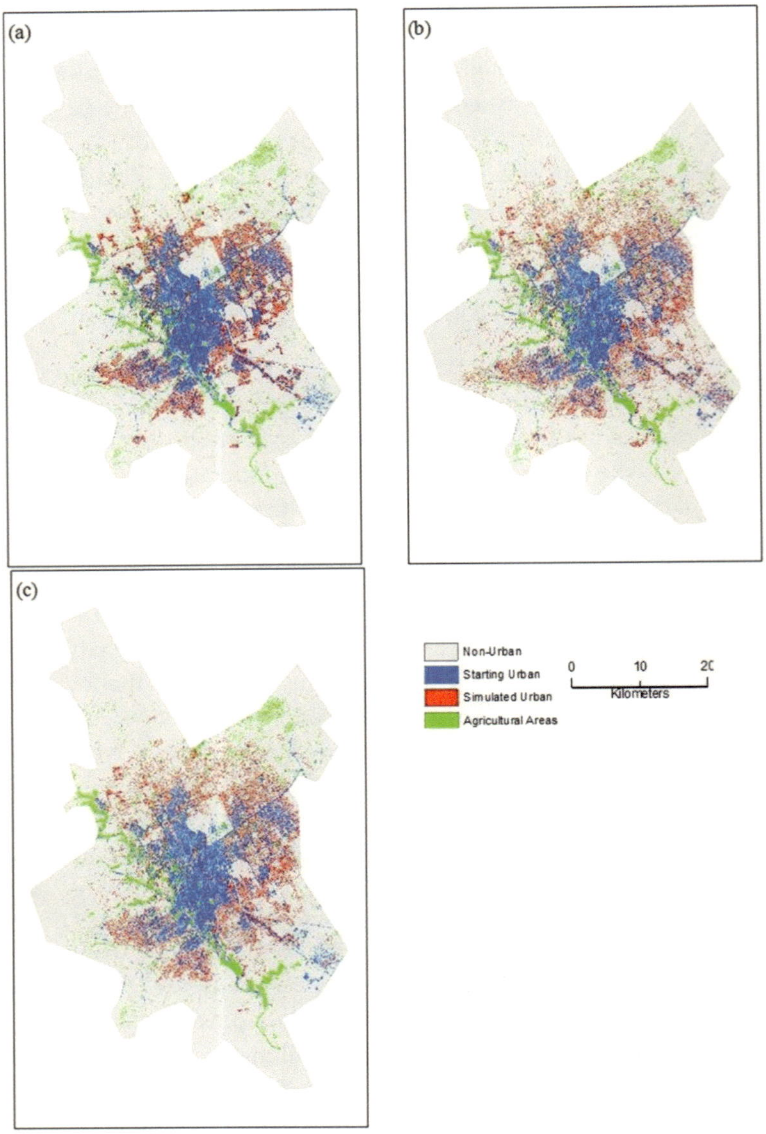

Figure 1. Model simulations from the FCUGM for the period 1987 – 1997 for the three scenarios: (a) M1-S4; (b) M2-S4; and (c) M3-S1.

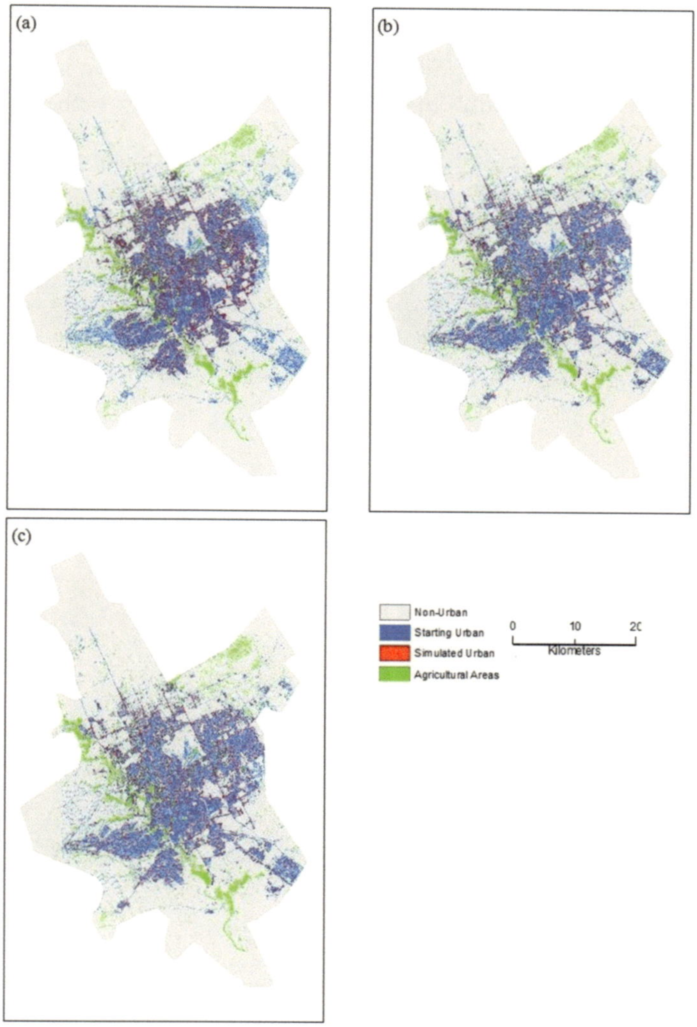

Figure 2. Model simulations from the FCUGM for the period 1997 – 2005 for the three scenarios: (a) M1-S4; (b) M2-S4; and (c) M3-S1.

In contrast to the two individual periods (UGB I and UGB II), the simulated urban growth over the combined period UGB I +II shows a more consistent pattern in terms of trend and direction of growth. This is not surprising since the simulation is for a period of 18 years, where more macroscopic urban growth patterns can be identified. The three model simulations produced a broadly similar direction of urban growth where the highest growth took place to the east of the city followed by a moderate growth to the south west and south east and a low growth to the north and south for the reasons noted above. However, there is a notable variation between the three scenarios in terms of urban morphological pattern. M1-S4 produced highly compact urban patterns while M2-S4 and M3-S1 both generated more dispersed patterns. The patterns produced by M3-S1 contained less noise (i.e. unrealistic scattered urban lands) compared to M2-S4, which can be clearly viewed in the north eastern part of the city. However, the non-uniform dispersal of lands, as shown in these simulations, is one of the characteristics of Riyadh's historical pattern of urban growth.

Overall the model outputs verify that the model is replicating the main processes and drivers as would be expected given knowledge of policies and city structure in the past. In the following sections, more formal methods of model validation are considered.

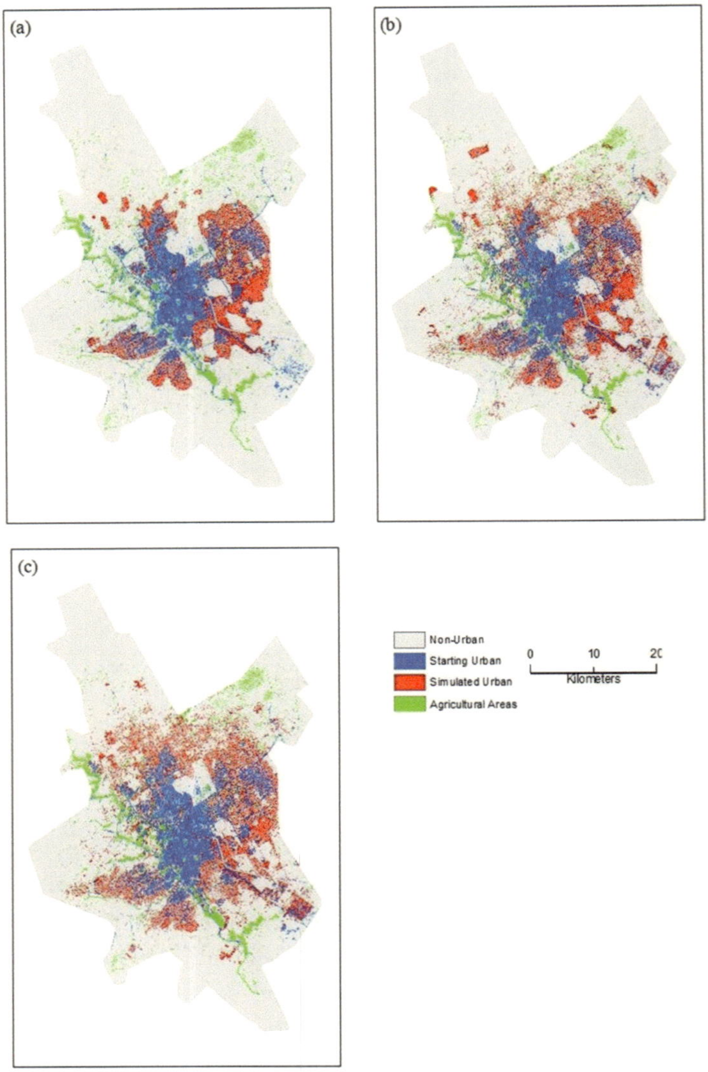

Figure 3. Model simulations from the FCUGM for the period 1987 – 2005 for the three scenarios: (a) M1-S4; (b) M2-S4; and (c) M3-S1.

3. Methods of CA Validation

Seven different methods are described in this chapter; these approaches have all been used to validate the FCUGM model for the city of Riyadh. These include: visual validation; measures of accuracy; urban cell correspondence; the Lee-Sallee index; a spatial pattern measure; a spatial district measure; and multi-resolution validation. The first method, or visual validation, compares the observed results and simulated images by overlaying one image on top of the other and comparing the patterns qualitatively. Such an approach has been used in a number of studies to compare the overall spatial distribution and urban patterns of observed and simulated images, see e.g. [25, 36-39]. Visual comparison by itself may be prone to bias as it is based on the judgment of the researcher or planner. For this reason, more objective methods are required such as those described below. However, visual examination is still an essential part of the validation process since the human brain is particularly good at recognising spatial patterns (and highlighting missing ones), which a more automated or global method would not adequately capture [40].

One of the most common methods for assessing the performance of urban CA models quantitatively is through the calculation of an error or confusion matrix. This approach has been widely used by several authors to compare simulated results against the actual ones for urban CA models [21, 25, 38-39, 41]. The error matrix is a square array, where the rows and columns represent the number of categories whose classification accuracies are being assessed. Typically, the columns represent the observed data and the rows indicate the simulated data. Table 2 shows the error matrix for evaluating the FCUGM where the cells that are categorized in agreement with their observed data are located along the major diagonal of the matrix from the upper left to the lower right. These include urban areas that were simulated and are also observed, i.e. the true urban areas (TU) and areas that are not urban in both the observed and simulated data (true not urban or TNU). The cells off the diagonal represent errors that are underestimated (FNU or false non-urban) or overestimated (FU or false urban) in the simulated image when compared to the observed image.

		Observed Image		
		Urban	**Non-Urban**	**Overall**
	Urban	TU	FNU	TU+FNU
Simulated Image	Non-Urban	FU	TNU	FU+TNU
	Overall	TU+FU	FNU+TNU	TU+FU+TNU+FNU

Table 2. Error matrix of the FCUGM. **TU** = True Urban, **FU** = False Urban, **TNU** = True Non-Urban and **FNU** = False Non-Urban.

From this error matrix, the accuracy can be calculated, which assesses the overall performance of the model by calculating the proportion of the total number of simulated cells that match the corresponding ones in the observed image using Equation 7. In addition the percentages of agreement and disagreement can be calculated as expressed in Equations 8 and 9:

$$\text{Accuracy }(\%) = (TU + TNU) \ / \ (TU + FU + FNU + TNU) \tag{7}$$

$$\text{Agreement }(\%) = ((TU + TNU) \ / \ (TU + FU + FNU + TNU))*100 \tag{8}$$

$$\text{Disagreement }(\%) = ((FU + FNU) \ / \ (TU + FU + FNU + TNU))*100 \tag{9}$$

However, if the study area includes a large number of non-urban cells and a small number of urban cells, the accuracy measure might overstate the model performance due to the high number of non-urban simulated cells that match the non-urban observed ones (i.e. true non-urban (TNU) in Table 2). Such a situation renders it difficult to differentiate between the true performances of different simulations as they might yield similarly high values of accuracy. A validation measure which overcomes this problem is the urban cell correspondence (UCC), since it considers only the True Urban and False Urban cells from the error matrix, as outlined in Equation 10:

$$UCC = \frac{TU}{(TU + FU)} \tag{10}$$

Another problem with the error matrix is that it is not able to assess and estimate the form and shape of patterns because it is based on independent comparisons between pairs of cells. Once such measure that does take shape into account and which has been used frequently for assessing the urban shape produced by CA models is the Lee-Sallee Index (LSI) [18, 38-39, 42-43]. The LSI is calculated as the ratio of the intersection between the observed and simulated urban areas against the union of these areas in the two images as follows:

$$LSI = \sum (S_{ij} \cap O_{ij}) / \sum (S_{ij} \cup O_{ij}) \tag{11}$$

where S_{ij} is a simulated urban cell ij and O_{ij} is an observed urban cell ij .

Another validation measure that considers shape is the spatial pattern measure (SPM). Most cell-by-cell based analyses like those described above ignore the underlying presence of neighbourhoods. In the case of the SPM, a cell is regarded as erroneous if the category in the observed map differs from the category in the simulated map, irrespective of whether the category is found in the neighbouring cell or nowhere near the cell. In this sense, the SPM evaluates the performance based on the agreement within a neighbourhood. If a simulated cell and its corresponding observed urban cell have the same number of adjacent urban neighbours within a predefined neighbourhood, then the cell in question gets a value of 1, indicating that this simulated cell and its neighbours have the same simulated spatial pat-

http://dx.doi.org/10.5772/51708

tern as the observed one. Finally, the total number of correct cells is summed and compared against the results generated by the cell-by-cell analysis. In practice, a pre-designed kernel matrix is moved across the whole study area which simultaneously compares the number of neighbours for each cell both in the simulated and observed images. When the number of neighbours (cells) is the same for this particular cell, a value of 1 is assigned to the output image. This can be expressed mathematically as shown below:

$$\text{IF } \sum\Omega\, S_{ij} = \sum\Omega\, O_{ij};\ \text{then } SPM_{ij} = 1;\ \text{otherwise } SPM_{ij} = 0 \tag{12}$$

where $\Omega\, S_{ij}$ is the number of simulated urban cells ij within a neighbourhood Ω; and $\Omega\, O_{ij}$ is the number of observed urban cells ij within a neighbourhood Ω. To calculate this measure, a special kernel matrix is designed as a neighbourhood measure to mimic the common urban block shape in Riyadh. The general urban pattern can be characterised as a grid-iron pattern. The most common shape and size of urban blocks in the contemporary and future districts of Riyadh are rectangular shapes of 180m length and 60m width. In the FCUGM (with a cell size of 20m), this is equivalent to 9 cells in length and 3 cells in width. Thus, a neighbourhood with a rectangular shape of 180m in length and 60m in width is used to validate the performance of the model in terms of spatial pattern. The SPM compares the number of developed land cells within this neighbourhood shape and size in both the simulated and observed images.

A measure that captures the spatial district structure (SDS) is also used to validate the structural similarity between the simulated and observed urban growth in terms of urban neighbourhood (Figure 4a). It would also be possible to assess this in terms of urban sub-neighbourhood (Figure 4b) and urban block (Figure 4c), where the boundaries of these zones are shown for the city of Riyadh in Figure 4. Figure 5 shows what these structures look like when zooming into a section of the city. In this chapter, only the spatial structure of the urban neighbourhood is examined.

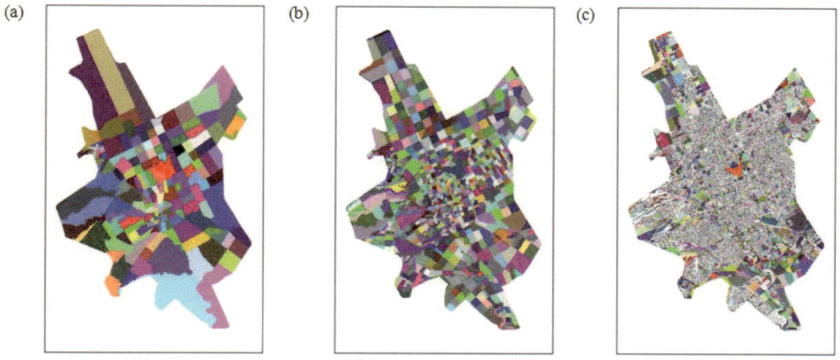

Figure 4. The boundaries of three spatial structures in the city of Riyadh: (a) urban neighbourhoods; (b) urban sub-neighbourhoods; and (c) urban blocks.

The final validation method considers the effect of spatial scale or resolution on the model results. The effects of scale have been considered in previous studies of urban growth modelling by [40, 44-45]. For example, in [40], a multiple-resolution comparison was conducted between the reference and modelled images by demonstrating a pixel aggregation procedure by which four adjacent pixels were averaged at increasingly coarser levels of resolution. To investigate the influence of spatial resolution on the outputs from the FCUGM model, a similar multiple-resolution validation experiment was conducted to that of [40]. The model output from simulation M3-S1 over the period UGB I+II and the observed image for the corresponding period were aggregated from higher to lower levels of spatial resolution whereby four neighbouring pixels were averaged at each coarser resolution. Thus, cells at the next level up had twice the width and height of the previous cell size. The initial cell size was 20 m and the experiments were conducted for 40, 80, 160, 320 and 640 m pixel sizes.

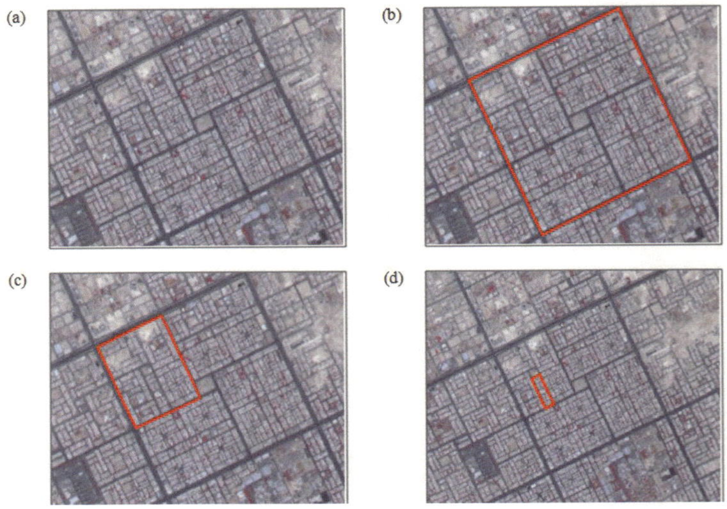

Figure 5. a) A section of the city of Riyadh with delineations for (b) urban neighbourhood; (c) urban sub-neighbourhood; and (d) an urban block.

4. Results

This section provides the results from the application of the seven validation methods as described in section 3.

4.1. Visual Validation of Urban Growth Patterns

The simulated images were overlaid on the observed patterns of development for each of the three time periods and for the three model simulations. Figure 6 shows the overlaid outputs for the period UGB I (1987-1997) for M1-S4, M2-S4 and M3-S1 while Figures 7 and 8 show the same comparison but for UGB II (1997-2005) and UGB I+II (1987-2005) respectively. In the comparison of the images, four main categories were mapped:

i. non-urban match (non-urban in observation and simulation);

ii. urban match (urban in observation and simulation);

iii. underestimated (urban in observation but non-urban in simulation); and

iv. overestimated (non-urban in the observation but urban in the simulation).

The first two classes indicate that the simulation is correct while the latter two are incorrect. Two other classes have been added to facilitate the comparison:

i. starting urban (i.e. already developed lands before the year of the simulation); and

ii. agricultural areas.

For the period UGB I (1987 – 1997), the urban development for the three scenarios in most areas of the city such as north, north east or south west is relatively well estimated (as shown in red). However, areas located at the immediate edges of boundaries of urbanised areas are overestimated (as shown in yellow). This is not surprising because those cells are adjacent to urban land and nearby to attractions, which are more likely to be urban than non-urban. Although the model was able to simulate the pattern or distribution of the developed land of the city reasonably well, it is clear that the FCUGM was not able to reproduce all of the actual urban development that took place, for example, at the extreme south eastern edge of the city (right-bottom corner of Figure 6, coloured in black), which resulted in an underestimation of these lands. Additionally, some small clusters at the extreme edge of the mid-east, west and south west of the city are also underestimated. This underestimation could be attributed to the fact that these areas are widely scattered from one another and from the boundaries of the other urbanised areas, and they are located at some distance from most attractions (e.g. the town centre, developed lands and other services), which in turn were assigned a low possibility of being developed. Thus these areas would have been simulated as non-urban. Another possible explanation is misclassification of the satellite images during the image processing procedure. However, this underestimation is reasonably small, indicating that the model was able to capture the majority of chaotic and fragmented development that occurred during this period.

In contrast to UGB I (1987 – 1997), during the period UGB II (1997 – 2005) (as shown in Figure 7), the correctly estimated urban areas are hard to distinguish and detect, because most of the developments are in small urbanised clusters located within the boundaries of already developed areas. Moreover, this particular period was characterised by significant levels of 'leapfrog' development, which might explain why most of the areas in the maps are coloured blue (starting urban) and the urban match that is coloured in red is marginal and scarcely to be seen. However, M1-S4 and M3-S1 seem to have estimated the urban development reasonably well. It is very hard to detect any urban matching in the M2-S4 simulation, which might suggest that the topographical constraints factor can be considered as a significant influence during this period. This is corroborated by the fact that each of the simulations that included this factor (such as M1-S4 and M3-S1) produced better results than M2-S4.

With respect to UGB I+II as shown in Figure 8, the main result of this analysis is that there is a good visual similarity between the maps, and the simulation results resemble the real city. It can be noted that urban development is largely estimated by the three simulations where M3-S1 has estimated most of the urban development followed by M2-S4 and M1-S4. However, some clusters of land cells are underestimated, mainly in the peripheral areas, showing a different shape in comparison with the actual city. This particular area (coloured in black) is under-estimated highly, moderately and slightly by M1-S4, M2-S4 and M3-S1 respectively. The locations of these cells are very difficult to model since they are located in a highly non-linear and chaotic pattern (e.g. they are far from already developed lands, distant from attractions and services, etc.). Furthermore, it can be noted that M3-S1 was capable of reproducing such complex features to a large extent. This can be attributed to that fact that in this particular simulation, the three urban growth driving forces (TSF, UAAF and TCF) are embedded in each single fuzzy rule, while in M2-S4 and M1-S4 only two and one of these factors are embedded, respectively. This explains why M3-S1 performed well over all periods. It can also be noted that few cells are overestimated compared with the other two periods (i.e. UGB I, UGB II).

Thus overall, the visual analysis of the simulated images shows that they compare well with the patterns that actually occurred in Riyadh during these periods for most of the three simulations, which is a positive reflection of the model's ability to simulate urban growth in the past.

4.2. Accuracy Assessment and Spatial Statistical Measures

An accuracy assessment is another commonly used validation method where the first step is to calculate the error matrix as shown in Table 3 for the three simulations over the three time periods. It can be seen from Table 3-A that the observed urban development during the period UGB I (1987-1997) was about 261,000 cells. The FCUGM simulated around 265,000, 303,000 and 269,000 urban cells in M1-S4, M2-S4 and M3-S4, respectively. Amongst those simulated cells, about 135,000, 152,000 and 142,000 cells were correctly simulated and matched the observed image. However, 129,000, 151,000 and 128,000 were overestimated, and approximately 125,000, 109,000 and 119,000 were underestimated. For the period UGB II (1997-2005), the results were less good as shown in Table 3-B. The simulated urban cells that were generated by the simulations M1-S4, M2-S4 and M3-S4 were only 82,000, 10,000 and 108,000 compared with 237,000 observed ones. In contrast, the simulated results for both periods together UGB I+II (1987-2005) (Table 3-C) showed an improvement and resulted in a higher correspondence of urban cells compared with the two preceding periods (UGB I and UGB II). The urban cells that were correctly matched reached 222,000, 343,000 and 355,000 compared with 464,000 urban observed cells.

From the error matrix, the accuracy measures and the UCC were calculated as shown in Table 4. The LSI is also provided. The results show that the overall accuracy of all simulations is quite high, ranging between 0.890 for simulation M2-S4 UGB II and 0.937 for scenario M3-

http://dx.doi.org/10.5772/51708

S1 UGB I+II. However, these high values of accuracy are mainly achieved through the high matching of non-urban cells, of which there are a very large number in this test area (i.e. it ranges between 3,250,000 and 3,450,000). This implies the need to use a measure that allows for better discrimination between the different simulations, i.e. the UCC, which considers only the matching of the urban cells. Note that the accuracy drops across all simulations, resulting in 0.053 (lowest) and 0.743 (highest) for M2-S4 during UGB II and M3-S1 during UGB I+II, respectively. The UCC measure reveals that the FCUGM simulated the urban growth more accurately over the period UGB I+II (ranging between 0.635 – 0.743) followed by UGB I (0.500 – 0.525), while over the period UGB II, the model produced the poorest results (0.053 – 0.376).

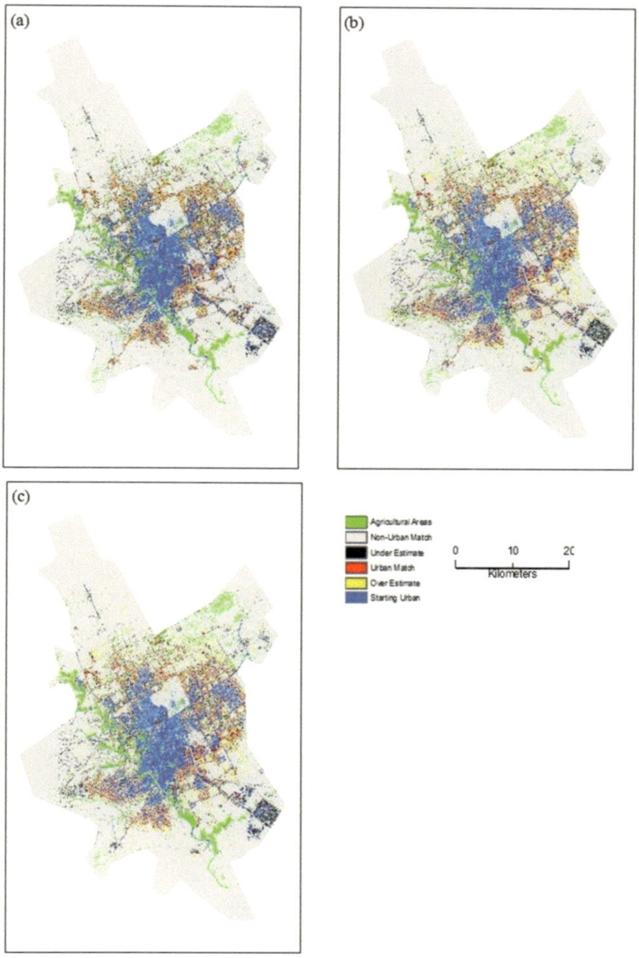

Figure 6. Comparison of the simulated (FCUGM) versus observed cells for the period UGB I (1987 – 1997) for: (a) M1-S4; (b) M2-S4; and (c) M3-S1.

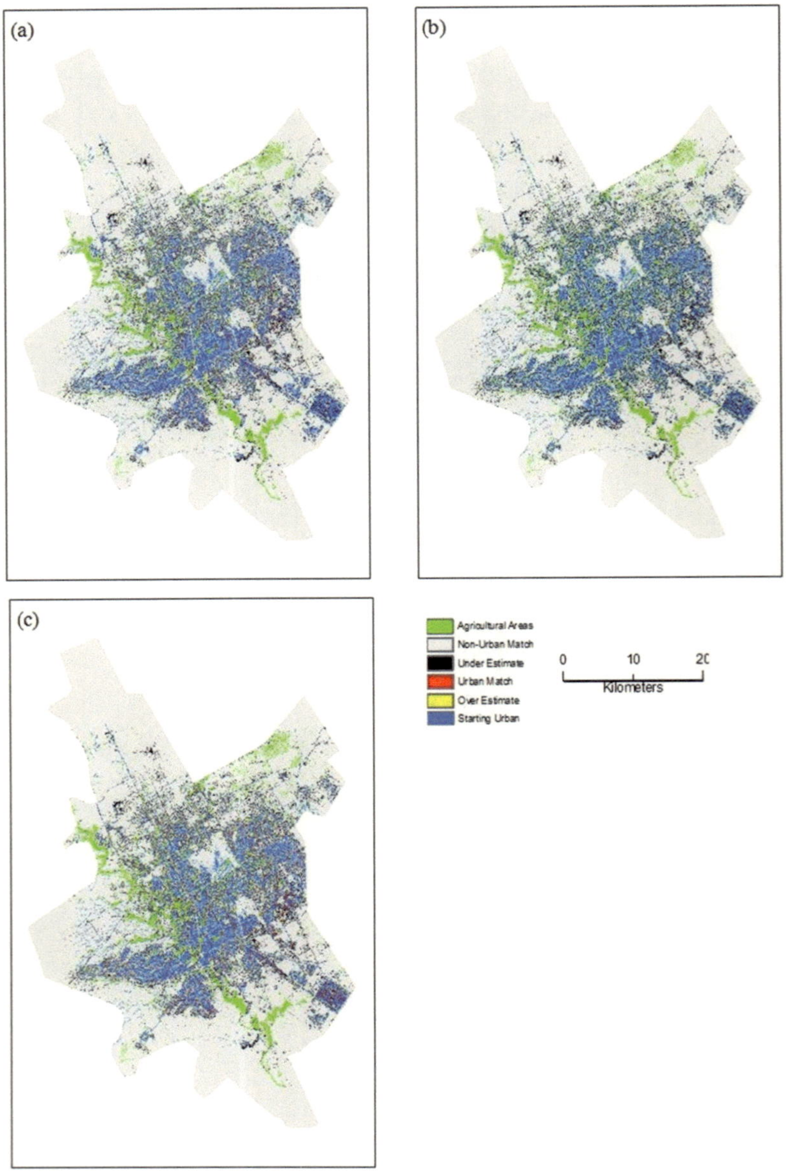

Figure 7. Comparison of the simulated (FCUGM) versus observed cells for the period UGB II (1997 – 2005) for: (a) M1-S4; (b) M2-S4; and (c) M3-S1.

The M3-S1 simulation over all periods yielded the most accurate results compared to the other two simulations, achieving UCC accuracies of 0.743, 0.525 and 0.376 for the periods UGB I +II, UGB I and UGB II, respectively. In contrast, M2-S4 produced the poorest performance across the two periods UGB I and UGB II with a UCC accuracy of 0.500 and 0.053, respectively, while over the period UGB I+II, this simulation performed better than M1-S4 but worse than M3-S1. The M1-S4 simulation produced moderately accurate results with UCC values of 0.635, 0.511 and 0.373 for the three periods UGB I+II, UGB I and UGB II, respectively.

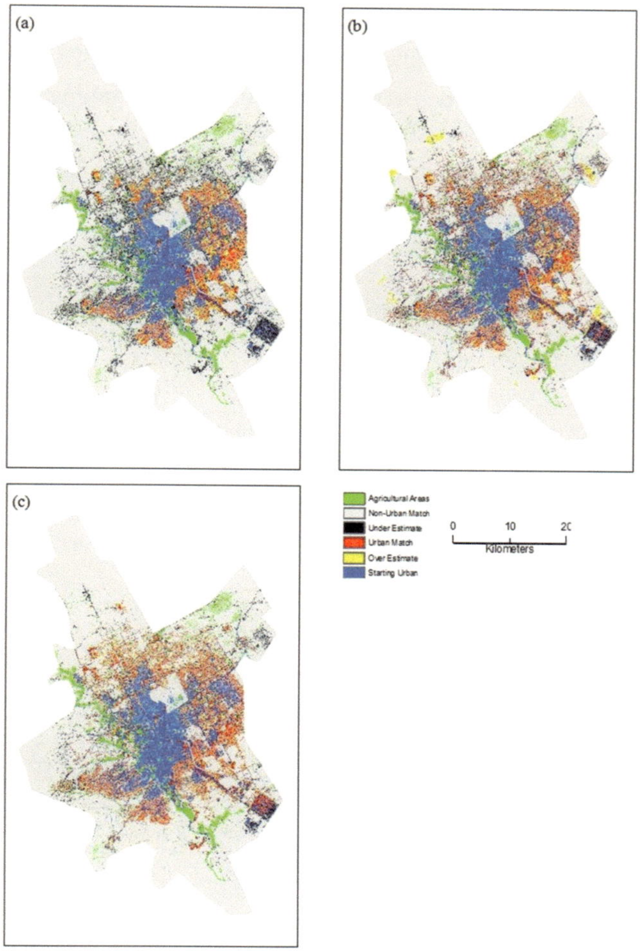

Figure 8. Comparison of the simulated (FCUGM) versus observed cells for the period UGB I+II (1987 – 2005) for: (a) M1-S4; (b) M2-S4; and (c) M3-S1.

With respect to the agreement between the shape of the simulated and observed images in the form of the LSI, Clark and Gaydos (1998) reported that the practical accuracy of the LSI is only around 0.3 while Cheng and Masser (2004) reported values of 0.383 for their model simulations. However, LSI values of greater than 0.35 were achieved in six out of nine simulations from the FCUGM, indicating a better performance than other CA urban growth models. It can also be noted that the LSI and UCC are highly related to one another where a correlation coefficient of 0.969 was obtained between the two measures for all simulations. Thus, simulations with high UCC are more likely to achieve high LSI, indicating a consistency in performance and stability between the spatial shape measure and the cell-by-cell accuracy measure.

The accuracy of the LSI produced by the FCUGM was relatively good with the majority above 0.35. During the period UGB I+II, the model was reasonably good at capturing the shape of the simulated urban areas with values ranging between 0.375 and 0.602. In contrast, the poorest LSI was produced for the period UGB II with values falling to between 0.024 and 0.259. The LSI during the period UGB I was acceptable, ranging between 0.347 and 0.364. The simulation M3-S1 during the period UGB I+II generated the highest shape matching, whilst simulation M2-S4 over the period UGB II showed the poorest performance.

(a): UGB I				Observed	
			Urban	Non-Urban	Overall
		Urban	135,934	129,948	265,882
M1-S4	Simulated	Non-Urban	125,405	3,309,700	3,435,105
		Overall	261,339	3,439,648	3,700,987
				Observed	
			Urban	Non-Urban	Overall
		Urban	151,902	151,773	303,675
M2-S4	Simulated	Non-Urban	109,437	3,287,875	3,397,312
		Overall	261,339	3,439,648	3,700,987
				Observed	
			Urban	Non-Urban	Overall
		Urban	141,904	128,060	269,964
M3-S1	Simulated	Non-Urban	119,435	3,311,588	3,431,023
		Overall	261,339	3,439,648	3,700,987
(b): UGB II				Observed	
			Urban	Non-Urban	Overall
		Urban	81,630	135,234	216,864
M1-S4	Simulated	Non-Urban	155,936	3,328,187	3,484,123
		Overall	237,566	3,463,421	3,700,987
				Observed	
			Urban	Non-Urban	Overall
		Urban	10,099	178,113	188,212
M2-S4	Simulated	Non-Urban	227,467	3,285,308	3,512,775
		Overall	237,566	3,463,421	3,700,987

			Observed		
			Urban	Non-Urban	Overall
		Urban	108,066	178,113	286,179
M3-S1	Simulated	Non-Urban	129,500	3,285,308	3,414,808
		Overall	237,566	3,463,421	3,700,987
(c): UGB I+II				Observed	
			Urban	Non-Urban	Overall
		Urban	222,175	127,517	349,692
M1-S4	Simulated	Non-Urban	241,992	3,109,303	3,351,295
		Overall	464,167	3,236,820	3,700,987
				Observed	
			Urban	Non-Urban	Overall
		Urban	342,960	124,755	467,715
M2-S4	Simulated	Non-Urban	121,207	3,112,065	3,233,272
		Overall	464,167	3,236,820	3,700,987
				Observed	
			Urban	Non-Urban	Overall
		Urban	355,315	122,649	477,964
M3-S1	Simulated	Non-Urban	108,852	3,114,171	3,223,023
		Overall	464,167	3,236,820	3,700,987

Table 3. The error matrices for the three FCUGM simulations over the period: (a) UGB I (1987 – 1997); (b) UGB II (1997 – 2005); and (c) UGB I+II (1987 – 2005).

Simulation	**Agreement (%)**	**Disagreement (%)**	**Accuracy**	**UCC**	**LSI**
M1-S4 UGB I	93.1	6.9	0.931	0.511	0.347
M2-S4 UGB I	92.9	7.1	0.929	0.500	0.367
M3-S1 UGB I	93.3	6.7	0.933	0.525	0.364
M1-S4 UGB II	91.6	8.4	0.916	0.373	0.259
M2-S4 UGB II	89.0	11.0	0.890	0.053	0.024
M3-S1 UGB II	92.1	7.9	0.921	0.376	0.218
M1-S4 UGB I+II	90.0	10.0	0.900	0.635	0.375
M2-S4 UGB I+II	93.3	6.7	0.933	0.733	0.582
M3-S1 UGB I+II	93.7	6.3	0.937	0.743	0.605

Table 4. Statistical performance of the FCUGM for the three different simulations over the three periods of growth UGB I (1987 – 1977), UGB II (1997 – 2005) and UGB I+II (1987 – 2005).

4.3. Spatial Pattern Measure (SPM)

Tables 5 and 6 show the error matrix and statistical indices for the spatial pattern measure for the three FCUGM simulations over the three time periods. These measures include the percentage of agreement, disagreement, accuracy, UCC and LSI when considering the underlying neighbourhood (Equation 12). It can be seen from Tables 5 and 6 that the performance of the FCUGM taking the spatial pattern of neighbourhoods into account shows relatively positive results. For example, the percentage of agreement across all simulations lies between 88% and 94%. The UCC indicates a very high degree of matching between the simulated and observed urban lands with the UCC accuracy as high as 0.765 generated by simulation M3-S1 over the period UGB I+II, and a value of 0.542 generated by simulation M1-S4 and M2-S4 over the period UGB II. The least satisfactory performance was generated by M2-S4 during the period UGB II. In terms of the shape index, this measure shows fairly consistent results similar to the accuracy and the UCC. Those results with high values of UCC and accuracy also generated high shape agreements similar to the findings in section 4.2 where the underlying neighbourhood was not taken into account.

The performance of the different simulations based on both cell-by-cell and spatial pattern methods of validation are provided in Figure 9. If the validation measures from applying the SPM method produced better results than the cell-by-cell ones, this would be understandable since it is extremely difficult to simulate and predict the precise location of urban lands due to the complexity of the urban system. However, the results in Figure 9 indicate a high degree of consistency and stability in the model. From this it can be inferred that the FCUGM has simulated urban growth based on both local and neighbourhood configurations to a large extent.

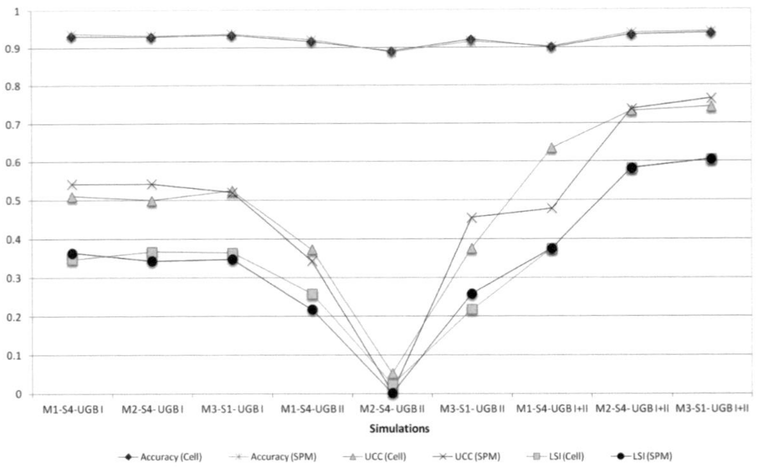

Figure 9. Comparison of the FCUGM performance between the cell-by-cell measures and spatial pattern measures for the different simulations and time periods UGB I (1987 – 1977), UGB II (1997 – 2005) and UGB I+II (1987 – 2005)

(a) UGB I				Observed	
			Urban	Non-Urban	Overall
		Urban	141,904	128,060	269,964
M1-S4	Simulated	Non-Urban	119,435	3,600,558	3,719,993
		Overall	261,339	3,728,618	3,989,957
				Observed	
			Urban	Non-Urban	Overall
		Urban	141,902	151,773	293,675
M2-S4	Simulated	Non-Urban	119,437	3,611,426	3,730,863
		Overall	261,339	3,763,199	4,024,538
				Observed	
			Urban	Non-Urban	Overall
		Urban	135,934	129,948	265,882
M3-S1	Simulated	Non-Urban	125,405	3,630,959	3,756,364
		Overall	261,339	3,760,907	4,022,246
(b) UGB II				Observed	
			Urban	Non-Urban	Overall
		Urban	81,630	135,234	216,864
M1-S4	Simulated	Non-Urban	155,936	3,328,187	3,484,123
		Overall	237,566	3,463,421	3,700,987
				Observed	
			Urban	Non-Urban	Overall
		Urban	99	178,113	178,212
M2-S4	Simulated	Non-Urban	237,464	3,285,308	3,522,772
		Overall	237,563	3,463,421	3,700,984
				Observed	
			Urban	Non-Urban	Overall
		Urban	108,066	178,113	286,179
M3-S1	Simulated	Non-Urban	129,500	3,285,308	3,414,808
		Overall	237,566	3,463,421	3,700,987
(c) UGB I+II				Observed	
			Urban	Non-Urban	Overall
		Urban	222,175	127,517	349,692
M1-S4	Simulated	Non-Urban	241,992	3,393,273	3,635,265

		Overall	464,167	3,520,790	3,984,957
				Observed	
			Urban	Non-Urban	Overall
		Urban	342,960	124,775	467,735
M2-S4	Simulated	Non-Urban	121,207	3,401,015	3,522,222
		Overall	464,167	3,525,790	3,989,957
				Observed	
			Urban	Non-Urban	Overall
		Urban	355,315	122,649	477,964
M3-S1	Simulated	Non-Urban	108,852	3,403,130	3,511,982
		Overall	464,167	3,525,779	3,989,946

Table 5. The error matrix for the FCUGM using the spatial pattern measure for the period: (a) UGB I (1987 – 1997); (b) UGB II (1997 – 2005); and (c) UGB I+II (1987 – 2005).

Simulation	Agreement (%)	Disagreement (%)	Accuracy	UCC	LSI
M1-S4 UGB I	93.7	6.3	0.937	0.542	0.364
M2-S4 UGB I	93.2	6.8	0.932	0.542	0.343
M3-S1 UGB I	93.6	6.4	0.936	0.520	0.347
M1-S4 UGB II	92.1	7.9	0.921	0.343	0.218
M2-S4 UGB II	88.7	11.3	0.887	0.004	0.002
M3-S1 UGB II	91.6	8.4	0.916	0.454	0.259
M1-S4 UGB I+II	90.2	9.8	0.902	0.478	0.375
M2-S4 UGB I+II	93.8	6.2	0.938	0.738	0.582
M3-S1 UGB I+II	94.1	5.9	0.941	0.765	0.605

Table 6. Statistical performance of the spatial pattern measure for three FCUGM simulations and three time periods: UGB I (1987 – 1977), UGB II (1997 – 2005) and UGB I+II (1987 – 2005).

4.4. Spatial District Structural Measure

Figure 10 presents the results of the spatial structure indicator, which plots the number of developed areas in each district against the observed ones for the city of Riyadh over the three periods UGB I, II and I+II producing a profile of development by district ID. During the periods UGB I+II and UGB I, the simulation results generated similar patterns to the observed while, in contrast, the simulation results over the period UGB II underestimated large areas for districts with IDs between 47-50, 75-90 and 110-150.

http://dx.doi.org/10.5772/51708

With respect to the simulations, the model results generated from simulations M2-S4 and M3-S1 show good matching with the observed data, while M1-S4 moderately underestimated some actual developed areas. During the period UGB II, simulation M3-S1 performed better than the other two simulations (M1-S4 and M3-S1), while over the period UGB I, the three simulations produced similar moderate levels of urban matching.

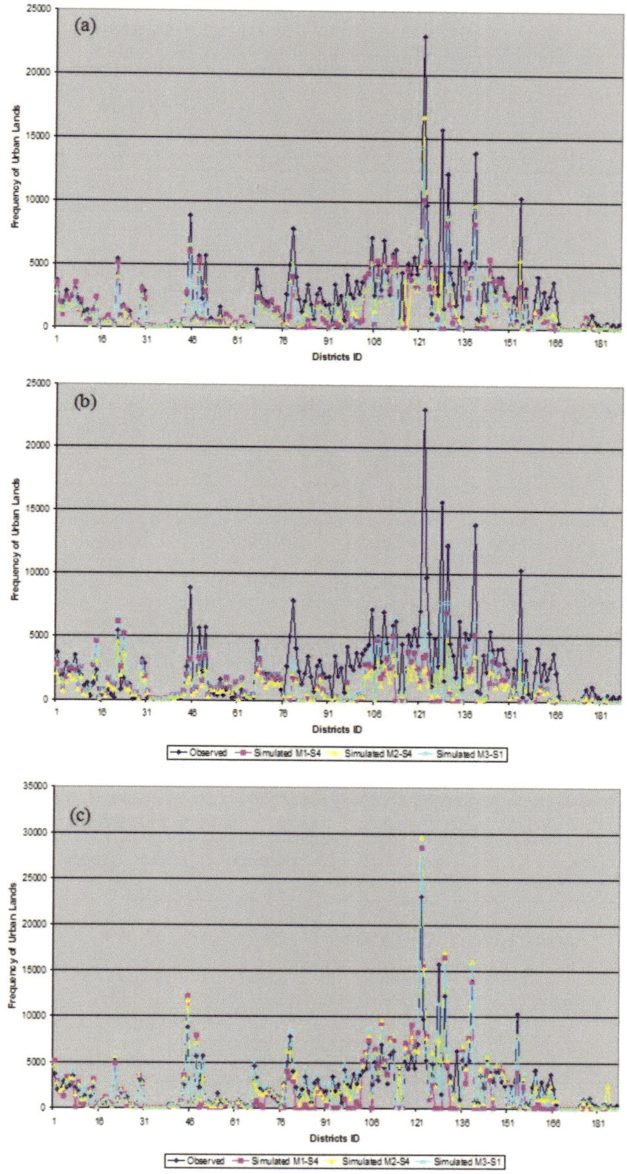

Figure 10. The development profiles by the districts in Riyadh for (a) UGB I (1987 – 1977); (b) UGB II (1997 – 2005); and (c) UGB I+II (1987 – 2005).

4.5. Spatial Multi-Resolution Validation

Table 7 shows the error matrix for the FCUGM for simulation M3-S1 over the period UGB I +II (1987 – 2005) at the original and five increasingly coarser spatial resolutions while Table 8 presents the statistical indicators derived from the error matrix.

Cell Size				Observed	
			Urban	Non-Urban	Overall
		Urban	355,315	122,649	477,964
20 (Original)	Simulated	Non-Urban	108,852	3,114,171	3,223,023
		Overall	464,167	3,236,820	3,700,987
				Observed	
			Urban	Non-Urban	Overall
		Urban	144,635	33,206	177,841
40	Simulated	Non-Urban	27,264	890,363	917,627
		Overall	171,899	923,569	1,095,468
				Observed	
			Urban	Non-Urban	Overall
		Urban	361,127	8,430	369,557
80	Simulated	Non-Urban	6,738	222,551	229,289
		Overall	367,865	230,981	598,846
				Observed	
			Urban	Non-Urban	Overall
		Urban	9,120	2,045	11,165
160	Simulated	Non-Urban	1,721	55,577	57,298
		Overall	10,841	57,622	68,463
				Observed	
			Urban	Non-Urban	Overall
		Urban	2,269	538	2,807
320	Simulated	Non-Urban	380	13,933	14,313
		Overall	2,649	14,471	17,120
				Observed	
			Urban	Non-Urban	Overall
		Urban	579	137	716
640	Simulated	Non-Urban	104	3,459	3,563
		Overall	683	3,596	4,279

Table 7. The error matrix of the FCUGM for simulation M3-S1 over the period UGB I+II (1987 – 2005) at the original and five coarser spatial resolutions.

http://dx.doi.org/10.5772/51708

Cell Size (m)	Agreement (%)	Disagreement (%)	Accuracy	UCC	LSI
20	93.744	6.256	0.937	0.743	0.605
40	94.454	5.455	0.944	0.841	0.705
80	97.467	2.543	0.974	0.981	0.959
160	94.499	6.251	0.944	0.841	0.707
320	94.637	5.363	0.946	0.856	0.711
640	94.367	5.633	0.943	0.847	0.706

Table 8. Statistical performance of the FCUGM for simulation M3-S1 over the period UGB I+II (1987 – 2005) at the original and five coarser spatial resolutions

The results show that there are improvements to all the measures reported in Table 8 as the cell size increases from 20 m to a higher resolution. However, some of these improvements are very small and they remain relatively stable as the resolution continues to increase. For example, the accuracy at a 20m resolution is 93.7%, while accuracies at higher resolutions are all around 94%. The only exception is at 80 m where the performance according to all measures is the highest. In terms of urban cell matching, the lowest performance (0.841) was found at 40 and 160 m while moderate UCC accuracies (0.856 and 0.847) were found at spatial resolutions of 320 and 640 m respectively. Thus, the UCC does not appear to improve very much with a coarser spatial resolution and is likewise quite stable at higher resolutions. With respect to matching the shape between the output of the model and the actual urban image, the LSI also indicates similar values at the higher resolutions with the exceptional performance at a resolution of 80 m. Overall the results suggest that the simulated urban images produced by the FCUGM are not that sensitive to spatial resolution, which indicates that a significant feature of the model is its stability and consistency of accuracy over various cell sizes.

5. Discussion and Conclusions

Simulating the main processes and drivers of urban growth is a challenging area; researchers are increasingly turning to individual-based models to handle the complexity of these systems. To have any confidence in the outputs of these models, rigorous calibration and validation tests need to be applied. Within this chapter, a series of different measures were used to validate the FCUGM, a complex CA model, for the city of Riyadh. While no one validation method was found to 'outperform' the others, there was great benefit in using a combination of several approaches. Three different simulations of the FCUGM applied to three different time periods of urban growth were considered. It is clear from the results that the characteristics and patterns of urban development over a particular time period have a large influence on the performance of the model and the resulting accuracy of a given simulation. For example, over UGB II, urban development has mainly followed a pattern of infilling of urban growth, i.e. the non-urban areas surrounded by urban areas were converted to urban, while very limited development took place on the margins or fringe areas of the city. This type of development exhibits a highly non-linear pattern, where the new potential developed land occurs in very small clusters that are surrounded by very large urban clusters. Consequently, the simulation results over this period were the least satisfactory when compared with the other two time periods. It is worth noting that this pattern was generated as a result of applying the urban growth limit regulations (as advocated by the planning local authority of Riyadh) to prevent urban sprawl. The urban growth pattern over the periods UGB I and UGB I+II can be characterised by a pattern of edge-expansion, where the newly developed urban areas spread out from the fringes or margins of existing urban patches. This feature was modeled in a satisfactory manner during these two periods of growth.

Similarly, the characteristics of the simulation are another factor that can have a significant impact on the results, which was clearly supported by consistency across the different validation measures when examining the three simulations, i.e. simulation M3-S1 produced the best spatial simulation over all of the periods followed by M1-S4 and M2-S4. It is worth noting that the three urban growth factors, i.e. transportation, urban density and attractiveness, and topographical constraints, were part of all three simulations M1-S4, M2-S4 and M3-S1. However, the difference between these model instances has to do with the form of the fuzzy rules and how many factors are combined in each rule. M1-S4 embeds only one factor, M2-S4 embeds two factors and M3-S1 combines all three factors in each fuzzy rule. Embedding all factors into the fuzzy rules and combining these via the AND operator appears to have produced the best performing model. However, M1-S4, with only one factor per fuzzy rule, generally outperformed M2-S4 with two factors in each rule but containing all three factors in the model with more rules needed to capture all the possible pairs of factors. Perhaps restricting the model to rules with only two factors produced a model that was actually more complex than the simple M1-S4 and even the M3-S1 simulation, but less able to capture urban growth as adequately.

Overall there was consistency between the measures regarding which model instance performed better and for which growth periods. The visual inspection provided an overall qualitative assessment that would not have been possible using any of the quantitative measures and is therefore always recommended as a method of model validation. The accuracy measures are very sensitive to the number of non-urban cells and should mostly likely not be used or reported in conjunction with the UCC, which took only urban cells into account. This measure provides a much better assessment of model performance. The measures that took shape or underlying neighbourhood into account are also valuable. In this case, they provided a consistent message regarding model performance but they could help to identify models that are good global predictors but are not spatially or locally very good. Finally the analysis at multiple resolutions provides a good indication of model stability across spatial scales and should be implemented as a minimum measure of validation as advocated in [40].

While the validation techniques used in this work provided a comprehensive assessment of the model outputs, there are other techniques available, e.g. fractal dimensional analysis [34, 46]. However, this approach has limitations, e.g. two maps that seem different may have

http://dx.doi.org/10.5772/51708

identical fractal dimensions. Thus, this measure tells us very little about how similar the two maps may be in terms of local structures. Although the approach reflects how much space is filled correctly across a range of scales, it does not seem to be valid when dealing with non-urban situations [1]. However, other approaches involving comparison with null models require further investigation [40]. What remains clear from this study and the current state of validation approaches in the CA urban modelling literature is that there is no one best method or set of approaches available for validating CA urban growth models. Many different methods are available and the best approach appears to be validation using multiple measures. Ultimately, these measures must be linked to confidence in the model performance and the ability to simulate future growth especially when they move from an academic and experimental environment to real world applications by planners.

Author details

Khalid Al-Ahmadi[1], Linda See[2,3] and Alison Heppenstall[4*]

*Address all correspondence to: a.j.heppenstall@leeds.ac.uk

1 King Abdulaziz City for Science and Technology (KACST), Riyadh, Saudi Arabia

2 Ecosystems Services and Management Programme, International Institute of Applied Systems Analysis (IIASA), Laxenburg, Austria

3 Centre for Applied Spatial Analysis (CASA), University College London, London, UK

4 School of Geography, University of Leeds, Leeds, UK

References

[1] White, R., & Engelen, G. (2000). High Resolution Integrated Modelling of the Spatial Dynamics of Urban and Regional Systems. *Computers, Environment and Urban Systems*, 24, 383-440.

[2] Batty, M. (1995). New Ways of Looking at Cities. *Nature*, 574.

[3] Portugali, J. (2000). Self-Organization and the City. Berlin: Springer-Verlag.

[4] Allen, PM. (1997). Cities and Regions as Self-organizing Systems: Models of Complexity. Amsterdam Gordon and Breach Science.

[5] Batty, M., & Longley, P. (1994). Fractal Cities: A Geometry of Form and Function. London Academic Press.

[6] Wilson, AG. (2000). Complex Spatial Systems: The Modeling Foundations of Urban and Regional Analysis. Harlow Pearson Education.

[7] Batty, M. (2003). The Emergence of Cities: Complexity and Urban Dynamics. *Centre for Advanced Spatial Analysis, University College London, Working paper 64,* http://www.casa.ucl.ac.uk/cellularmodels.pdf.

[8] Wu, F. (1998). An Experiment on the Generic Polycentricity of Urban Growth in a Cellular Automatic City. *Environment and Planning B.*, 25, 731-752.

[9] Batty, M. (1997). The Computable City. *International Planning Studies.*, 2, 155-173.

[10] White, R., & Engelen, G. (1994). Cellular Dynamics and GIS: Modelling Spatial Complexity. *Geographical Systems*, 1, 237-253.

[11] Couclelis, H. (1985). Cellular Worlds: A Framework for Modelling Micro-macro Dynamics. *Environment and Planning A*, 17, 585-596.

[12] Wolfram, S. (1994). Cellular Automata and Complexity. Reading MA:, Addison-Wesley.

[13] Toffoli, T., & Margolus, N. (1987). Cellular Automata Machines. *Cambridge MA: The MIT Press.*

[14] Batty, M., & Xie, Y. (1994). From Cells to Cities. *Environment and Planning B*, 21, 31-48.

[15] Wu, F. (1996). A Linguistic Cellular Automata Simulation Approach for Sustainable Land Development in a Fast Growing Region. *Computers Environment, and Urban Systems.*, 20, 367-387.

[16] Wu, F. (1998). Simulating Urban Encroachment on Rural Land with Fuzzy-logic-controlled Cellular Automata in a Geographical Information System. *Journal of Environmental Management*, 53, 293-308.

[17] Wagner, D. F. (1997). Cellular Automata and Geographic Information Systems. *Environment and Planning B.*, 24, 219-234.

[18] Clarke, K. C., & Gaydos, L. J. (1998). Loose-coupling a Cellular Automaton Model and GIS: Long-term Urban Growth Prediction for San Francisco and Washington/Baltimore. *International Journal Geographical Information Sciences.*, 12, 699-714.

[19] Torrens, P. M. (2000). How Cellular Models of Urban Systems Work. CASA Centre for Advanced Spatial Analysis, University College London, Working Paper 28, http://www.casa.ucl.ac.uk/publications/workingPaperDetail.asp?ID=28.

[20] Torrens, P. M. (2000). How Land-Use Transport Models Work. *Centre for Advanced Spatial Analysis, University College London, Working Paper 20,* http://www.casa.ucl.ac.uk/publications/workingPaperDetail.asp?ID=20.

[21] Li, X., & Yeh, A. (2001). Calibration of Cellular Automata by using Neural Networks for the Simulation of Complex Urban System. *Environment and Planning A.*, 33(8), 1445-1462.

[22] Wu, F, & Martin, D. (2002). Urban Expansion Simulation of Southeast England using Population Surface Modeling and Cellular Automata. *Environment and Planning A.*, 34(10), 1855-1876.

[23] Yeh, A., & Li, X. (2002). Neural-network Based Cellular Automata for Simulating Multiple Land Use Changes using GIS. *International Journal Geographical Information Sciences.*, 16, 323-343.

[24] Li, X., & Yeh, A. (2000). Modelling Sustainable Urban Development by the Integration of Constrained Cellular Automata and GIS. *International Journal of Geographical Information Systems.*, 14, 131-152.

[25] Wu, F. (2002). Calibration of Stochastic Cellular Automata: The Application to Rural-urban land Conversions. *International Journal of Geographical Information Systems.*, 16(8), 795-818.

[26] Engelen, G., & White, R. (2008). Validating and Calibrating Integrated Cellular Automata Based Models of Land Use Change. *In: The Dynamics of Complex Urban Systems.*, Albeverio S, Andrey D, Giordano P, Vancheri A (Eds.), 185-211, Heidelberg, Physics-Verlag.

[27] Torrens, P. M. (2011). Calibrating and Validating Cellular Automata Models of Urbanization. *In: Urban Remote Sensing: Monitoring, Synthesis and Modeling in the Urban Environment.*, Yang, X. (Ed.), 335-345, Chichester, John Wiley & Sons.

[28] Openshaw, S., & Openshaw, C. (1997). Artificial Intelligence in Geography. New York NY: John Wiley and Sons.

[29] Al-Ahmadi, K., Heppenstall, A. J., Hogg, J., & See, L. (2009a). A Fuzzy Cellular Automata Urban Growth Model (FCAUGM) for the City of Riyadh, Saudi Arabia. Part 1: Model Structure and Validation. *Applied Spatial Analysis.*, 2(1), 65-83.

[30] Al-Ahmadi, K., Heppenstall, A. J., Hogg, J., & See, L. (2009b). A Fuzzy Cellular Automata Urban Growth Model (FCAUGM) for the City of Riyadh, Saudi Arabia. Part 2: Scenario Analysis. *Applied Spatial Analysis.*, 2(2), 85-105.

[31] Al-Ahmadi, K., See, L., Heppenstall, A. J., & Hogg, J. (2009c). Calibration of a Fuzzy Cellular Automata Model of Urban Dynamics in Saudi Arabia. *Ecological Complexity*, 6(2), 80-101.

[32] Rykiel, E. J. (1996). Testing Ecological Models: The Meaning of Validation. *Ecological Modeling.*, 90, 229-244.

[33] Santé, I., Garcia, A. M., Miranda, D., & Crecente, R. (2010). Cellular Automata Models for the Simulation of Real-world Urban Processes: A Review and Analysis. *Landscape and Urban Planning*, 96(2), 108-122.

[34] White, R., & Engelen, G. (1993). Cellular Automata and Fractal Urban Form: A Cellular Modelling Approach to the Evolution of Urban Land-use. *Environment and Planning A*, 25(8), 1175-1199.

[35] Soares-Filho, B., Coutinho-Cerqueira, G., & Lopes-Pennachin, C. (2002). DINAMICA-Stochastic Cellular Automata Model Designed to Simulate the Landscape Dynamics in an Amazonian Colonization Frontier. *Ecological Modelling.*, 154, 217-235.

[36] Clarke, K. C., Hoppen, S., & Gaydos, L. (1997). A Self-modifying Cellular Automaton Model of Historical Urbanization in the San Francisco Bay Area. *Environment and Planning B.*, 24(2), 247-261.

[37] Ward, D. P., Murray, AT, & Phinn, S. R. (2000). A Stochastically Constrained Cellular Model of Urban Growth. *Computers, Environment and Urban Systems.*, 24, 539-558.

[38] Barredo, J. I., Demicheli, L., Lavalle, C., Kasanko, M., & Mc Cormick, N. (2004). Modelling Future Urban Scenarios in Developing Countries: An Application Case Study in Lagos, Nigeria. *Environment and Planning B.*, 31(1), 65-84.

[39] Cheng, J., & Masser, I. (2004). Understanding Spatial and Temporal Process of Urban Growth: Cellular Automata Modeling. *Environment and Planning B.*, 31, 167-194.

[40] Pontius, R., Huffaker, D., & Denman, K. (2004). Useful Techniques of Validation for Spatially Explicit Land-change Model. *Ecological Modeling.*, 179(4), 445-461.

[41] Wu, F., & Webster, C. J. (1998). Simulation of Land Development through the Integration of Cellular Automata and Multi-criteria Evaluation. *Environment and Planning B.*, 25, 103-126.

[42] Lee, D., & Sallee, T. (1974). Theoretical Patterns of Farm Shape and Central Place Location. *Journal of Regional Science*, 14(3), 423-430.

[43] Jantz, C., & Goetz, S. (2005). Analysis of Scale Dependencies in an Urban Land-use Change Model. *International Journal of Geographical Information Science.*, 19, 271-241.

[44] Kok, K., & Veldkamp, A. (2001). Evaluating Impact of Spatial Scales on Land Use Pattern Analysis in Central America. *Agricultural, Ecosystems and Environment.*, 85, 205-221.

[45] Kok, K., Farrow, A., Veldkamp, A., & Verburg, P. (2001). A Method and Application of Multi-scale Validation in Spatial and Land Use Models. *Agricultural, Ecosystems and Environment.*, 85, 223-238.

[46] Frankhauser, P., & Sadler, R. (1991). Fractal Analysis of Agglomerations. In: Natural Structures: Principles, Strategies, and Models in Architecture and Nature. M. Hilliges (Ed.), 57-65, Stuttgart: University of Stuttgart.

Chapter 3

Cellular Automata for Pattern Recognition

Sartra Wongthanavasu and Jetsada Ponkaew

Additional information is available at the end of the chapter

http://dx.doi.org/10.5772/52364

1. Introduction

Cellular Automata (CA) are spatiotemporal discrete systems (Neumann, 1966) that can model dynamic complex systems. A variety of problem domains have been reported to date in successful CA applications. In this regard, digital image processing is one of those as reported by Wongthanavasu et. al. (Wongthanavasu et al., 2003; 2004; 2007) and Rosin (Rosin, 2006).

Generalized Multiple Attractor CA (GMACA) is introduced for elementary pattern recognition (Ganguly et al., 2002; Maji et al., 2003; 2008). It is a promising pattern classifier using a simple local network of Elementary Cellular Automata (ECA) (Wolfram, 1994), called attractor basin that is a reverse tree-graph. GMACA utilizes a reverse engineering technique and genetic algorithm in ordering the CA rules. This leads to a major drawback of computational complexity, as well as recognition performance. There are reports in successful applications of GMACA in error correcting problem with only one bit noise. It shows the promising results for the restricted one bit noise, but becomes combinatorial explosion in complexity, using associative memory, when a number of bit noises increases.

Due to the drawbacks of complexity and recognition performance stated previously, the binary CA-based classifier, called Two-class Classifier Generalized Multiple Attractor Cellular Automata with artificial point (2C2-GMACA), is presented. In this regard, a pattern recognition of error correcting capability is implemented comprehensively in comparison with GMACA. Following this, the basis on CA for pattern recognition and GMACA's configuration are presented. Then, the 2C2-GMACA model and its performance evaluation in comparison with GMACA are provided. Finally, conclusions and discussions are given.

2. Cellular Automata for Pattern Recognition

Elementary Cellular Automata (ECA) (Wolfram, 1994) is generally utilized as a basis on pattern recognition. It is the simplest class of one dimension (1d) CA with n cells, 2 states and 3 neighbors. A state is changed in discrete time and space ($S_i^t \rightarrow S_i^{t+1}$; where S_i^t is the present state and S_i^{t+1} is the next state for the ith cell) by considering it nearest neighbor (S_{i-1}^t, S_i^t, S_{i+1}^t) of the present state.

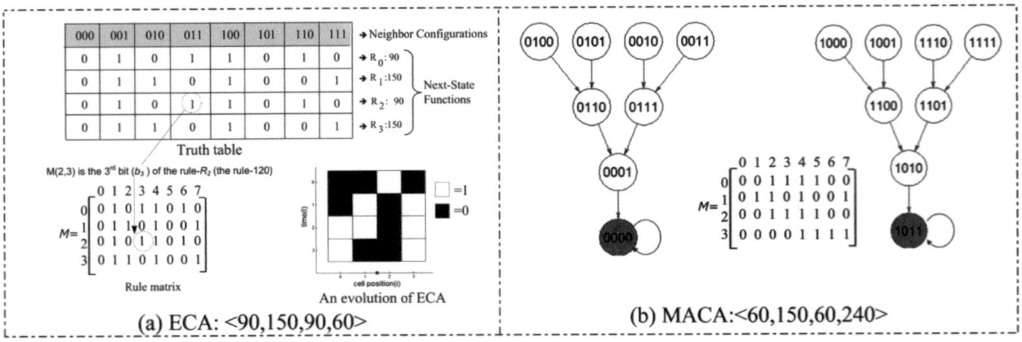

Figure 1. Elementary Cellular Automata (ECA) and Generalized Multiple Attractor Cellular Automata (GMACA).

For n-cell ECA, the next state function ($S_i^t \rightarrow S_i^{t+1}$) can be represented by a rule matrix (M) with size $|n\text{x}8|$ and the nearest neighbour configuration (S_{i-1}^t, S_i^t, S_{i+1}^t) of the present state. Suppose an n-cell ECA ($S_0^t S_1^t S_2^t \ldots S_{n-1}^t$) at time 't' is changed in discrete time by a rule vector $<R_0, R_1, \ldots, R_{n-1}>$. A truth table is a simplified form of the rule vector as illustrated in Fig. 1(a). It comprises the possible 3 neighbor values of S_{i-1}^t S_i^t S_{i+1}^t from 000 to 111, and the next states for the rule R_i; where i=0, 1, 2..., n-1. Each rule is represented in binary numbers (b_7 b_6 b_5 b_4 $b_3 b_2 b_1 b_0$). If the binary numbers are decoded into decimal, it must equal to the number R_i such as '01011010' for the rule-90. Simultaneously, A rule matrix (M) can also be represented the rule vector.

Let $M(i,j)$ be an element of the matrix at the ith (i=0,1,2,...,n-1) row and the jth (j=0,1,2,...,7) column. The $M(i,j)$ is contained b_j of the rule-R_i. For example, M(2,3) is b_3 of the rule R_2 (the rule-90) that is '1'. Consequently, the next state (S_i^{t+1}) for the i th cell is represented by the $M(i,j)$ as the following:

$$S_i^{t+1} = M(i, j_i) \tag{1}$$

where;

S_i^{t+1} is the next state of the ith cell.

j_i is the 3 neighbouring values ($S_{i-1}^t S_i^t S_{i+1}^t$) of the present state at the ith cell decoded in decimal.

The next state (S^{t+1}) for *n*-cell ECA calculated is also defined by the rule matrix *M* as following:

$$\begin{aligned} S^{t+1} &= (S_0^{t+1}, S_1^{t+1}, \ldots, S_{n-1}^{t+1}) \\ &= (M(0, j_0), M(1, j_1) \ldots, M(n-1, j_{n-1})) \\ &= (M, S^t) \end{aligned} \tag{2}$$

Suppose a system designed with a rule matrix (*M*) comprises a set of solutions *Y*= $\{y_i \mid y_i \in \{0,1\}^n\}$ and an input *x*; $x \in \{0,1\}^n$, where *i =1, 2…, N*. Consequently, the pattern classifiers based on the evolution of the ECA is defined as following

$$S^{t+1} = \begin{cases} (M, S^t), if\ S^t \notin Y \\ S^t\ and\ stop, otherwise \end{cases} \tag{3}$$

For an input x , it must be identified a solution from *Y* using the equation (3). Firstly, the present state (S^t) will be set to x . Then, the next state (S^{t+1}) will be generated using the rule matrix *M* until it reaches some solution ($S^t \in Y$). The structure for pattern classification using ECA can be represented by a simple local network called attractor basin. It consists of a cyclic and non-cyclic states. The cyclic state contains a pivotal point which is a solution to classification problem, while the transient states (all possible inputs) are contained in the non-cyclic states. The attractor cycle lengths (height) in the GMACA (Oliveira, et al., 2006; Sipper, 1996) are greater than or equal to one, while Multiple Attractor Cellular Automata (MACA) (Das, et al., 2008; Maji, et al., 2003; Sipper, 1996) is limited to one. In Fig. 1(b), two attractor basins of 4-bit pattern of MACA with null boundary condition are designed with a rule vector <60, 150, 60, 240>. The target solution patterns are 0000 and 1011, respectively. The rule vector is ordered by the evolution of heuristic search using simulated annealing algorithm.

3. Generalized Multiple Attractor Cellular Automata

This section gives the detailed configuration of GMACA and its application in ECC. Suppose *an n*-bit pattern is sent in a communication system. Let *X* be the sender's pattern and *Y* be the receiver's pattern. Thus, the number of different bits between *X* and *Y* is determined by Hamming distance (*r*) defined as follows:

$$r = \sum_{i=0}^{n-1} |x_i - y_i| \tag{4}$$

where $X = x_0 x_1 \dots x_{n-1}; x_i \in \{0,1\}$ and $Y = y_0 y_1 \dots y_{n-1}; y_i \in \{0,1\}$.

The number of possible error patterns (p_r) for a given r of n-bit communication can be expressed as follow:

$$p_r = \binom{n}{r} \tag{5}$$

Then, the number of all possible error patterns (p_{All}) for a given r_{max}, where $r_{max} \in (0, n)$ is the maximum permissible noise, is given by:

$$p_{All} = \sum_{r=0}^{r_{\max}} \binom{n}{r} \tag{6}$$

The maximum permissible noise (r_{max}) is the highest value of r allowed to occur in the communication system. The Hamming distance model of a message (pattern) and it errors are also represented by an attractor basin—that is, the messages is a pivotal point while the errors are transient states. Thus, the error correcting codes can be solved by the Generalized Multiple Attractor Cellular Automata (GMACA).

Figure 2. Two-Class Classifier GMACA with artificial point (2C2-GMACA): <232,212,178,142 >.

Suppose a communication system comprises k original messages of n-bit data and the maximum permissible noise r_{max}. If error messages are corrected using the GMACA, thus a satisfied rule vector is required. The rule vector is a result of a reverse engineering technique. Firstly, k attractor basins are randomly constructed with the number of nodes for each attractor basin equals p_{All}. Then original messages are randomly mapped into pivotal points while its possible errors are also randomly mapped into transient states at the same attract basin. Finally, the search heuristics, such as simulated annealing (SA) and genetic algorithm (GA) (Holland, 1992; Shuai, et al., 2007; Jie, et al., 2002) have been taken to explore the optimal structure. The search heuristics then iteratively changes directions and height of the attractor basins until the satisfied rule vector is acquired.

As reported in Ganguly, et al., 2002, Maji, et al., 2003 and Maji, et al., 2008, the GMACA provides the best performance of pattern recognition if it is trained with the r_{max} having a value of 1. Although percentage of recognition in testing is high when deals with the r_{max} equals 1, it sharply decreases the recognition performance when the r_{max} is greater than 1.

4. Proposed 2C2-GMACA Model

Due to the drawbacks of recognition performance resulting from the increasing r_{max} and search space complexity in rule ordering, the proposed method, called Two-class Classifier Generalized Multiple Attractor Cellular Automata with artificial point (2C2-GMACA) (Ponkaew, et al., 2011; Ponkaew, et al., 2011), is introduced. The 2C2-GMACA is designed based on two class classifier architecture basis. In this regard, two classes are taken to process at a time and a solution is binary answer +1 or -1, which is a pointer to the class label of solution. There are two kinds of attractor basins: a positive attractor basin that returns the +1 as the result and a negative attractor basin, otherwise.

Suppose a system consists of patterns (x_i, y_i), where $x_i \in \{0,1\}^n$ is the ith pattern, and $y_i \in \{L^+, L^-\}$ is the ith class label and $i=1,2,\ldots N$. Let L^+ and L^- be a class label of the positive and negative attractor basins, respectively. Given $x \in \{0,1\}^n$ as an input, the x must be assigned a class label which is a solution to the pattern recognition. The 2C2-GMACA begins with setting the present state (S^t) to x . Then, the S^t will be evolved with the equation (2) to the next state (S^{t+1}). Next, the binary decision function will take S^{t+1} and artificial point *(A)* as parameters as the equation (7) to assign the class.

$$f(S^{(t+1)}, A) = sgn(\sum_{i=0}^{n-1} S_i^{t+1}.A_i - \sum_{i=0}^{n-1} \bar{S}_i^{t+1}.A_i) \tag{7}$$

where

$sgn(\_)$ denotes the sign function.

S_i^{t+1} represents the next state for the ith cell.

A_i represents the artificial point for the ith cell.

$\bar{S}_i^{t+1}$ represents a bit complement of the next state for the ith cell.

(.) denotes "AND" logical operator.

Finally, the x is considered to be a member of the positive attractor basin and returns L^+ if $f(S^{t+1}, A) = +1$, and returns L^-, otherwise.

Example 1: Consider two attractor basins of 4-bit recognizer of 2C2-GMACA with periodic boundary condition given in Fig. 2, they are designed by a rule vector <232,212,178,142> representing in a matrix M, and an artificial point (A) of '0001'. Suppose a class label of the positive (L^+) and the negative attractor basins (L^-) are '1101' and '0010', respectively. For an input x' ='1100', firstly the present state $(S^t; t=0)$ is set to x' and then evolved with the given rule vector to the next state $(S^{t+1}; t+1=1)$ by the equation (2), resulting

$$S^1 = (S_0^0, S_1^0, S_2^0, S_3^0) = (M(0, j_0), M(1, j_1), M(2, j_2), M(3, j_3)) \tag{8}$$

where j_i is the 3 neighbour values ($S_{i-1}^t S_i^t S_{i+1}^t$) for the ith cell decoded in decimal. That is, j_0= $(011)_2$=3, j_1= $(110)_2$=6, j_2= $(100)_2$=4 and j_3= $(001)_2$=1. Thus, the above equation is replaced with the j_i in decimal as following

$$= (M(0,3), M(1,6), M(2,4), M(3,1)) = 1111 \tag{9}$$

Finally, the binary decision function will process the S^{t+1} , which equals "1111" using the artificial point A=0001 as co-parameters resulting in the following

$$f(S^{t+1}, A) = sgn\left(\sum_{i=0}^{n-1} S_i^{t+1}.A_i - \sum_{i=0}^{n-1} \bar{S}_i^{t+1}.A_i\right) = sgn\left((1.0+1.0+1.0+1.1) - \left(\bar{1}.0+\bar{1}.0+\bar{1}.0+\bar{1}.1\right)\right) = +1 \tag{10}$$

The function returns 1 meaning that the input x' is a member of positive attractor basin and then the label '1101' is assigned as the solution.

4.1. 2C2-GMACA with Associative and Nonassociative Memories

Given a set of patterns $Y = \{y_1, y_2 \ldots, y_k\}$ represents original messages; where $y_i \in \{0,1\}^n$ and i=1,2...,k. 2C2-GMACA takes two patterns { y_i , y_j }: $y_i \neq y_j$ and $y_i, y_j \in Y$ to process at a time. For associative memory learning, all possible transient states of the y_i and y_j are generated using the equation (6) with the maximum permissible noise (r_{max}), while all transient states are randomly generated $r \in [0, r_{max}]$ for non-associative memory. Then, all states of y_i and y_j are mapped into the leaf nodes of the positive and negative attractor basins, respectively. After two attractor basins are completely constructed, it will be synthesized by a majority voting technique to arrive at the rule vector. In other word, the rule vector is determined in only one time step which is different from GMACA in that it is iteratively determined through the evolution of heuristic search. In this regard, complexity is the main drawback excluding recognition performance.

According to a binary classifier, 2C2-GMACA conducts multiclass classification by DDAG (Decision Directed Acyclic Graph), One-versus-All, One-versus-One, etc., for example. However, this paper focuses on DDAG approach [28]. Suppose that a set of three patterns $\{y_1, y_2, y_3\}$, where $y_i \in \{0,1\}^n$ and i=1, 2, 3, is constructed using the DDAG scheme. Thus, total number of binary classifier is $(3 \bullet 2/2) = 3$. That is, (1 vs 3), (1 vs 2) and (2 vs 3) and the number of levels is $\lceil log_2 3 \rceil = 2$. A root node is (1 vs 3) contained in the 0th-level. Then, (1 vs 2) and (2 vs 3) are contained in the 1st-level. Finally, the solutions {3, 2, 1} are labeled in the leaf nodes of the 2nd-level. In order to assign a class label for an unknown input $x \in \{0,1\}^n$, it is first evaluated at the root node. The node is exited through the left edge if the binary decision function is -1. On the other hand, it is exited via the right edge if the binary decision function is +1. The x is evaluated until it reaches final level. At this point, a leaf node connecting to the edge of the binary decision function is assigned as the solution.

4.2. Design of Rule Vector

A majority voting rule is utilized to synthesize a rule vector for two attractor basins. It is one time step process which is different from a reverse engineering technique (Maji, et al., 2003; Maji, et al., 2008) using in GMACA. Reverse engineering technique continues reconstructing attractor basins randomly until arriving at the rule vector with the lowest collision. In this regard, 2C2-GMACA's time complexity for ordering the rule is simply O(1). However, it must search for an optimal artificial point which applies evolutionary heuristic search. The 2C2-GMACA synthesis scheme comprises three phases as follows.

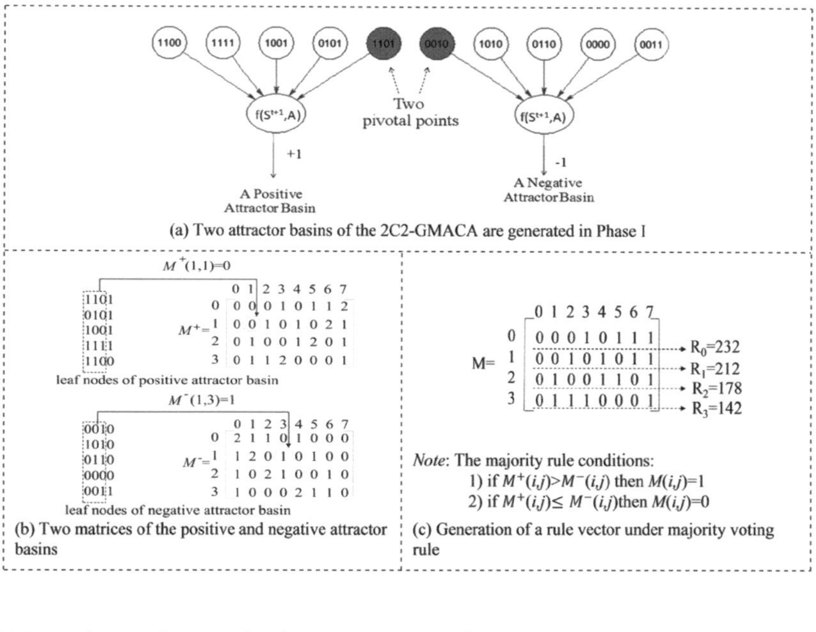

(a) Two attractor basins of the 2C2-GMACA are generated in Phase I

(b) Two matrices of the positive and negative attractor basins

(c) Generation of a rule vector under majority voting rule

Figure 3. GMACA synthesize scheme under the majority voting rule.

Phase I--- Two attractor basins, namely, positive and negative attractor basins, are generated. In this phase, two patterns { y_l , y_m }, where $y_l \neq y_m$ and y_l, $y_m \in Y$ are chosen from a set of learnt patterns to process according to the multiclass classification scheme [28]. Suppose y_l is assigned to a class label of L^+. Thus, the y_m is a class label of L^-. Then, transient states of the y_l and y_m are generated into the leaf nodes of the positive and negative attractor basins, respectively.

Example 1: Fig. 3(a) represents two attractor basins based on associative memory learning of 4 bit patterns with r_{max}=1. Suppose Y={1101, 0010} is a set of learnt patterns. The 2C2-GMA-CA takes two patterns {y_1=1101, y_2=0010} to process according to the multiclass classification algorithm. Let a class label of the positive (L^+) and negative (L^-) attractor basins be '1101' and '0010', respectively. Then, two sets of noisy patterns with r_{max}=1 are generated resulting in {1101, 0101, 1001, 1111, 1100} and {0010, 1010, 0110, 0000, 0011}, respectively. Then, all patterns are mapped into leaf nodes of attractor basins corresponding with its label as shown in Fig. 3(a).

Phase II--- Let M^+ and M^- be matrices with size |nx8|, and $M^+(i,\ j)$ and $M^-(i,\ j)$, where i=0,1,2,...,n-1 and j=0,1,2,...,7, be an element of the matrices M^+ *and* M^-, respectively. The $M^+(i,\ j)$ represents numbers of nodes from the positive attractor basin where the 3 neighbors, ($S^t_{i-1}S^t_iS^t_{i+1}$), for the ith cell is decoded in decimal satisfying the jth column. The negative attractor basin considers the $M^-(i,\ j)$ under the similar condition with the positive one.

Example 2: As shown in Fig. 3(b), two matrices M^+ *and* M^- are constructed with size |4x8|, each element of which is represented the numbers of nodes from corresponding attractor basin. For example, $M^+(1,\ 1)$ represents an element of matrix M^+ at the *1* [st] row and the *1* [st] column; it is a total number of leaf nodes from the positive attractor basin where 3 neighbors ($S^t_0S^t_1S^t_2$) of the *1* [st] cell decoded in decimal equal to *1*, i.e. j=1=001_2=($S^t_{i-1}S^t_iS^t_{i+1}$)$_2$ where i=1.

Phase III--- Rule matrix *M* is determined. The matrix *M* with size |nx8| is the simplified form of the rule vector (*RV*), while an element *M* (*i, j*) represents the next state for the *i* [th] cell, where the 3 neighbor ($S^t_{i-1}S^t_iS^t_{i+1}$) of the cell decoded in decimal equal to *j*. The *M* is designed by comparing between $M^+(i,\ j)$ and $M^-(i,\ j)$, where i=0,1,2,...,n-1 and j=0,1,2,...,7, due to the following conditions:

1) if $M^+(i,\ j) > M^-(i,\ j)$ then $M(i,\ j)=1$

2) if $M^+(i,\ j) \leq M^-(i,\ j)$ then $M(i,\ j)=0$

Fig. 3(c) shows that a rule vector <232, 212, 178, 142> is obtained by the majority voting technique. The rule vector (matrix rule) is utilized to evolve the given pattern in one time step to the pattern at the next time step which becomes one of parameters of the binary decision function.

4.3. Design of Artificial Point

An artificial point (A) takes a major role in the binary decision function. It interprets the next state (S^{t+1}) in features space to be a pointer identifying the class label of solution. In this respect, Genetic Algorithm (GA) (Holland, 1992; Buhmann, et al., 1989) is implemented to determine the optimal artificial point. A chromosome with n genes in GA represents an n-bit artificial point as follows:

$$chromosome = \left[b_0 \, b_1 \, b_2 \ldots \, b_{n-1} \right] \tag{11}$$

Selection is done by using a random pairing approach and a traditional single point cross-over is also performed by random at the same point of the n element array of the selected two parents. Mutation makes a small change in the bits in the list of a chromosome with a small percentage. The fitness function is calculated as a cost for each chromosome. It is created from a true positive (TP) and a false positive (FP) of the confusion matrix (Simon, et al., 2010) calculated by the below equation (8). The fitness function is given as following

$$Fitness = 1 - \frac{TP}{TP + FP} \tag{12}$$

The search space complexity for rule ordering of the 2C2-GMACA is the all possible patterns of the artificial point, *000…000 to 111….111*, which is 2^n, i.e. $O(2^n)$.

5. Performance Evaluation

This section reports performance evaluation of the proposed method in comparison with GMACA on a set of measured matrices consisting of search space and classification complexities, recognition percentage, evolution time for rule ordering, and effects of the number of pivotal point, permissible noises, p-parameter, pattern size on error correcting problem.

5.1. Reduction of Search Space

Given a set of learnt patterns $Y = \{y_1, y_2 \ldots, y_k\}$, where $y_i \in \{0,1\}^n$ and i=1,2…,k, is original messages. The 2C2-GMACA and GMACA based associative memory learning will generate all transient states using the equation (6) with the maximum permissible noise (r_{max}). Then, the transient states are constructed to be attractor basins.

Theorem 1: In training phase, a search space complexity of the GMACA (S_{GMACA}) depends on parameters of bit patterns (n), the maximum permissible noise (r_{max}) and the maximum permissible height (h_{max}), while the search space complexity of 2C2-GMACA ($S_{2C2\text{-}GMACA}$) depends only on a parameter n.

Proof: From the set $Y=\{y_1, y_2 \ldots, y_k\}$, GMACA constructs k attractor basins randomly until a satisfied rule vector is acquired. Thus, the search space of the GMACA (S_{GMACA}) is all possible patterns of k attractor basins defined by

$$S_{GMACA} = G^k \tag{13}$$

where G is the number of learnt patterns in each attractor basin previously defined by Cayley 's formula (Maji, et al., 2003) as follows:

$$G = p^{p-2} \tag{14}$$

where p is the number of possible transient states calculated from (6). Therefore, the above equation is defined following

$$S_{GMACA} = [\sum_{r=0}^{r_{\max}} \binom{n}{r}^{\sum_{r=0}^{r_{\max}} \binom{n}{r} - 2}]^k \in O(n!) \tag{15}$$

It shows that search space complexity of GMACA is factorial growth $O(n!)$, which depends on parameters n and r_{max}. In real world application, it must face a severe search space in which the search heuristics cannot reach the optimal solution if n or r_{max} is considered at a high number. In this regard, GMACA tries to examine the optimal values of the r_{max} and h_{max}. GMACA shows that the search space complexity can be reduced to $O(n^n)$ if the r_{max}=1 as shown following

$$S_{GMACA} = (n+1)^{kn-k} \in O(n^n) \tag{16}$$

The search space complexity in Maji, et al., 2003 and Maji, et al., 2008 is examined under the h_{max}=*2* and the r_{max}=*1* as described below.

$$S_{GMACA} = n^k \in O\left(n^c\right); c > 1 \tag{17}$$

For the proposed 2C2-GMACA, the search space is the number of possible patterns (G) of artificial point: *000…000 to 111….111*—that is; 2^n. Due to DDAG approach for multiclass classification algorithm, the machine consists of $k(k\text{-}1)/2$ binary classifier. Thus, the search space complexity of the 2C2-GMACA ($S_{2C2\text{-}GMACA}$) is:

$$\begin{aligned} S_{2C2-GMACA} &= \frac{k(k-1)}{2} G \\ &\cong k^2(2^n) \in O(2^n) \end{aligned} \tag{18}$$

When comparing the search space complexity between GMACA and 2C2-GMACA, we found that GMACA can only be implemented if it is considered at the h_{max}=2 and r_{max} =1, while 2C2-GMACA can be implemented whatsoever with the exact solution through heuristic search. This corresponds to the reports in Maji, et al., 2003 and Maji, et al., 2008, the GMACA provides the best performance of pattern recognition when it is trained with the r_{max}=1 and h_{max}=2. However, the percentage of recognition in testing is also high if the Hamming distance of patterns is less than or equal to 1 and it is decreased sharply when the Hamming distance is greater than 1.

5.2. Reduction of Classification Complexity

Theorem 2: In worst case scenario of learning based on associative memory model, the classification complexity of *n*-bit pattern for GMACA is $O(n^2)$, while 2C2-GMACA is $O(n)$.

Proof: In general, time spent in classifying *n* nodes of GMACA depends on an arrangement of nodes in attractor basins. At worst, the attractor basin is a linear tree. Thus, time for classifying *n* nodes is the summation of the number of traversal paths from each node to a pivotal point. For example, the number of traversal paths of a pivotal point is 0 while the nth-node is (n-1). This can be solved by arithmetic series (S_n). Given the common different *d* is 1 and an initial term (a_1) is 0, the equation in determining the summation is given as follows.

$$\begin{aligned} S_n &= \frac{n}{2}[2a_1 + (n-1)d] \\ &= \frac{n}{2}[2(0) + (n-1)(1)] \\ &= (\frac{n^2}{2} - \frac{n}{2}) \in O(n^2) \end{aligned} \tag{19}$$

As being designed the height of attractor basis of 2C2-GMACA is limited to 1, the time of classifying *n* nodes is n , *ie*. $O(n)$.

5.3. Performance Analysis of 2C2-GMACA on Associative Memory

Pattern classifiers based on an associative memory is independent from the number of patterns to be learnt, because all possible distorted patterns are generated into learning system. Suppose a set of pivotal points $Y = \{y_1, y_2 \ldots, y_k\}$, where $y_i \in \{0,1\}^n$ and i=1, 2…, *k*, is original messages. 2C2-GMACA takes two pivotal points { y_l , y_m }, where y_l, $y_m \in Y$, $y_l \neq y_m$ and *l*, *m*=1, 2…,*k*, to process at a time using the DDAG scheme. Thus, the number of classifiers of the 2C2-GMACA is $k \bullet (k - 1)/2$, while GMACA takes all pivotal points to process at once.

5.3.1. Recognition and Evolution Time

This section reports recognition rate and evolution time for rule ordering between 2C2-GMACA and GMACA based on associative memory. Table 1 presents the recognition rate at different sizes of bit patterns (*n*) and the number of attractor basins (*k*). It generates patterns with maximum permissible noise in training phase (r_{max}) and testing with different sizes of noise r; $r \in (1, r_{max})$. Table 2 presents the evolution time in second for the genetic algorithm in determining the well-fitting attractor basins and artificial point with different values of n and k. The results show that 2C2-GMACA is superior to GMACA both recognition performance and times spent in rule ordering. This corresponds the previous mention that search space is the major problem of GMACA for ordering the rules when deals with high number of r_{max}.

5.3.2. Effects of Number of Pivotal Points and Pattern Size

A pivotal point in 2C2-GMACA represents an original message in communication systems. Fig. 4 shows the effects of the number of pivotal points (k) in the recognition performance of the proposed 2C2-GMACA based on associative memory learning at a particular r_{max} and bit pattern. It shows that if is trained by r_{max}= 3 the recognition rate is almost 100% when the number of bit noises (r) is not greater than 5 no matter of the number of classes (k), and declined sharply when the number of bit noises increases. The less the number of classes, the better the recognition performance. Fig. 5 shows the effects of the number of bit pattern in recognition performance of the 2C2-GMACA based on associative memory learning by fixing r_{max} and the number of classes (k). In this regard, when the number of bit noises in testing increases, the recognition of different number of bit patterns decreases in distinguishable manner. The more the number of bit patterns, the less the recognition performance.

5.4. Performance Analysis of 2C2-GMACA on Non-Associative Memory

The memory capacity becomes a serious problem of pattern classifier based on an associative memory learning if the classfier deal with the high values of n, r_{max} and k. It generates a large number of transient states. In ordet to solve this problem, the 2C2-GMACA based on non-associtive memory is presented. The transient states will be generated by randomly choosing bit noise $r \in (0, r_{max})$, the number of which is limited into some number $p; p \in I^+$.

5.4.1. Effects of Maximum Permissible Noise and P-Parameter

In order to examine the effects of the maximum permissible noise r_{max} on the error correcting problem of 2C2-GMACA based non-associative memory, two pivotal points are randomly generated and then the number of transient states is limited to some number $p; p \in I^+$. Thus, the transient states are randomly generated from the equation (6) using $r \in (0, r_{max})$ until the number of states equals to p. This method is called uniform distribution learning. Fig. 6 shows the effects of the r_{max} at $1/4 \bullet n$, $2/4 \bullet n$ and $3/4 \bullet n$; where n=100 and n is bits pattern. The number of pivotal points (k) and transient states (p) is fixed to 2 and 2000, respectively. Results are plotted in the inverted bell curve. It shows that the 2C2-GMACA has the lowest capability in range of $r \in (0 , 1/2 \bullet n)$ if it is trained by the $r_{max} \approx 3/4 \bullet n$, which opposed to the r_{max}= $1/2 \bullet n$. However, overall average percentage of the r_{max} $\approx 3/4 \bullet n$ is the highest value.

The effects of the number of transient states (p ; $p \in I^+$) for two attractor basins (k=2) are examined and shown in Fig. 7. During the training phase, the number of bit pattern (n) is set to 100, while the maximum permissible noise (r_{max}) is set nearly to $3/4 \bullet n \approx 75$. Then, the percentage of recognition is observed at different numbers of p---that is 2000, 4000 and 10000. The results show that the average percentage of recognition is highest if it is trained with the highest number of p. However, it is memory consumptions as already mentioned.

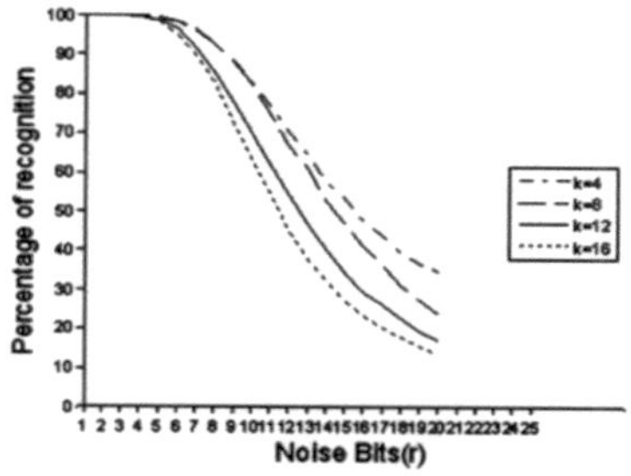

n=50 and r_{max}=3

Figure 4. The effect of k-parameter on the percentage of recognition of 2C2-GMACA based on associative memory.

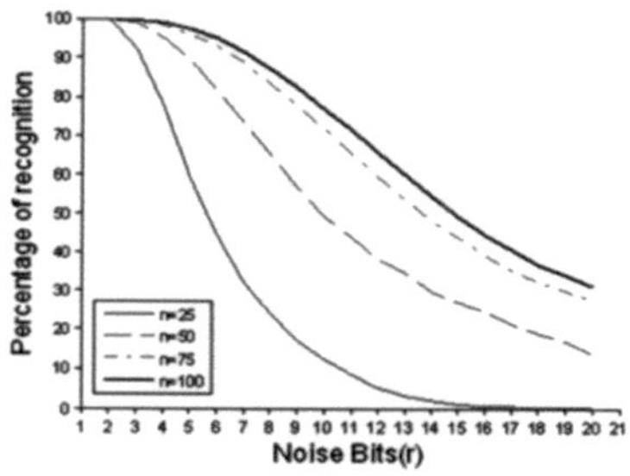

k=15 and r_{max}=2

Figure 5. The effect of n-parameter on the percentage of recognition of 2C2-GMACA based on associative memory.

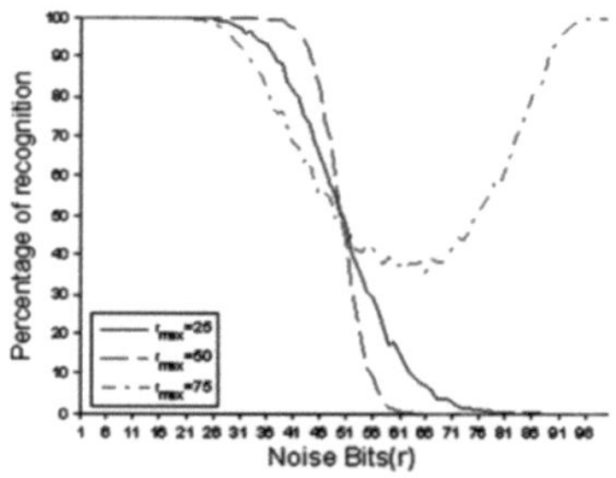

n=100, k=2 and p=2000

Figure 6. The effect of r_{max} parameter on the percentage of recognition of 2C2-GMACA based on non-associative memory.

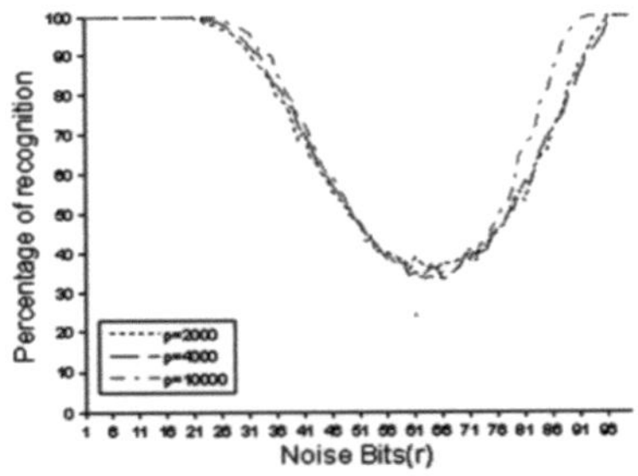

n=100, k=2 and r_{max}=75

Figure 7. The effect of *p*-parameter on the percentage of recognition of 2C2-GMACA based on non-associative memory.

6. Conclusions and Discussions

This chapter presents a non-uniform cellular automata-based algorithm with binary classifier, called Two-class Classifier Generalized Multiple Attractor Cellular Automata with artificial point (2C2-GMACA), for pattern recognition. The 2C2-GMACA is built around the simple structure of evolving non-uniform cellular automata called attractor basin, and classify the patterns on the basis of two-class classifier architecture similar to support vector machines. To reduce computational time complexity in ordering the rules, 2C2-GMACA is limited the height of attractor basin to 1, while GMACA can have its height to n, where n is a number of bit pattern. Genetic algorithm is utilized to determine the CA's best rules for classification. In this regard, GMACA designs one chromosome consists of k-genes, where k is a number of classes (target patterns) to be classified. This leads to abundant state spaces and combinatorial explosion in computation, especially when a number of bit noises increases. For the design of 2C2-GMACA, a chromosome represents an artificial point which is consists of n-bit pattern. Consequently, the state space is minimal and feasible in computation in general pattern recognition problem. The 2C2-GMACA reduces search space for ordering a rule vector from GMACA which is $O(n^n)$ to $O(1)+O(2^n)$. In addition, multiple errors correcting problem is empirically experimented in comparison between the proposed method and GMACA based on associative and non-associative memories for performance evaluation. The results show that the proposed method provides the 99.98% recognition rate superior to GMACA which reports 72.50% when used associative memory, and 95.00% and 64.30% when used non-associative memory, respectively. For computational times in ordering the rules through genetic algorithm, the proposed method provides 7 to 14 times faster than GMACA. These results suggests the extension of 2C2-GMACA to other pattern recognition tasks. In this respect, we are improving and extending the 2C2-GMACA to cope with complicated patterns in which state of the art methods, SVM, ANN, etc., for example, poorly report the classification performance, and hope to report our findings soon.

http://dx.doi.org/10.5772/52364

Author details

Sartra Wongthanavasu[1*] and Jetsada Ponkaew[2]

*Address all correspondence to: wongsar@kku.ac.th

1 Machine Learning and Intelligent Systems (MLIS) Laboratory, Department of Computer Science, Faculty of Science, Khon Kaen University, Khon Kaen, Thailand

2 Cellular Automata and Knowledge Engineering (CAKE) Laboratory, Department of Computer Science, Faculty of Science, Khon Kaen University, Khon Kaen, Thailand

References

[1] Neumann, J.V. (1966). Theory of Self-Reproducing Automata. University of Illinois Press.

[2] Wongthanavasu, S., & Sadananda, R. (2003). A CA-based edge operator and its performance evaluation. *Journal of Visual Communication and Image Representation*, 14, 2, 83-96.

[3] Wongthanavasu, S., & Lursinsap, C. (2004). A 3D CA-based edge operator for 3D images. *in Image Processing*, ICIP'04. 2004 International Conference on, 2004, 235-238.

[4] Wongthanavasu, S., & Tangvoraphonkchai, V. (2007). Cellular Automata-Based Algorithm and its Application in Medical Image Processing. *Image Processing*, ICIP 2007. IEEE International Conference on, 2007, 41-44.

[5] Rosin, P.L. (2006). Training cellular automata for image processing. *IEEE Transactions on Image Processing*, 15(7), 2076-2087.

[6] Wolfram, S. (1994). Cellular automata and complexity: collected papers. Addison-Wesley Pub. Co.

[7] Delgado, O.G., Encinas, L.H., White, S.H., Rey, A.M.d. and Sanchez, G.R.,. (2005). Characterization of the reversibility of Wolfram cellular automata with rule number 150 and periodic boundary conditions. *INFORMATION*, 8(4), 483-492.

[8] Das, S., & Chowdhury, D. R. (2008). An Efficient n x n Boolean Mapping Using Additive Cellular Automata. *Proceedings of the 8th international conference on Cellular Automata for Reseach and Industry*, Yokohama, Japan Springer-Verlag,, 168-173.

[9] Maji, P., Shaw, C., Ganguly, N., Sikdar, B.K., & Chaudhuri, P.P. (2003). Theory and application of cellular automata for pattern classification. *Fundam. Inf.*, 58(3-4), 321-354.

[10] Chady, M., Chady, a. M., & Poli, R. (1997). Evolution of Cellular-automaton-based Associative Memories. *Technical Report CSRP-97-15*, University of Birmingham, School of Computer Science, May.

[11] Ganguly, N., Maji, P., Sikdar, B.K., & Chaudhuri, P.P. (2002). Generalized Multiple Attractor Cellular Automata (GMACA) For Associative Memory. *International Journal of Pattern Recognition and Artificial Intelligence, Special Issue: Computational Intelligence for Pattern Recognition*, 16(7), 781-795.

[12] Maji, P., Ganguly, N., & Chaudhuri, P.P. (2003). Error correcting capability of cellular automata based associative memory. *Systems, Man and Cybernetics, Part A: Systems and Humans, IEEE Transactions on*, 33(4), 466-480.

[13] Maji, P., & Chaudhuri, P.P. (2008). Non-uniform cellular automata based associative memory: Evolutionary design and basins of attraction. *Information Sciences*, 178(10), 2315-2336.

[14] Niloy, G., Maji, P., Sikdar, B.K., & Chaudhuri, P.P. (2004). Design and characterization of cellular automata based associative memory for pattern recognition. *Systems, Man, and Cybernetics, Part B: Cybernetics, IEEE Transactions on*, 34(1), 672-678.

[15] Tan, S.K., & Guan, S.U. (2007). Evolving Cellular Automata to Generate Nonlinear Sequences with Desirable Properties. *Applied Soft Computing*, 7(3), 1131-1134.

[16] Shannon, C.E., & Weaver, W. (1949). The Mathematical Theory of Communication. *Univ. of Illinois Press Urbana*.

[17] de Oliveira, P.P.B., Bortot, J.C., & Oliveira, G.M.B. (2006). The best currently known class of dynamically equivalent cellular automata rules for density classification. *Neurocomputing*, 70(1-3), 35-43.

[18] Sipper, M. (1996). Co-evolving Non-Uniform Cellular Automata to Perform Computations.

[19] Holland, J.H. (1992). Adaptation in natural and artificial systems. MIT Press.

[20] Oh, H. (2001). Application of a Heuristic Search to the Deadlock Avoidance Algorithm that Achieves the High Concurrency. *INFORMATION*, 4(4).

[21] Shuai, D., Dong, Y., & Shuai, Q. (2007). A new data clustering. approach Generalized cellular automata. *Information Systems*, 32(7), 968-977.

[22] Jie, Y., & Binggang, C. (2002). Study on an Improved Genetic Algorithm. *INFORMATION*, 5(4).

[23] Ponkaew, J., Wongthanavasu, S., & Lursinsap, C. (2011). A nonlinear classifier using an evolution of Cellular Automata,. *Intelligent Signal Processing and Communications Systems (ISPACS)*, 2011 International Symposium on, 1-5.

[24] Ponkaew, J., Wongthanavasu, S., & Lursinsap, C. (2011). Two-class classifier cellular automata. *Industrial Electronics and Applications (ISIEA)*, 2011 IEEE Symposium on, 354-359.

[25] Buhmann, J., Divko, R., & Schulten, K. (1989). Associative memory with high information content. *Physical Review A*, 39(5), 2689-2692.

[26] Simon, D., & Simon, D.L. (2010). Analytic Confusion Matrix Bounds for Fault Detection and Isolation Using a Sum-of-Squared-Residuals Approach. *Reliability, IEEE Transactions on*, 59(2), 287-296.

Chapter 4

Using Cellular Automata and Global Sensitivity Analysis to Study the Regulatory Network of the L-Arabinose Operon

Advait A. Apte, Stephen S. Fong and Ryan S. Senger

Additional information is available at the end of the chapter

http://dx.doi.org/10.5772/52085

1. Introduction

The field of computational biologyhas grown significantly in recent years, allowing researchers to investigatecomplex biological systems *in silico.* In this chapter, a new method of combining cellular automata (CA) with global sensitivity analysis (GSA) is introduced. This method has the potential to determine which mechanisms of a regulated biological network contribute to characteristics such as stability and responsiveness. For dynamic models of biochemical reactions and networks, determining the correct values ofthe kineticparameters that govern the system is often problematic[12, 13, 19, 29, 30, 33, 36, 46, 47, 49, 50, 55, 57]. This isoften due to the difficulty ofobtaining accurate experimental measurements ofvital kineticconstants[6, 10, 17, 21, 32, 37]. This is currently the case for biochemical reactions occurring in complex environments *in vivo* that cannot be approximated through more simple experiments*in vitro*.Complex gene regulatory networks are a prime example.Modelling these systems using aCA approach allows researchers to easily change kineticparameter values (individuallyand in combination) to study their effects on system function[4, 7, 8, 25, 38, 51]. Since the overall system function (i.e., the output molecule or action) is something that can be measured easily, CA modelling provides a method for determining "difficult-to-measure" parameters using "easy-to-measure" observations of the system being studied.However, the real challenge after conducting a CA study with combinatorial parameter variation is interpreting the results. It has been found that GSAis an extremely useful tool for identifying the parameters that most significantly affect overall model performance[9, 11, 16, 24, 28, 31, 44, 45, 56]. In this chapter,a new approach that combinesCA and GSA is applied for analysing regulatory mechanisms of the L-arabinose (*ara*) operon. In particular, the influence of the negative autoregulatory (NAR) action of the transcription factor AraC on system dynamics and stability is calculated. The purpose of this chapter is to provide instruction through a detailed example of how to apply CA and GSA simultaneously to analysea biological network that must be studied *in vivo*. An in-depth explanation of GSA and the regulatory elements of the *ara* operon are provided in the Introduction. Detailed descriptions of CA model building and system parameters as well as a comprehensive GSA tutorial are presented in the Materials and Methods section.Computational experiments illuminating the influence of the NAR mechanism on the studied regulatory network are presented and discussed throughout the rest of thechapter.

1.1. Global sensitivity analysis

GSA uses Monte Carlo simulations to calculate the outputs of a model over the entire range of all input parameters [39, 40]. This variance-based method calculates the contribution of each input parameter to the total variability of the model output. In other words, GSA is used to determine which inputs most significantly influence the output. This provides the investigator one or multiple targets that can be manipulated to effectively engineer the system. GSA differs significantly from the traditionally used method of partial gradient-based sensitivity analysis (SA). With traditional SA, the change in a model output is calculated by allowing only one parameter to vary, while keeping others constant. This variance in the model output is likely to change if all other parameters are held constant at different values. The GSA approach takes this into account and enables the consideration of multiple parameters simultaneously over the entire range of each parameter. To consider the model output variance caused by only a single parameter is a "first-order" analysis. Two parameters may be considered simultaneously to develop a measure of their interactions in a "second-order" analysis. Or, a single parameter can be considered with is interactions with all other parameters in the model. This is called the "total effect index" [39, 40]. Thus, another significant advantage of GSA over SA is that GSA accounts for the influence and interactions between input parameters over the entire input space. A simplified tutorial of GSA has been published for a deterministic ammonia emissions model [35]. The GSA methods are also presented in detail in this chapter for the *ara* operon model system.

1.2. The L-arabinose operon

Transcriptional regulation networks are largely made up of recurring regulatory patterns called network motifs. These network motifs have been shown to carry out many signal transduction functions[2, 3, 27, 48]. One of the most abundantly found network motifs is thenegative autoregulation (NAR) motif. In an NAR motif, a transcription factor (TF) negatively regulates the promoter of its own gene or operon. This has been found to

1. dramatically increase response acceleration and

2. increase the stability of the gene product concentration response to noise [26, 41].

The L-arabinose system is an example of an NAR network.L-arabinose,which is a five-carbon sugar foundin plant cell walls, is used as a carbon source by many organisms. The *ara* operon contains genes encoding enzymes leading to L-arabinose catabolism. The selective usage of the *ara* operon isone of the best-studied gene regulation systems and is well-characterized[5, 15, 22, 23, 34, 42, 52, 59]. The entire arabinose system consists of the following:

1. the system specific transcription factor (TF) *araC,*
2. the arabinose transporters (*araE, araFGH,* and *araJ*), and
3. the *ara* operon containing the arabinose catalytic enzymes, *araBAD.*

Ultimately, the *ara* operon is responsible for the conversion of arabinose to D-xylulose-5-phosphate, which then enters the pentose phosphate pathway. The AraC TF regulates the *ara* operon [1, 14, 18, 20, 26, 52, 54, 59].Recent studies have shown that *araC*and the *ara* operon share a common regulatory protein,cAMP Receptor Protein (CRP),which is activated by cAMP. AraC both activates and represses the *ara* operonusing a DNA looping mechanism. As a negative regulator, AraC isde-activated by L-arabinose, allowing transcription of the *ara* operon. AraC represses its own promoter through a NAR motif[1, 14, 26, 43, 58].

1.3. Goals of the Modelling Effort

In this research, the overall influence of NAR on the dynamics of a regulated biological network was studied by applying a unique combination of CA and GSA. Here, the expression of *araBAD* was calculated in the

1. presence and
2. absence of NAR by AraC.

The CA approach was used to simulate this network given altered kinetic rate constants and initial concentrations. Then, the GSA approach was applied to determine which of these parameters most directly influence *araBAD* expression. When applied to the

1. presence and
2. absence of NAR, the difference in GSA results give clues to the influence of the NAR mechanism in regulating the system dynamics.

In the case studied in this research, NAR was found to equally distribute model sensitivity across all input parameters. This dramatically increases stability and responsivenessof the regulatory network. The approach presented in this chapter of combining CA and GSA can be applied to virtually any biologicalnetwork using the methods presented in this chapter.

2. Methods

2.1. Model Construction

The *ara* operon model was constructed using NetLogo simulation environment [53]. To perform a CA simulation, individual (agents) (i.e., interacting molecules) were allowed to move among (cells) (i.e., spatial locations) inside the simulation environment and undergobiochemical reactions with other agents in their Von Neumann neighbourhood. In all simulations, a two-dimensional16 x 16 matrix of cells was used as the simulation environment, and 10 time steps were executed. Whether a reaction occurs between interacting agents is governed by probability. The agents of the *ara* operon model are:

1. L-arabinose,
2. cAMP,
3. AraC (the TF regulator),
4. CRP, and
5. AraBAD (representing gene products of the *ara* operon).

Characteristics and reaction rules for individual agents were predefined at model initialization in NetLogo. Basal expression levels for CRP, AraC, and AraBAD were set at 10, 0, and 0 cells respectively.The number of agents occupying cells represents concentration in agent based modelling. For example, CRP was present in 10 cells of the simulation environment upon initializing the simulation. Specifics of the varied model parameters are discussed in detail in the next section. These included

1. the concentrations of L-arabinose and cAMP,
2. the probabilities of biochemical reactions, and
3. NAR by ArgC.

Monte Carlo methods were used to select 2000 values of each parameter to perform CA simulations. This was followed by 1000 independent iterations of the model to perform GSA. The CA simulation records activation of the *ara* operon measured as number of AraBAD agents present in cells at the end of the simulation. Simulations are also often run to record the number of model "events" required to reach a specified concentration of an agent of interest (e.g., AraBAD). Independent simulations use different values of the varied parameters, resulting in different values of the targeted agent. Two common approaches use

1. a set number of model events to derive a target agent or
2. a different number of model events required to reach a specified concentration of the target agent.

The first approach was used in this study. Two different scenarios for NAR byAraC regulation were simulated in this research:

1. AraC is not allowed to negatively autoregulate its own promoter and
2. NAR by AraC is allowed.

These simulations seek to understand the influence of the NAR mechanism on overall rigidity and robustness of the *ara* operon regulatory network.

http://dx.doi.org/10.5772/52085

2.2. System parameters

A mathematical model was created to simulate the dynamics of *ara* operon activation in the presence and absence of NAR by AraC. CA was applied by allowing critical parameters to vary over thousands of simulations of the system. GSA was then applied to the results to determine which system parameters most influence *ara* operon activation.The following parameters were taken into consideration while building and simulating the model. The upper and lower bounds of the parameters and a description of their functions are described in detail below.

Simulation	**1**	**2**	**...**	**1000**
Parameter				
conc_cAMP	105	188	...	32
conc_arabinose	159	179	...	244
rate_CRP_activate	0.019	0.103	...	0.500
rate_araC_activate	0.418	0.391	...	0.406
rate_araBAD_activate	0.577	0.326	...	0.445
rate_araC_autoreg	0	0	...	0
Output (Y_1)	**9**	**3**	**...**	**296**

Table 1. The *M1* matrix of GSA.

1. *conc_arabinose*: The initial concentration of L-arabinose was allowed to vary between 1 and 250 cells. Upon binding,L-arabinoseactivates the TF and autoregulatorAraC.Unbound AraC inhibits transcription of the *ara* operon.

2. *conc_cAMP*: Initial concentration of the second messenger cAMP was allowed to vary between 1 to 250cells. cAMP binds to CRP causing its activation. The cAMP-CRP positively regulates transcription of the *ara* operon.

3. *rate_CRP_activate*: This parameter controls the probability of CRP activation by cAMP. This parameter was varied between 0 and 1 for the simulations described in this chapter. This probability parameter represents the rate of activation of CRP.

4. *rate_araC_activate*: This parameter controls the probability of AraC activation by L-arabinose and was allowed to vary between 0 and 1.This probabilityultimately controlsthe activity of the *araC*gene and transcription of the *ara* operon.

5. *rate_araBAD_activate*: This parameter controls the probability of *araBAD* activation by CRP and was allowed tovary between 0 and 1.

6. *rate_araC_autoreg*: This parameter controls the NARbyAraC protein and was allowed tovary between 0 and 1.Thisrepresents the rate at which AraC supresses its promoter.

2.3. Global sensitivity analysis

GSA was performed on the *ara* operon activation model described in this chapter. The following step-by-step tutorial is given to combine CA with GSA.

The procedure starts with the derivation of the *M1* and *M2* matrices shown in Tables 1 and 2, respectively. To build each table, 1000 CA simulations were run given random values of the system parameters. For each simulation, the model output (activated *araBAD*or expressed AraBAD) was calculated and recorded. The estimated unconditional means ($\hat{E}_Y$) and estimated unconditional variances ($\hat{V}_Y$) of the model outputs were calculated for both matrices according to the following, where *N* is the number of simulations (i.e., 1000 for this study).

$$\hat{E}_{Y_1} = \frac{1}{N}\sum_{i=1}^{N} Y_1^{(i)} \qquad \hat{E}_{Y_2} = \frac{1}{N}\sum_{i=1}^{N} Y_2^{(i)} \tag{1}$$

$$\hat{V}_{Y_1} = \frac{1}{N-1}\sum_{i=1}^{N}\left(Y_1^{(i)}\right)^2 - \left(\hat{E}_{Y_1}\right)^2 \qquad \hat{V}_{Y_2} = \frac{1}{N-1}\sum_{i=1}^{N}\left(Y_2^{(i)}\right)^2 - \left(\hat{E}_{Y_2}\right)^2 \tag{2}$$

Next, the *P* matrix was created for the calculation of the first-order sensitivity index for each model parameter. To illustrate this example, the model parameter *conc_cAMP*was used. The *P* matrix for this case is shown in Table 3.

The *P* matrix consists of the *conc_cAMP*parameter values from matrix *M2*, and all other parameters are assigned their values from *M1*. Then model outputs were calculated for the *P* matrix using these new inputs. Thus, 1000 more simulations are required for each parameter a first-order sensitivity index is desired. The first-order sensitivity index (S_{conc_cAMP}) was calculated by the following.

$$U_P = \frac{1}{N-1}\sum_{i=1}^{N} Y_1^{(i)} Y_P^{(i)} \tag{3}$$

$$S_{conc\_cAMP} = 1 - \left(\frac{U_p - \hat{E}_{Y1}\hat{E}_{Y2}}{\hat{V}_{Y1}}\right) \tag{4}$$

Next, the total effect index was calculated by creation of the *R* matrix for each parameter. The first-order index describes the influence of a single parameter on the model output directly. The total effect index takes into account all interactions of a parameter with all other parameters when determining the effect on model output.

Simulation	**1**	**2**	**...**	**1000**
Parameter				
conc_cAMP	190	189	...	227
conc_arabinose	67	212	...	208
rate_CRP_activate	0.887	0.281	...	0.671
rate_araC_activate	0.638	0.413	...	0.693
rate_araBAD_activate	0.530	0.620	...	0.891
rate_araC_autoreg	0	0	...	0
Output (Y_2)	**608**	**93**	**...**	**3043**

Table 2. The *M2* matrix of GSA.

Simulation	**1**	**2**	**...**	**1000**
Parameter				
conc_cAMP (M2)	190	189	...	227
conc_arabinose (M1)	159	179	...	244
rate_CRP_activate (M1)	0.019	0.103	...	0.500
rate_araC_activate (M1)	0.418	0.391	...	0.406
rate_araBAD_activate (M1)	0.577	0.326	...	0.445
rate_araC_autoreg (M1)	0	0	...	0
Output (Y_P)	**12**	**196**	**...**	**6**

Table 3. The *P* matrix of GSA.

The *R* matrix is shown in Table 4 for the *conc_cAMP*parameter example. To build the *R* matrix, the parameter values from *M1* for *conc_cAMP*were used along with parameter values from *M2* for all other parameters. An additional 1000 CA simulations are required to calculate the model outputs for the *R* matrix. The calculation of the total effect index for rcAMP ($S_{T(conc\_cAMP)}$) was calculated as follows.

$$U_R = \frac{1}{N-1}\sum_{i=1}^{N} Y_1^{(i)} Y_R^{(i)} \tag{5}$$

$$S_{T(conc\_cAMP)} = 1 - \left(\frac{U_R - \hat{E}_{Y1}^2}{\hat{V}_{Y1}} \right) \quad (6)$$

3. Results

The CA modeling of the *ara* operon was performed for two cases

1. without NAR (i.e., negative autoregulation) by AraC and
2. with NAR by AraC (as is observed experimentally).

GSA was applied to both cases in order to determine how the NAR mechanism impacts overall system dynamics. To simulate the model without NAR, the parameter *rate_araC_autoreg* was held constant at 0. The results of the GSA calculations derived from Eqs. 1-6 and the values in Tables 1-4 are given in Table 5. This case was simulated without NAR by AraC.

Simulation	**1**	**2**	**...**	**1000**
Parameter				
conc_cAMP (M1)	105	188	...	32
conc_arabinose (M2)	67	212	...	208
rate_CRP_activate (M2)	0.887	0.281	...	0.671
rate_araC_activate (M2)	0.638	0.413	...	0.693
rate_araBAD_activate (M2)	0.530	0.620	...	0.891
rate_araC_autoreg (M2)	0	0	...	0
Output (Y_R)	**288**	**519**	**...**	**324**

Table 4. The *R* matrix of GSA.

The first-order sensitivity indices for each system parameter for the *ara* operonmodel without NAR by AraCare reported in Fig. 1. These values are reported as a percentage of the summation of all first-order index values. When interactions between single parameters are not taken into consideration, the probability of CRP activation was found to be the single most important parameter significantly influencing the *araBAD*activation(29.58%).All other parameters show similar influence (~17%). The total effect indices for the *ara* operon model without NAR by AraC is shown in Fig. 2. When all the interactions between all parameters were considered, probability of CRP activation (*rate_CRP_activate* parameter) was shown to have most influence (29.47%) over *araBAD*activation. The more noticeable result is the small contribution from the initial concentration of L-arabinose (*conc_arabinose* parameter). This is

http://dx.doi.org/10.5772/52085

significant because the *ara* operon is known to require the presence of L-arabinose to be active in the cell.

Calculation	Value
$\hat{E}_{Y_{1_1}}$(estimated unconditional mean of *M1*)	256.78
$\hat{E}_{Y_{1_2}}$(estimated unconditional mean of *M2*)	228.49
$\hat{V}_{Y_1}$(estimated unconditional variance of *M1*)	309411.56
$\hat{V}_{Y_2}$(estimated unconditional variance of *M2*)	N/A
U_P	4210.45
S_{conc_cAMP}(first-order sensitivity index of conc_cAMP)	0.18
U_R	83451.88
$S_{T(conc\_cAMP)}$(total effect index of conc_cAMP)	0.94

Table 5. GSA calculations for the *rcAMP* parameter

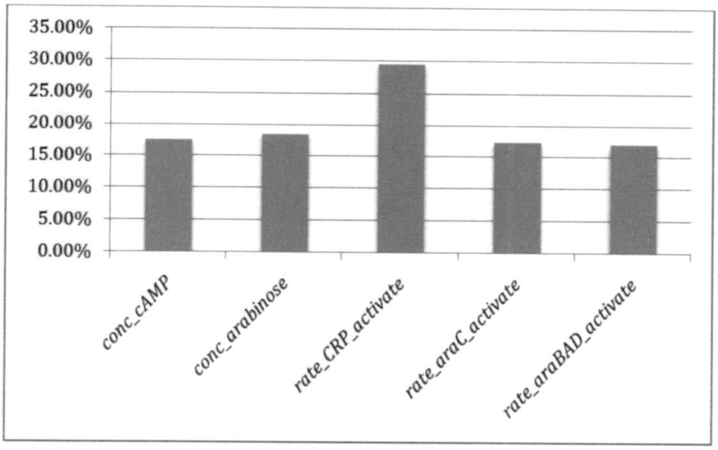

Figure 1. First-order indices calculated by GSA for the case without NAR by AraC.

The first-order indices for each parameter for the *ara* operonmodel with NAR by AraC are reported in Fig. 3. By activating the NAR role of AraC, the first-order indices show very close index values for all parameters (~16.5%). In other words, the NAR reduced the excessive influence of CRP activation over *araBAD*activation. The total effect indices are shown in Fig. 4. A pattern similar to that revealed by first-order indices was obtained. All total effect indices were also similar for all parameters (~16.5%).Adding the NAR by AraCto the regulation network dramatically increased the influence of L-arabinose concentration on *araBAD*activation.

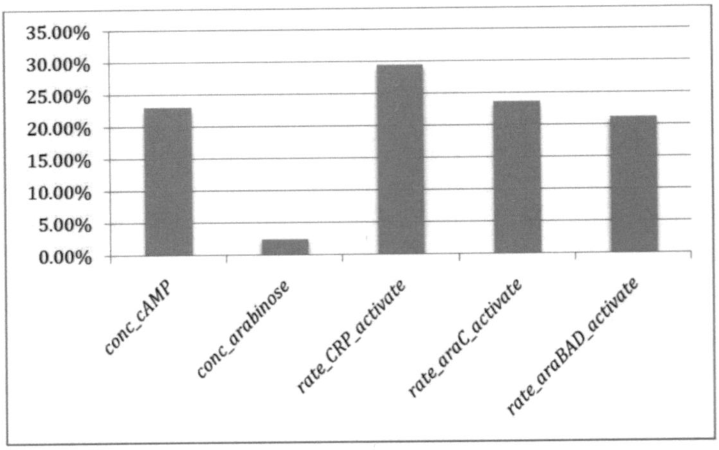

Figure 2. Total effect indices calculated by GSA for the case without NAR by AraC.

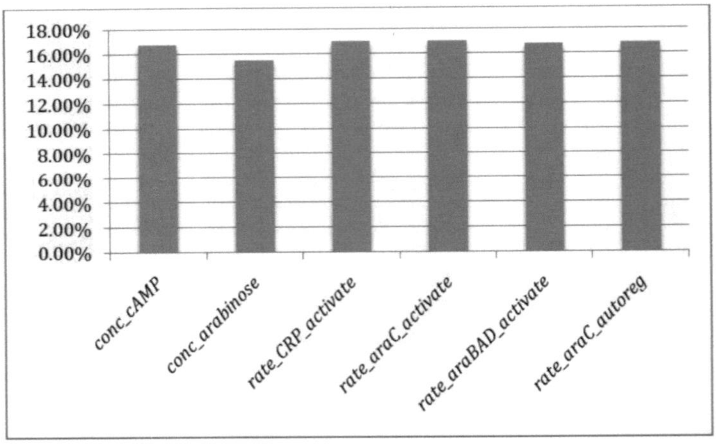

Figure 3. First-order indices calculated by GSA for the case with NAR by AraC.

4. Discussion

In this study, a unique combination of CA and GSA were used to study the parameters that influence the dynamics of the *ara* operon regulatory network. The results of the GSA study revealed the degree to which individual parameters affect the output of a biological model.GSA was used to explorethe influence of NAR on the regulatory network by calculating the impact of parameter variance on model output.Comparing first-order and total effect sensitivity indices with and without NAR by AraC elucidates the roles NAR plays in the signaling network. These include

1. increasing network stability and
2. increasing the response of the network to L-arabinose concentrations.

Equal distribution of variation among all parameters suggests that the NAR mechanism increases network robustness,providing protection against random perturbations (both biological and environmental) of the system.

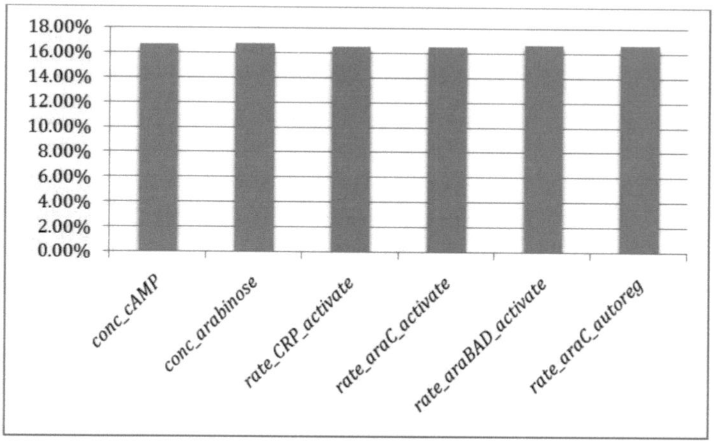

Figure 4. Total effect indices calculated by GSA for the case with NAR by AraC.

GSA has shown that parameter sensitivity indices can provide useful insight in interpreting the results of CA simulations.Thus, the combination of CA and GSA provides a valuable tool for the identification of source of output variability. In the case of the *ara*operon, all model parameters showed to contribute equally to the variance of *araBAD*activationlevel. While all the systemparameters are important and can significantly influence *araBAD*activation, those parameters with higher first-order sensitivities can have profound effects on regulation of the *ara* operon if NAR function by AraC is lost. This scenario demonstrates the potential of CA and GSA for identifying targets for manipulating highly interconnected gene regulatory networks.

Author details

Advait A. Apte[1], Stephen S. Fong[2] and Ryan S. Senger[1*]

1 Department of Biological Systems Engineering, Virginia Tech, Blacksburg, VA, USA

2 Department of Chemical and Life Science Engineering, Virginia Commonwealth University, Richmond, VA, USA

References

[1] Akel, E., Metz, B., Seiboth, B., & Kubicek, C. P. (2009). Molecular regulation of arabinan and L-arabinose metabolism in Hypocrea jecorina (Trichoderma reesei). *Eukaryotic cell.*, 8, 1837-44.

[2] Alon, N., Dao, P., Hajirasouliha, I., Hormozdiari, F., & Sahinalp, S. C. (2008). Biomolecular network motif counting and discovery by color coding. *Bioinformatics.*, 24, i241-9.

[3] Apte, A., Cain, J., Bonchev, D., & Fong, S. (2008a). Cellular automata simulation of topological effects on the dynamics of feed-forward motifs. *Journal of Biological Engineering*, 2, 2.

[4] Apte, A. A., Cain, J. W., Bonchev, D. G., & Fong, S. S. (2008b). Cellular automata simulation of topological effects on the dynamics of feed-forward motifs. *Journal of Biological Engineering*, 2, 2.

[5] Beverin, S., Sheppard, D. E., & Park, S. S. (1971). D-Fucose as a gratuitous inducer of the L-arabinose operon in strains of Escherichia coli B-r mutant in gene araC. *Journal of Bacteriology*, 107, 79-86.

[6] Califano, A. (2011). Striking a balance between feasible and realistic biological models. *Science translational medicine*, 3, 103ps39.

[7] Chavoya, A., Andalon-Garcia, I. R., Lopez-Martin, C., & Meda-Campana, M. E. (2010). Use of evolved artificial regulatory networks to simulate 3D cell differentiation. *Bio Systems*, 102, 41-8.

[8] Chavoya, A., & Duthen, Y. (2008). A cell pattern generation model based on an extended artificial regulatory network. *Bio Systems.*, 94, 95-101.

[9] Chhatre, S., Francis, R., Newcombe, A. R., Zhou, Y., Titchener-Hooker, N., King, J., & Keshavarz-Moore, E. (2008). Global Sensitivity Analysis for the determination of parameter importance in bio-manufacturing processes. *Biotechnology and applied biochemistry*, 51, 79-90.

[10] Chou, I. C., Martens, H., & Voit, E. O. (2006). Parameter estimation in biochemical systems models with alternating regression. *Theoretical biology & medical modelling.*, 3, 25.

[11] Ciavatta, S., Lovato, T., Ratto, M., & Pastres, R. (2009). Global uncertainty and sensitivity analysis of a food-web bioaccumulation model. *Environmental toxicology and chemistry SETAC.*, 28, 718-32.

[12] Coelho, F. C., Codeco, C. T., & Gomes, M. G. (2011). A Bayesian framework for parameter estimation in dynamical models. *PLoS ONE*, 6, e19616.

[13] Cuenod, C. A., Favetto, B., Genon-Catalot, V., Rozenholc, Y., & Samson, A. (2011). Parameter estimation and change-point detection from Dynamic Contrast Enhanced MRI data using stochastic differential equations. *Mathematical biosciences*, 233, 68-76.

[14] Desai, T. A., & Rao, C. V. (2010). Regulation of arabinose and xylose metabolism in Escherichia coli. *Applied and Environmental Microbiology*, 76, 1524-32.

[15] Englesberg, E., Squires, C., & Meronk, F. Jr. (1969). The L-arabinose operon in Escherichia coli B-r: a genetic demonstration of two functional states of the product of a regulator gene. *Proceedings of the National Academy of Sciences of the United States of America*, 62, 1100-7.

[16] Feng, X. J., Hooshangi, S., Chen, D., Li, G., Weiss, R., & Rabitz, H. (2004). Optimizing genetic circuits by global sensitivity analysis. *Biophysical journal.*, 87, 2195-202.

[17] Frangi, A. F., Coatrieux, J. L., Peng, G. C., D'Argenio, D. Z., Marmarelis, V. Z., & Michailova, A. (2011). Editorial: Special issue on multiscale modeling and analysis in computational biology and medicine--part-1. *IEEE transactions on bio-medical engineering*, 58, 2936-42.

[18] Greenblatt, J., & Schleif, R. (1971). Arabinose C protein: regulation of the arabinose operon in vitro. *Nature: New biology*, 233, 166-70.

[19] Hadeler, K. P. (2011). Parameter identification in epidemic models. *Mathematical biosciences*, 229, 185-9.

[20] Hendrickson, W., & Schleif, R. F. (1984). Regulation of the Escherichia coli L-arabinose operon studied by gel electrophoresis DNA binding assay. *Journal of molecular biology*, 178, 611-28.

[21] Hinkelmann, F., Murrugarra, D., Jarrah, A. S., & Laubenbacher, R. (2011). A mathematical framework for agent based models of complex biological networks. *Bulletin of mathematical biology.*, 73, 1583-602.

[22] Irr, J., & Englesberg, E. (1971). Control of expression of the L-arabinose operon in temperature-sensitive mutants of gene araC in Escherichia coli B-r. *Journal of Bacteriology*, 105, 136-41.

[23] Kolodrubetz, D., & Schleif, R. (1981). Regulation of the L-arabinose transport operons in Escherichia coli. *Journal of molecular biology*, 151, 215-27.

[24] Li, G., Rabitz, H., Yelvington, P. E., Oluwole, O. O., Bacon, F., Kolb, C. E., & Schoendorf, J. (2010). Global sensitivity analysis for systems with independent and/or correlated inputs. *The journal of physical chemistry.*, A114, 6022-32.

[25] Machado, D., Costa, R. S., Rocha, M., Ferreira, E. C., Tidor, B., & Rocha, I. (2011). Modeling formalisms in Systems Biology. *AMB Express*, 1, 45.

[26] Madar, D., Dekel, E., Bren, A., & Alon, U. (2011). Negative auto-regulation increases the input dynamic-range of the arabinose system of Escherichia coli. *BMC Systems Biology*, 5, 111.

[27] Mangan, S., & Alon, U. (2003). Structure and function of the feed-forward loop network motif. *Proceedings of the National Academy of Sciences of the United States of America*, 100, 11980-5.

[28] Marino, S., Hogue, I. B., Ray, C. J., & Kirschner, D. E. (2008). A methodology for performing global uncertainty and sensitivity analysis in systems biology. *Journal of theoretical biology*, 254, 178-96.

[29] Mente, C., Prade, I., Brusch, L., Breier, G., & Deutsch, A. (2011). Parameter estimation with a novel gradient-based optimization method for biological lattice-gas cellular automaton models. *Journal of mathematical biology*, 63, 173-200.

[30] Miro, A., Pozo, C., Guillen-Gosalbez, G., Egea, J. A., & Jimenez, L. (2012). Deterministic global optimization algorithm based on outer approximation for the parameter estima- tion of nonlinear dynamic biological systems. *BMC bioinformatics*, 13, 90.

[31] Mishra, S., Deeds, N., & Ruskauff, G. (2009). Global sensitivity analysis techniques for probabilistic ground water modeling. *MishraS.DeedsN.RuskauffG. 2009. Global sensitivity analysis techniques for probabilistic ground water modeling. Ground water.*, 47, 730-47.

[32] Mogilner, A., & Odde, D. (2011). Modeling cellular processes in 3D. *Trends in cell biology*, 21, 692-700.

[33] Neftci, E. O., Toth, B., Indiveri, G., & Abarbanel, H. D. (2012). Dynamic State and Parameter Estimation Applied to Neuromorphic Systems. *Neural computation.*

[34] Ogden, S., Haggerty, D., Stoner, C. M., Kolodrubetz, D., & Schleif, R. (1980). The Escherichia coli L-arabinose operon: binding sites of the regulatory proteins and a mechanism of positive and negative regulation. *Proceedings of the National Academy of Sciences of the United States of America*, 77, 3346-50.

[35] Ogejo, J. A., Senger, R. S., & Zhang, R. H. (2010). Global sensitivity analysis of a process-based model for ammonia emissions from manure storage and treatment structures. *Atmospheric Environment*, 44, 3621-3629.

[36] Olufsen, M. S., & Ottesen, J. T. (2012). A practical approach to parameter estimation applied to model predicting heart rate regulation. *Journal of mathematical biology.*

[37] Qu, Z., Garfinkel, A., Weiss, J. N., & Nivala, M. (2011). Multi-scale modeling in biology: how to bridge the gaps between scales? *Progress in biophysics and molecular biology.*, 107, 21-31.

[38] Rosenfeld, S. (2011). Critical self-organized self-sustained oscillations in large regulatory networks: towards understanding the gene expression initiation. *Gene regulation and systems biology*, 5, 27-40.

[39] Saltelli, A., Chan, K., & Scott, M. (2000). Sensitivity Analysis. *Wiley.*

[40] Saltelli, A., Ratto, M., Andres, T., Camplongo, F., Cariboni, J., Gatelli, D., Saisana, M., & Tarantola, S. (2008). Global Sensitivity Analysis:. *The Primer. Wiley.*

[41] Sarkar, R. R., Maithreye, R., & Sinha, S. (2011). Design of regulation and dynamics in simple biochemical pathways. *Journal of mathematical biology*, 63, 283-307.

[42] Schimz, K. L., Lessmann, D., & Kurz, G. (1974). Proceedings: Aspects of regulation of the pathways for D-glucose 6-phosphate, D-galactose, and L-arabinose in Pseudomonas fluorescens. *Hoppe-Seyler's Zeitschrift fur physiologische Chemie.*, 355, 1249.

[43] Schleif, R. (2010). AraC protein, regulation of the l-arabinose operon in Escheric hia coli, and the light switch mechanism of AraC action. *FEMS microbiology reviews.*, 34, 779-96.

[44] Sheridan, R. P. (2008). Alternative global goodness metrics and sensitivity analysis: heuristics to check the robustness of conclusions from studies comparing virtual screening methods. *Journal of Chemical Information and Modeling*, 48, 426-33.

[45] Sin, G., Gernaey, K. V., Neumann, M. B., van Loosdrecht, M. C., & Gujer, W. (2011). Global sensitivity analysis in wastewater treatment plant model applications: prioritizing sources of uncertainty. *Water research*, 45, 639-51.

[46] Sumner, T., Shephard, E., & Bogle, I. D. (2012). A methodology for global-sensitivity analysis of time-dependent outputs in systems biology modelling. *Journal of the Royal Society, Interface / the Royal Society.*

[47] Tashkova, K., Korosec, P., Silc, J., Todorovski, L., & Dzeroski, S. (2011). Parameter estimation with bio-inspired meta-heuristic optimization: modeling the dynamics of endocytosis. *BMC Systems Biology.*

[48] Taylor, R. J., Siegel, A. F., & Galitski, T. (2007). Network motif analysis of a multimode genetic-interaction network. *Genome biology*, 8, R160.

[49] Tian, L. P., Liu, L., & Wu, F. X. (2010). Parameter estimation method for improper fractional models and its application to molecular biological systems. *Conference proceedings :... Annual International Conference of the IEEE Engineering in Medicine and Biology Society. IEEE Engineering in Medicine and Biology Society. Conference 2010*, 1477-80.

[50] Toni, T., & Stumpf, M. P. (2010). Parameter inference and model selection in signaling pathway models. *Methods in molecular biology.*, 673, 283-95.

[51] Tyson, J. J., & Mackey, M. C. (2001). Molecular, metabolic, and genetic control: An introduction. Chaos. ., 11, 81-83.

[52] Wilcox, G., Meuris, P., Bass, R., & Englesberg, E. (1974). Regulation of the L-arabinose operon BAD in vitro. *The Journal of biological chemistry*, 249, 2946-52.

[53] Wilensky, U. Netlogo. (1999). Center for Connected Learning and Computer-Based Modeling. *Northwestern University, Evanston, IL.*

[54] Winfield, M. D., Latifi, T., & Groisman, E. A. (2005). Transcriptional regulation of the 4-amino-4-deoxy-L-arabinose biosynthetic genes in Yersinia pestis. *The Journal of biological chemistry*, 280, 14765-72.

[55] Yang, X., Dent, J. E., & Nardini, C. (2012). An S-System Parameter Estimation Method (SPEM) for biological networks. *Journal of computational biology a journal of computational molecular cell biology.*, 19, 175-87.

[56] Yoon, J., & Deisboeck, T. S. (2009). Investigating differential dynamics of the MAPK signaling cascade using a multi-parametric global sensitivity analysis. *PLoS ONE*, 4, e4560.

[57] Zhan, C., & Yeung, L. F. (2011). Parameter estimation in systems biology models using spline approximation. *BMC Systems Biology*, 5, 14.

[58] Zhang, L., Leyn, S. A., Gu, Y., Jiang, W., Rodionov, D. A., & Yang, C. (2012). Ribulokinase and transcriptional regulation of arabinose metabolism in Clostridium acetobutylicum. *Journal of Bacteriology*, 194, 1055-64.

[59] Zubay, G., Gielow, L., & Englesberg, E. (1971). Cell-free studies on the regulation of the arabinose operon. *Nature: New biology*, 233, 164-5.

Chapter 5

Cellular Learning Automata and Its Applications

Amir Hosein Fathy Navid and
Amir Bagheri Aghababa

Additional information is available at the end of the chapter

http://dx.doi.org/10.5772/52953

1. Introduction

Cellular Automata are mathematical models for systems consisting of large number of simple identical components with local interactions. Cellular Automata is a non-linear dynamical system in which space and time are discrete. It is called cellular because it is made up of cells like points in a lattice or like squares of checker boards, and it is called automata because it follows a simple rule.

Informally, a d-dimensional Cellular Automata consists of an infinite d-dimensional lattice of identical cells. Each cell can assume a state from a finite set of states. The cells update their states synchronously on discrete steps according to a local rule [4]. The new state of each cell depends on the previous states of a set of cells, including the cell itself, and constitutes its neighbourhood. The state of all cells in the lattice is described by a configuration. A configuration can be described as the state of the whole lattice [11].

Cellular Automata provided a potential solution and is probably the most popular technique to model the dynamics of many processes, since they can predict complex global space pattern dynamic evolution using a set of simple local rules.

However, Cellular Automata is usually associated to bi-dimensional matrixes of rectangular identical cells that are not the most adequate to model and tessellate a real world geographic area.

Regular grids, or more particularly: rectangular grids are the standard grid structure that is used in previous Cellular Automata studies. Broadly, a regular grid assumes that the structure of the cell grid and the number of neighbours are homogenous for every location in the cellular space. This assumption seems highly implausible as an empirical description of the geographical or social space that underlies the processes typically studied in Cellular Automata modelling, like opinion formation or neighbourhood segregation. However, to our knowledge there are virtually no insights into how regular vs. irregular grid structures affect cellular dynamics [14].

Cellular Automata extensions using Voronoi spatial models have been previously proposed to overcome this problem. In these approaches one uses convex cells with different sizes and shapes that can provide a much more adequate terrain partition.

A different problem lies in the fact that, on regular Cellular Automata, each cell has a finite set of possible states, and transition between states is a crisp function of present cell state and neighbour cells state. Crisp data modelling and crisp transition mechanisms have known limitations when one trying to model and simulate real-world processes where uncertainty and imprecision is present and cannot simply be ignored [28].

The most prominent reason is that Cellular Automata can be seen as multi-agent system based on locality with overlapping interaction structures. In this perspective, Cellular Automata is attractive as a modelling framework that may provide a better understanding of micro/macro relations.

We will give some background specific to the study of cellular automata, and then background from other fields that are necessary for the work here [17].

We will then conclude with some potential questions that merit future investigation, and where appropriate we will discuss potential consequences of such questions.

2. Irregular Cellular Automata

Practically all social science applications of cellular modelling use a regular grid as the underlying network structure. More in particular, the standard grid structure used is a rectangular regular grid. Other regular grids could be hexagonal or triangular structures. In general, we denote grids as regular where all inner cells (i.e. cells that are not at the border of the grid) have the same number of neighbours, whatever our neighbourhood definition may be - von Neumann neighbourhood or a Moore neighbourhood of a given size. On a regular torus, this definition generalises even to border cells [7].

Regular Cellular Automata has cells with identical shape and size. Since geographic features in nature are usually not distributed uniformly, regular spatial tessellation obviously limits modelling and simulation potential of regular Cellular Automata. In order to overcome this limitation, several authors have extended the Cellular Automata model to irregular cells. The most successful approaches use the Voronoi spatial model [10].

A Cellular Automata is a system composed by several identical automata, physically organized as a 2 dimensional array of rectangular cells, where each cell is considered an automaton, A, with a set of rules, T, which gets its inputs from its own state and from neighboring cells states V:

$$A \sim (S,T,V) \tag{1}$$

Figure1 shows the regular cellular Automata with regular cells.

The Voronoi spatial model is a tessellation of space that is constructed by decomposing the entire space into a set of Voronoi regions around each spatial object. By definition, points in the Voronoi region of a spatial object are closest to the spatial object than to any other spatial object [5]. The generations of Voronoi regions can be considered as 'expanding' spatial objects at a unique rate until these areas meet each other. The mathematical expression of the Voronoi region is defined as:

$$V(p_i) = \{p \mid d(p,p_i) \leq d(p,p_j), j \neq i, j = 1...n\} \tag{2}$$

In this equation, the Voronoi region of spatial object *pi, V(pi)*, is the region defined by the set of locations *p* in space where the distance from *p* to the spatial object *pi, d(p, pi)*, is less than or equal to the distance from *p* to any other spatial object *pj*. In figure 2, the Voronoi based Cellular Automata is shown.

Voronoi region boundaries are convex polygons. Points along a common boundary between Voronoi regions are equidistant to the corresponding spatial objects. Objects which share a common boundary are neighbors to each other in the Voronoi spatial model [5, 12].

In this section, Irregular Cellular Automata has been defined in context but for a better understanding, we have also explained Voronoi diagrams concept and modelling irregular grid structures using a Voronoi diagram further in this section.

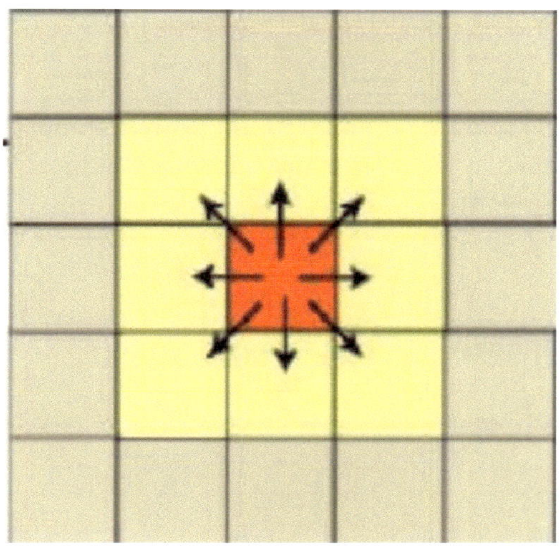

Figure 1. Regular Cellular Automata

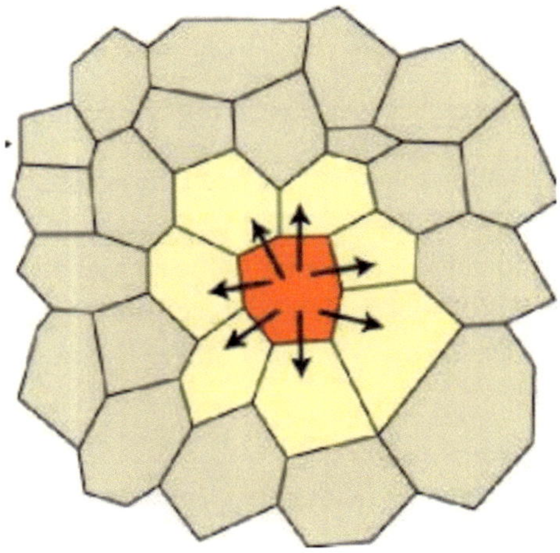

Figure 2. Voronoi Based Cellular Automata

2.1. Voronoi Diagrams

We begin with a description of elementary, though important, properties of the Voronoi diagram that will suggest some feelings for this structure. We also introduce notation used throughout this paper.

In this section, we introduce concepts of Voronoi Diagrams and describe necessary steps to create them. A naive approach to construct a Voronoi diagram is to determine the region for each point using Euclidean distance [16]. For points $p=(x_p, y_p)$ and $q=(x_q, y_q)$ in the plane, equation 3 denote their Euclidean distance.

$$d(p,q)=\sqrt{(x_p-x_q)^2+(y_p-y_q)^2} \tag{3}$$

By $\overline{pq}$, we denote the line segment from p to q. To draw Voronoi diagram, we use perpendicular bisectors of point set on the 2D space as it is shown in figure 3.

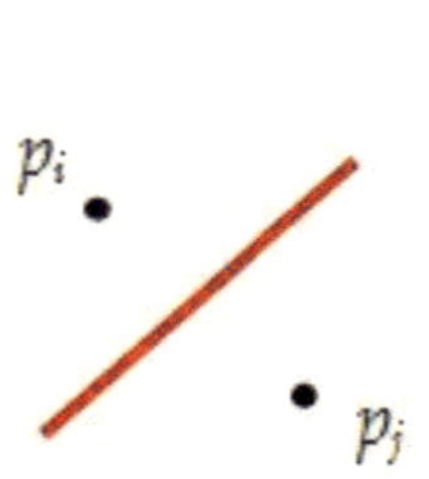

Figure 3. Divided plane with perpendicular bisector of two points

Given a set of S points $p_1, p_2, \ldots, p_n$ in the plane, a Voronoi diagram divides the plane into n Voronoi regions with the following properties:

- Each point p_i lies in exactly one region.
- If a point $q \notin S$ lies in the same region as p_i, then the Euclidian distance from p_i to q will be shorter than the Euclidian distance from p_j to q, where p_j is any other point in S.

The points $p_1, \ldots, p_n$ are called Voronoi sites. The Voronoi diagram for two sites p_i and p_j can be easily constructed by drawing the perpendicular bisector of line segment $\overline{p_i q}_j$.

Such diagrams would consist of two unbounded Voronoi regions, denoted by $V(p_i)$ and $V(p_j)$, in equation 4. In general, a Voronoi region $V(p_i)$ is defined as the intersection of $n-1$ half-planes formed by taking the perpendicular bisector of the segment for all where $i \neq j$.

$$V(p_i) = H(p_i p_1) \cap H(p_i p_2) \cap \ldots \cap H(p_i p_n) \tag{4}$$

In this notation, $H(p_i p_j)$ refers to the half-plane formed by taking the perpendicular bisector of $p_i p_j$ in figure 4. We know that the intersection of any number of half-planes forms a convex region bounded by a set of connected line segments. These line segments form the boundaries of Voronoi regions and are called Voronoi edges. The endpoints of these edges are called Voronoi vertices [8, 12].

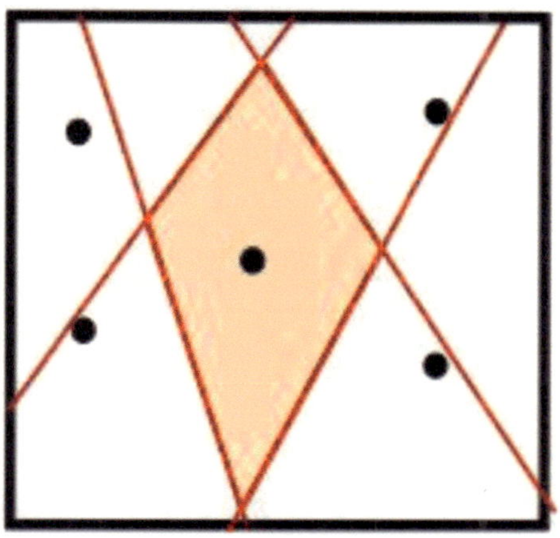

Figure 4. Create half-plane by perpendicular bisector

The points on Voronoi edges of Voronoi diagram are in equal distance of Voronoi sites p_i and p_j. You can see an example of Voronoi diagram in Figure 5.

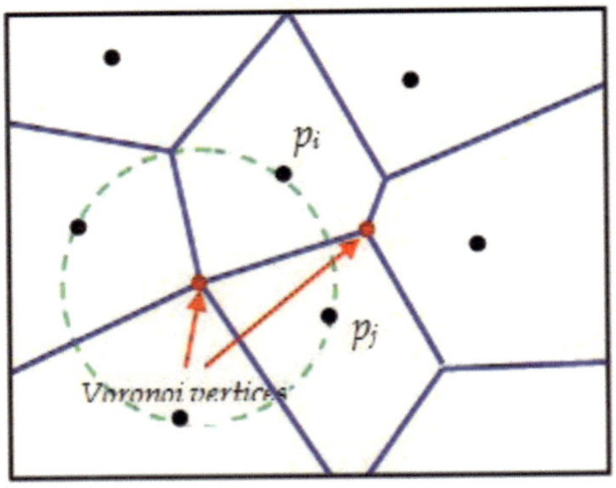

Figure 5. Voronoi diagrams of collection points on plane

Equation (5) shows the Voronoi region of p with respect to S, for $p,\ q \in S$.

$$V(p,S) = \bigcap_{q \in S, q \neq p} H(p,q) \tag{5}$$

Finally, the Voronoi diagram of S is defined by equation 6.

$$Voronoi(S) = \bigcup_{p,q \in S, p \neq q} \overline{V(p,S)} \cap \overline{V(q,S)} \tag{6}$$

By definition, each Voronoi region is the intersection of $n - 1$ open half-planes containing the site p.

2.2. Properties of Voronoi Diagrams

- The number of Voronoi vertices is at most $2n - 5$.
- The number of Voronoi edges is at most $3n - 6$.
- Each Voronoi vertex is the common intersection point of exactly three edges.
- If site $p_i \in S$ is the nearest neighbor of site $p_j \in S$, then the Voronoi regions $V(p_i)$ and $V(p_j)$ will share a common edge.
- Region $V(p)$ is unbounded iff p is an extreme point of S. That is, p will be part of the convex hull of S.

Given a triangle Δabc, the perpendicular bisector of each edge will intersect at a common point q called the circumcenter. The circumcenter is equi-distant from points a, b, c and these points all lie on a circle with q as its center. This circle is called the circumcircle for triangle Δabc [16].

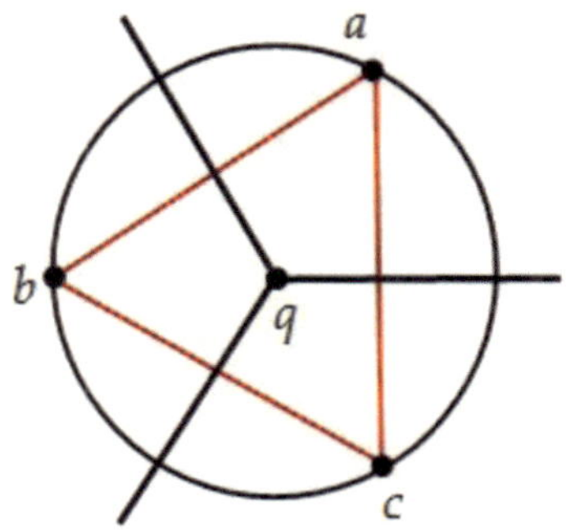

Figure 6. The circumcircle with circumcenter q

If a circumcircle is empty in its interior then in a Voronoi diagram:

- a, b, c would be Voronoi sites
- q would be a Voronoi vertex
- The perpendicular bisectors of Δabc would be Voronoi edges.

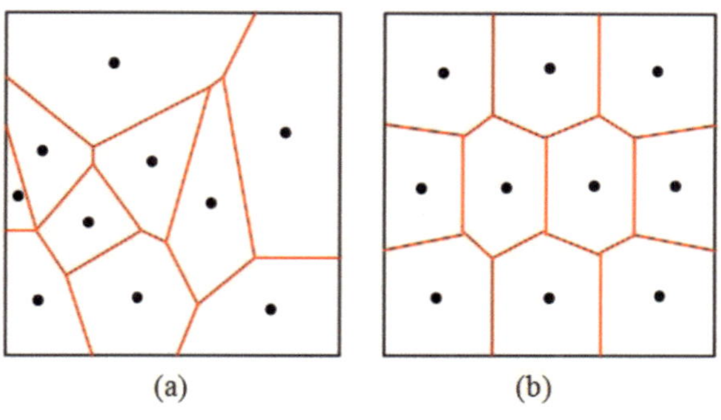

Figure 7. Voronoi Diagrams with (a) 10 random points (b) 10 simultaneous points

Figure 7 shows, on the left, the Voronoi regions corresponding to 10 randomly selected points in a square; the density function is constant. The dots are the Voronoi generators and the circles are the centroids of the corresponding Voronoi regions. Note that the generators and the centroids do not coincide. On the right, the 10 dots are simultaneously the generators for the Voronoi tessellation and the centroids of the Voronoi regions.

2.3. Constructing Voronoi Diagrams

2.3.1. Naive Approach

A naive approach to construct a Voronoi diagram is to determine the region for each site one at a time. Since each region is the intersection of *n− 1* half-planes, we can use an *O*(*n log n*) half-plane intersection algorithm to determine this region. Repeating for all *n* points, we have an *O*(*n*2 *log n*) algorithm.

2.3.2. Divide and Conquer

To construct a Voronoi diagram using the divide and conquer method, first partition the set of points *S* into two sets *L* and *R* based on x-coordinates. Next, construct the Voronoi diagrams for the left and right subset *V(L)*and *V(R)*. Finally, merge the two diagrams to produce *V(S)*. If the merge step can be carried out in linear time, then the construction of *V(S)* can be accomplished in *O*(*n log n*) time [16].

2.4. Irregular Grids in a Cellular Automaton

To model irregular grid structures, we use a Voronoi diagram. The crosses in Voronoi diagram are the generators of the grid. The edges of the resulting polygons are points with equal distance to their neighboring generators [10].

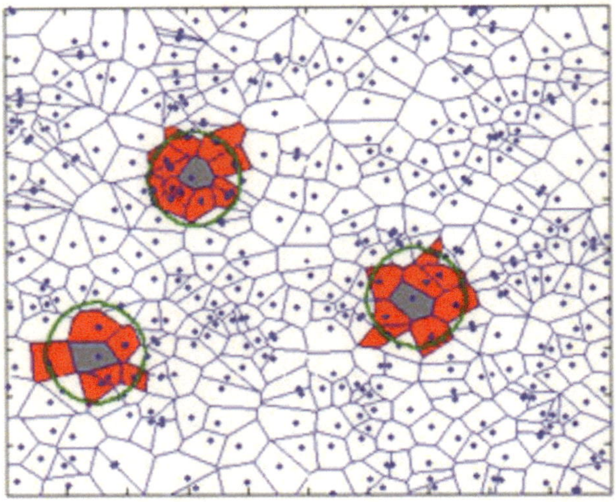

Figure 8. Neighborhoods of three different cells in an irregular field. Focal cells are gray and neighbor cells are red.

Figure 8 shows a decisive feature of irregular grids: even the cells inside the grid have different numbers of next neighbors. The figure shows locations of three different cells with 6, 8 and 12 next neighbors in an irregular grid. We define a next neighbor cell here as a cell that has a common border (not just a common edge) with the focal cell. Notice that this definition implies a von Neumann neighborhood on a rectangular grid. More in general, it has been found in simulation analyses that in a Voronoi graph, the number of neighbor cells varies between 3 and 14 [10].s

The idea of irregular cellular automata was suggested in mid 80s, but due to the computationally intensive operations required to search irregular neighborhood, it has been paid less attention to since then. In an informal way, Irregular Cellular Automata is a configuration of points in the space with no prior restriction. Each point has a number of other points as its neighbors such as figure 8. [8].

3. Learning Automata Concepts

In this section, we present the learning automata concept, cellular learning automata and irregular cellular learning automata.

3.1. Learning Automata

Learning Automaton is a simple entity which operates in an unknown random environment. In a simple form, the automaton has a finite set of actions to choose from, and at each stage its choice (action) depends upon its action probability vector. For each action chosen by the automaton, the environment gives a reinforcement signal with fixed unknown probability distribution. The automaton then updates its action probability vector depending on the reinforcement signal at that stage, and evolves to some final desired behavior [1].

Learning Automata is an abstract model which randomly selects one action out of its finite set of actions and performs it on a random environment. Environment, then evaluates the selected action and responses to the automata with a reinforcement signal. Based on the selected action and received signal, the automata updates its internal state and selects its next action. Figure 9 depicts the relationship between an automata and its environment.

Environment can be defined by the triple $E=\{\alpha, \beta, c\}$ where $\alpha=\{\alpha_1, \alpha_2 ..., \alpha_r\}$ represents a finite input set, $\beta=\{\beta_1, \beta_2, ..., \beta_r\}$ represents the output set, and $c=\{c_1, c_2, ..., c_r\}$ is a set of penalty probabilities where each element c_i of c corresponds to one input action α_i. Learning automata are classified into fixed structure stochastic, and variable structure stochastic [17, 18]. In the following, we consider only variable structure automata.

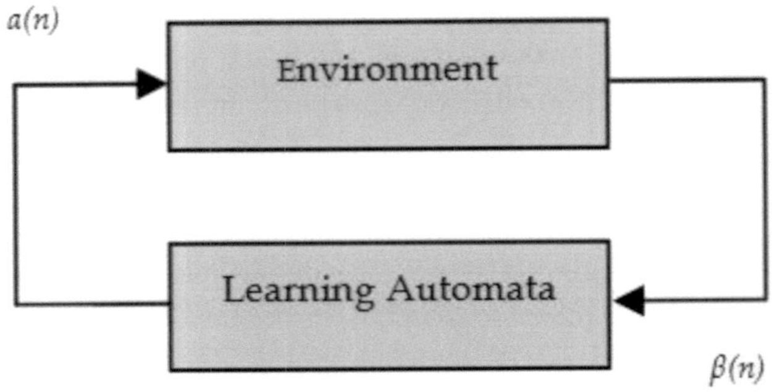

Figure 9. Relationship between learning automata and its environment

A variable structure automata is defined by the quadruple $\{\alpha, \beta, p, T\}$ in which $\alpha=\{\alpha_1, \alpha_2, \ldots, \alpha_n\}$ represents the action set of the automata, $\beta=\{\beta_1, \beta_2, \ldots, \beta_r\}$ represents the input set, $p=\{p_1, p_2, \ldots, p_r\}$ represents the action probability set, and finally $p(n+1)=T[\alpha(n), \beta(n), p(n)]$ represents the learning algorithm. This automaton operates as follows. Based on the action probability set p, automaton randomly selects an action α_i, and performs it on the environment. Having received the environment's reinforcement signal, automaton updates its action probability set based on equation (7) for favorable responses, and on equation (8) for unfavorable ones [18].

$$\begin{aligned} p_i(n+1) &= p_i(n) + a.(1-p_i(n)) \\ p_j(n+1) &= p_j(n) - a.p_j(n) \qquad \forall j \quad j \neq i \end{aligned} \tag{7}$$

$$\begin{aligned} p_i(n+1) &= (1-b).p_j(n) \\ p_j(n+1) &= \frac{b}{r-1} + (1-b)p_j(n) \qquad \forall j \quad j \neq i \end{aligned} \tag{8}$$

In these two equations, a and b are reward and penalty parameters, respectively. For $a = b$, learning algorithm is called L_{R-P}, for $a << b$, it is called $L_{R\varepsilon P}$, and for $b=0$ it is called L_{R-I}. For more information about learning automata the reader may refer to Learning automata that are, by design, "simple agents for doing simple things". The full potential of a Learning Automata is realized when multiple automata interact with each other. Interaction may assume different forms such as tree, mesh, array and etc. Depending on the problem that needs to be solved, one of these structures for interaction may be chosen. In most applications, full interaction between all Learning Automatons is not necessary and is not natural. Local interaction of Learning Automatons which can be defined in a form of graph such as tree, mesh, or array, is natural in many applications.

On the other hand, Cellular Automata are mathematical models for systems consisting of large numbers of simple identical components with local interactions. Cellular Automata and Learning Automata are combined to obtain a new model called Cellular Learning Automata (CLA). This model is superior to Cellular Automata because of its ability to learn and also is superior to single Learning Automata because it is a collection of Learning Automatons which can interact with each other.

3.2. Cellular Learning Automata

Cellular Learning Automata is a mathematical model for dynamical complex systems that consists of large number of simple components. The simple components have learning capability and act together to produce complicated behavioral patterns. A Cellular Learning Automata is a Cellular Automata in which a Learning Automata will be assigned to its every cell [4]. The learning automaton residing in each cell determines the state of the cell on the basis of its action probability vector. Like Cellular Automata, there is a rule that Cellular Learning Automata operates according to it. The rule of Cellular Learning Automata and the actions selected by the neighboring Learning Automatons of any cell determine the reinforcement signal to the Learning Automata residing in that cell. In Cellular Learning Automata, the neighboring Learning Automatons of any cell constitute its local environment. This environment is non-stationary because of the fact that it changes as action probability vectors of neighboring Learning Automatons vary [7].

The operation of cellular learning automata could be described as follows: At the first step, the internal state of every cell is specified. The state of every cell is determined on the basis of action probability vectors of the learning automata residing in that cell. The initial value of this state may be chosen on the basis of past experience or at random. In the second step, the rule of Cellular Learning Automata determines the reinforcement signal to each learning automaton residing in that cell. Finally, each learning automaton updates its action probability vector on the basis of supplied reinforcement signal and the chosen action. This process continues until the desired result is obtained (figure 10). Formally a d–dimensional Cellular Learning Automata is given below.

A d–dimensional cellular learning automata is a structure $A = (Z^d, \Phi, A, N, F)$, here

1. Z^d is a lattice of d–tuples of integer numbers.
2. Φ is a finite set of states.
3. A is the set of Learning Automatons each of which is assigned to each cell of the Cellular Automata.
4. $N = \{\bar{x}_1, \bar{x}_2, \ldots, \bar{x}_m\}$ is a finite subset of Z^d called neighborhood vector where $\bar{m}$ represents the number of neighboring cells and $\bar{x}_i \in Z^d$.

The neighborhood vector determines the relative position of the neighboring cells from any given cell u in the lattice Z^d. The neighbors of a particular cell u are set of cells $\{u+\bar{x}_i \mid i=1, 2, ..., \bar{m}\}$. We assume that there exists a neighborhood function $\bar{N}(u)$ mapping a cell u to the set of its neighbors according to equation (9).

$$\bar{N}(u) = \{u+\bar{x}_1, u+\bar{x}_2, \ldots, u+\bar{x}_{\bar{m}}\} \tag{9}$$

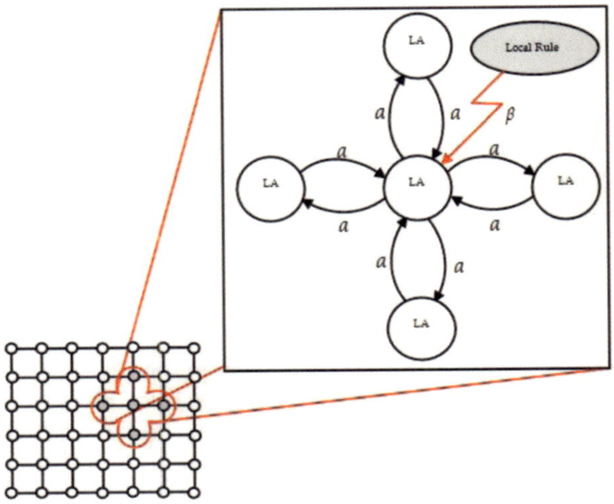

Figure 10. Cellular Learning Automata

A number of applications for Cellular Learning Automata have been developed recently such as rumor diffusion,image processing, modeling of commerce networks, fixed channel assignment in cellular networks, and VLSI Placement to mention a few (Beigy & Meybodi, 2004).

The Cellular Learning Automata can be classified into two types of *synchronous* and *asynchronous*. In synchronous Cellular Learning Automata, all cells are synchronized with a global clock and executed at the same time [10]. It is shown that the synchronous Cellular Learning Automata converges to a globally stable state for a class of rules called commutative rules. In some applications such as image processing, a type of Cellular Learning Automata in which the action of each cell in next stage of its evolution not only depends on the local environment (actions of its neighbors) but it also depends on the external environments.

3.3. Irregular Cellular Learning Automata

Irregular Cellular Learning Automata is a generalization of Cellular Learning Automata which removes the restriction of rectangular grid structure in traditional Cellular Learning Automata. This generalization is expected because there are applications which cannot be adequately modeled with rectangular grids [10].

In an informal way, Irregular Cellular Automata is a configuration of points in the space with no prior restriction. The few examples of Irregular Cellular Automata all use Voronoi polygons or the related Delaunay triangulation to divide space and determine the neighbors of each point. Voronoi polygons divide space into regions surrounding objects such that any point in an object's polygon is closer to that object than to any other object, while Delaunay triangulation is a triangulation of the points in a Voronoi diagram where the circumcircle of each triangle is an empty triangle.

An Irregular Cellular Learning Automata is a combination of Irregular Cellular Automata and Learning Automata (Figure 11). We define Irregular Cellular Learning Automata as an undirected graph in which each vertex represents a cell which is equipped with a learning automaton.

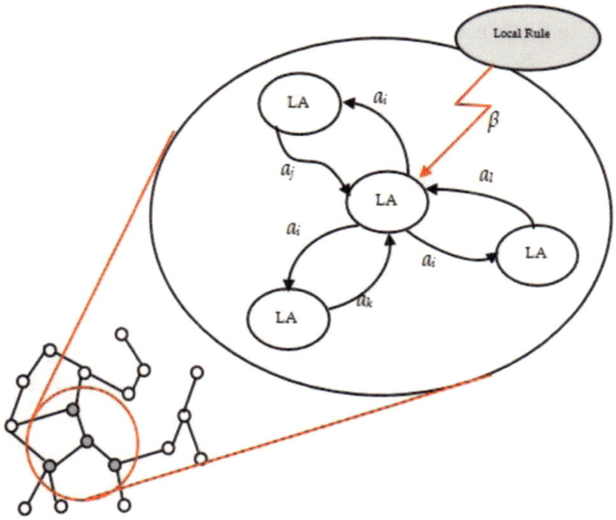

Figure 11. Irregular Cellular Learning Automata, LA means Learning Automata in each neighbor cell.

The Learning Automaton residing in a particular cell determines its state (action) on the basis of its action probability vector. Like Cellular Learning Automata, there is a rule that the Irregular Cellular Learning Automata operate according to it. The rule of the Cellular Learning Automata and the actions selected by the neighboring Learning Automatons of any particular Learning Automata determine the reinforcement signal to the Learning Automata residing in a cell. The neighboring Learning Automatons of any particular Learning Automata constitute the local environment of that cell. The local environment of a cell is non-stationary because the action probability vectors of the neighboring Learning Automatons vary during evolution of the Irregular Cellular Learning Automata.

An Irregular Cellular Learning Automata is formally defined below.

An Irregular Cellular Learning Automata is a structure $A = (G <E, V>, \Phi, A, F)$, where

- G is an undirected graph, with V as the set of vertices and E as the set of edges.
- Φ is a finite set of states.
- A is the set of Learning Automata each of which is assigned to one cell of the Irregular Cellular Learning Automata.
- $F : \underline{\Phi}_j \rightarrow \underline{\beta}$ is the local rule of the irregular cellular learning automata in each vertex j where $\underline{\Phi}_j = \{\Phi_i \,|(i,j) \in E\} + \{\Phi_j\}$ is the set of states of all neighbors of j,and β is the set of values that the reinforcement signal can take. β computes the reinforcement signal for Learning Automata based on the actions selected by the neighboring Learning Automata.

Note that in the definition of Irregular Cellular Learning Automata, no explicit definition of neighborhood of each cell is given. This is because neighborhood in Irregular Cellular Learning Automata is implicitly defined in definition of the graph G.

In what follows, we consider Irregular Cellular Learning Automata with n cells. The learning automaton A_i which has a finite action set α_i is associated to cell i (for $i=1, 2, \ldots, n$) of the Irregular Cellular Learning Automata. Let the cardinality of α_i be m_i. The state of the Irregular Cellular Learning Automata represented by $p= (p_1, p_2, \ldots, p_n)$, where $p_i=(p_{i1}, p_{i2}, \ldots, p_{imi})$ is the action probability vector of A_i. The operation of the Irregular Cellular Learning Automata takes place as the following iterations. At iteration k, each learning automaton chooses an action. Let $\alpha_i \in \alpha$ be the action chosen by A_i. Then all learning automata receive a reinforcement signal. Let $\beta_i \in \beta$ be the reinforcement signal received by A_i. This reinforcement signal is produced by the application of local rule $F(\Phi_i) \rightarrow \beta$. Finally, each Learning Automata updates its action probability vector on the basis of the supplied reinforcement signal and the chosen action by the cell. This process continues until the desired result is obtained.

There are some applications that apply Irregular Cellular Learning Automata such as Image Processing, Graph Coloring, Social Modeling, Clustering and Sensor network applications like Channel Assignment and Routing. In the following, we introduce a sensor network application.

4. Intrusion Detection in Wireless Sensor Network Using Irregular Cellular Learning Automata

4.1. Wireless Sensor Networks

A Wireless Sensor Network contains hundreds or thousands of sensor nodes. Basically, each sensor node comprises sensing, processing, transmission, mobilizer, position finding system, and power units (some of these components are optional like the mobilizer). By definition the nature of ad hoc networks is dynamically changing. Hence security is hard to achieve due to the dynamic nature of nodes. Routing protocols for WSNs are designed based on the assumption that all participating nodes are completely cooperative. In a closed MANET, all mobile nodes cooperate with each other towards a common destiny, such as emergency search/rescue or military and law enforcement operations. In an open MANET, different mobile nodes with different goals share their resources in order to ensure global connectivity [9, 15]. Lately, significant research efforts have focused on improving the security of ad hoc networks. In WSNs, nodes are both routers and terminals. Due to the lack of a routing infrastructure all the nodes have to cooperate to ensure successful communication. Clearly, cooperation means ensuring correct routing establishment mechanisms, the protection of routing information and the security of packet forwarding. One major challenge that was neglected previously is that of making wireless sensor network robust against MAC layer misbehaviors. Significant applications of WSNs include establishing survivable, efficient, dynamic communication for emergency/rescue operations, disaster relief. Security is a critical problem when implementing WSN. The fast detection of malicious nodes is vital in mobile ad hoc networks, since they rely on the cooperation of nodes for routing and forwarding. Also, cooperation of misbehaving nodes can seriously degrade the performance and jeopardize the functionality of network.

4.2. Intrusion Detection Protocols

The security difference between wired infrastructure networks and wireless sensor networks motivated researchers to model an intrusion detection system that can handle the new security challenges such as securing routing protocols [21]. We only list here some of the existent research work that is related to our approach.

Sterne et al. proposed a dynamic intrusion detection hierarchy that is potentially scalable to large networks with using clustering [24]. This method is similar with Kachirski and Guha, but it can be structured in more than two levels. Thus, nodes on first level are cluster-heads and nodes on the second level are leaf nodes. In this model, every node has the task of monitoring, logging, analyzing, properly responding to intrusions detection if there is enough evidence, and alert or report to cluster-heads. The cluster-heads, in addition, must also perform:

1. data fusion/integration and data filtering,
2. computations of intrusion, and
3. security management.

Sumalatha and Reddy proposed an approach for misbehavior detection [25]. Detection system is implemented based on fuzzy logic concept and the DSR has been used as routing protocol. Every node implements an instance of the detection system and runs it in two phases. In the initial phase, the detecting system learns about the normal behavior of nodes with respect to the DSR protocol. Then, the node may leave the protected environment and enters the second phase where node finds some of the nodes as malicious and captures each node parameters such as number of route requests, number of route replies and number of updates at each node in the network. These parameters are used for input of the fuzzy inference system and also are fuzzified at the beginning in order to make fuzzy values. To find the crisp value of the calculated trust, trust is assigned to each node in the ad hoc network. This process mainly contains fuzzification, inference by rule base construction and defuzzification processes. The Defuzzification is the process of conversion of fuzzy output set into a single number. In this approach, the authors have used these numbers to detect the malicious nodes in the network. In one of recent works, the authors suggested learning automata-based protocol for intrusion detection (LAID) in wireless sensor networks [27]. LAID functions in a distributed manner and uses the learning automata to optimize the selection of paths in which sampling has to be performed. The system, in essence, tries to identify or approximate the location of the attacker and, thus, it catches the malicious packets sent by the attacker. LAID protocol is not energy-aware and it may not be always practically ideal for resource-constrained networks such as distributed WSN.

Further, another learning automata-based intrusion detection protocol (S-LAID) has been proposed [28]. S-LAID functions in a distributed manner with each node functioning independently without any knowledge about the adjacent nodes. S-LAID assumes that the system budget is configured prior to its installation. In this protocol, the authors considered that sampling of a packet consumes energy. In S-LAID, each node continuously samples its interface at a minimum sampling budget. According to S-LAID algorithm if malicious packets are found and the detection rate is higher than the penalty threshold, then the sampling rate is increased. The learning functions calculate the sampling rate that should be used during the next instant by the automaton. In order to maintain efficiency and increase lifetime, the authors have bound the value by the sampling rate. They also have used the rate control algorithm to moderate the increase in the sampling rate.

4.3. Irregular Cellular Learning Automata-based Intrusion Detection Protocols

In this protocol, the entire network is divided into multiple clusters. Nodes are placed into clusters with one cluster-head for each cluster (Figure 12). Each cluster-head node is aware of its cluster information. The authenticity of a node is mostly determined by the nodes that are in same cluster. Each node has an IDS agent for detecting potential abnormalities in packets forwarding process. To reduce the overhead of intrusion detection process, nodes in a cluster will cooperate to select a cluster-head node based on learning automata residing in each node for handling the detection process for the whole cluster. Data packets may traverse between different clusters. The process of misbehaving nodes detection is performed in 3 sequential phases.

- Phase 1: Detection of misbehaving nodes by cluster-head node in same cluster.
- Phase 2: Confirmation of misbehaving nodes by neighbor nodes.
- Phase 3: Reward or penalize misbehaving node by neighbor nodes.

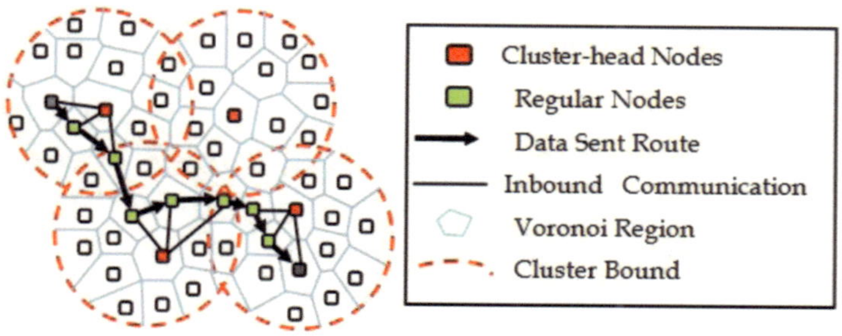

Figure 12. Network Model

To configure the routing in network, each node constructs its probability vector $\{p_1, p_2, \ldots, p_n\}$. Each node sends its *Id* and energy level to its cluster-head and neighbor nodes to form the clusters. Neighbor nodes construct their local routing tables upon receiving this packet. For each received packet, an entry for the node *Id* in the packet is created in routing table, and initial preference for that node is calculated as follows:

$$p(i) = \frac{EnergyLevel_i}{\sum_{j=1}^{m} EnergyLevel_j} \quad i \neq j \quad and \quad i = 1, 2, 3, \ldots \tag{10}$$

Where p_i is the probability of selecting the i_{th} neighbor node, $EnergyLevel_i$ is the energy level of the i_{th} neighbor node and m is the total number of neighbor nodes. Indeed each node in the network gets the preference of all nodes that are in the same clusters and sends this preference to its cluster-heads.

1. *Phase 1*

Systematically, in our protocol, we attach an IDS agent to each mobile node. These IDS agents run independently and monitor local activities to detect abnormal behaviors. We assume the local IDS agent is tamper resistant. Several software tamper resistance techniques have been proposed that are very hard to crack and suitable for our approach. In this method, we have considered two level architecture for each node. The first layer is the internal IDS agent. IDS agent can be divided into the following components: the data collection module (DCM), the data transmission quality (DTQ) module, the cluster aggregation and fusion module (CAFM), and the intrusion response module. A diagram is given in Figure 13.

The second layer is the ICLA. This layer is a combination of the detection engine module and learning automata residing in each node.

Data Collection Module (DCM)

The functionality of the data collection module is to collect security related data via monitoring local activities and local behaviors of neighbor nodes. We define misbehaving nodes as those that have aberrations in data exchange patterns. We have used the bucket as a specific count of packets that are transmitted from one node to the other. At the end of every bucket, Data collection modules send the gathered information and statistics to CAFM. This information determines the behavior of the node and its neighbors that are sending and receiving data packets.

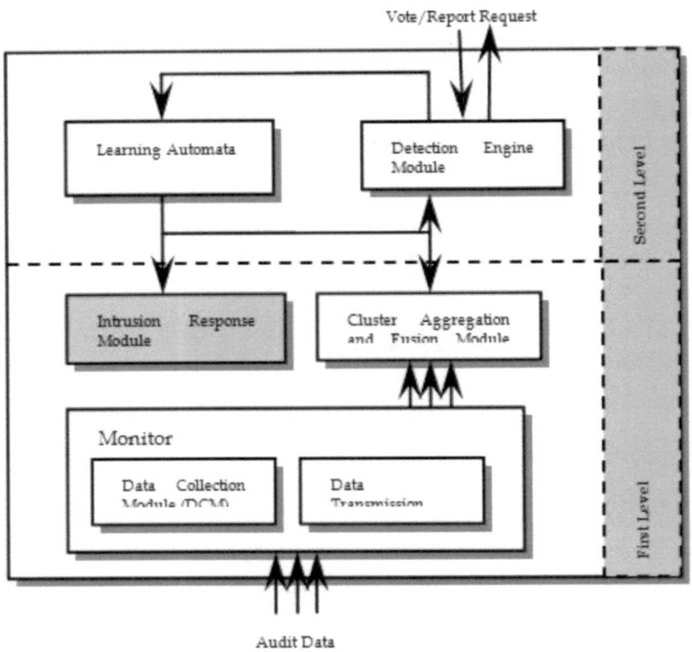

Figure 13. Internal Model for the IDS Agent

Data Transmission Quality (DTQ Function)

This module has a function to measure the quality of a communication node. In our Method, the DTQ function measures changes in the environment and sends a probability to a higher layer. This probability is calculated as follow:

$$p(i) = \lambda_1 \times \frac{STB_i(\ )}{Er(\ )} + \lambda_2 \frac{EnergyLevel_i}{IEnergy - N \times SEnergy}$$
$$i = 1, 2, 3, ... \tag{11}$$

In this function, $EnergyLevel_i$ is the level of the energy of the i_{th} neighbor node. *IEnergy* is the initial energy in each node, and *SEnergy* is the required energy to transmit data. N is the number of Data packets or the bucket size. *Er()* is probability of error in the channel. λ_1 and λ_2 declare the effect of nodal behavior and node's energy respectively. Also $STB_i()$ is the stability of the nodal behavior. This quantity is measured as follows:

$$STB_i = \frac{\sum_i numberoffcrwardedpackets}{\sum_i numberoffcrwardedpackets + \sum_i numberoffrecievedpackets} \tag{12}$$

Every node measures the number of received acknowledgments from the neighbor nodes it has tried to transmit to. This statistic is *STB()*.

2. *Phase 2*

Cluster Aggregation and Fusion Module (CAFM)

If a node is inter-cluster node or normal node, it sends the gathered data from the neighboring nodes to detection engine on second level. It can send the alarms and reports to its cluster-head based on voting request. While if the node is a cluster-head node, then the CAFM module receives the alarms and reports from inter-cluster nodes. Also, CAFM module of the cluster-head node allows the voting or prevents it by aggregation and fusion of the received alarms and reports. When the CAFM module of each cluster-head node receives the vote request packet, it votes for the suspect node. Voting process is performed base on the results that are calculated by the detection engine of inter-cluster nodes. At the end of the voting process, CAFM module of the cluster-head node sends the number of votes (V_m) to its detection engine.

Detection Engine Module

The detection engine identifies the misbehaving nodes according to the received information from CAFM module. The detection engine set a threshold (τ) according to equation (13). This threshold is determined based on the behavior and energy level of all nodes that are participating in voting process. In this equation, we use STB and energy level of each node because these values show the quality of node behavior properly.

$$\tau = \gamma_1 \times \frac{STB_i(\ )}{\sum_{j-1}^{M} STB_j(\ )} + \gamma_2 \times \frac{EnergyLevel_i}{\sum_{j-1}^{M} EnergyLevel_j} \quad (13)$$

$$i = 1, 2, \ldots$$

$$i \neq j$$

In equation (6), *STB* $_i$ *()* is the stability of the nodal behavior which can be calculated by equation (6). *EnergyLevel* $_i$ is the level of the energy of the *i* $_{th}$ neighbor node. *M* is the total number of nodes that participate in the voting. γ_1 and γ_2 are numbers between zero and one. According to the information of CAFM module, if the detection engine finds one or more values of *STB* in the table that are less than the threshold (τ), then it realizes that there may be one or more misbehaving nodes in its cluster. So it sends a vote request message about the suspect nodes to the CAFM module. In addition, the detection engine module makes a decision in cooperating with ICLA based on the number of vote response messages gathered by CAFM module. According to the results of voting, the node *M* is a well-behaving one and should be rewarded or it is a misbehaving one and should be punished.

3. *Phase 3*

CAFM module of the cluster-head will gather all the vote responses about suspect node *M*. CAFM module then sends the number of gathered vote response messages (V_{m}) to the detection engine module. According to the number of voting for the suspect node's authenticity, a decision is made as follow:

- If more than 80 percent of the participating nodes in the voting give a positive vote to suspect node *M*, then this node will be exclude from participating in the routing. Moreover, neighbor nodes of *M* add node *M* to their black lists.
- If less than 80 percent and more than 50 percent of the participating nodes in the voting give a positive vote to suspect node *M*, then this action will be penalized by learning automata residing in the node *N* with *b=0.2* according to L_{R-P} learning algorithm.
- If less than 50 percent and more than 30 percent of the participating nodes in the voting give a positive vote to suspect node *M*, then this action will be penalized by learning automata residing in the node *N* with *b=0.4* according to L_{R-P} learning algorithm.
- If less than 30 percent of the participating nodes in the voting give a positive vote to suspect node *M*, then this action will be rewarded by learning automata residing in the node *N* with *a=0.6* according to L_{R-P} learning algorithm.

Intrusion Response Module

The Intrusion Response Module efficiently penalizes misbehaving nodes based on updated statistics which are created and sent to intrusion response module by learning automata. The intrusion response module performs the following actions according to received statistics. First, it receives the updated *STB* values (equation 5) from the second layer and saves them in *STB* table. Second, if the specific node is a cluster-head node, the intrusion response module sends the order of penalization or dismissal of the suspected node to all cluster nodes. Therefore, misbehaving nodes won't be permitted to participate in routing process.

4.4. Evaluation the Proposed Protocol

In this section, we have implemented the proposed protocol by MATLAB and Glomosim simulator, a scalable discrete event simulator developed by UCLA.

Simulation settings

The network area size is 2000*2000 (in m2). The mobility model is the random waypoint model. The minimum speed is 5 m/s, and the maximum speed is 15 m/s. We have used the IEEE 802.11 for distributed wireless sensor networks as the MAC layer protocol. The number of nodes varies from 1000 to 3000 nodes. Radio bandwidth is 250000(in bps). Initial energy level of each node is 5(mW) and radio transmit power is 10 (in dBm). The size of all data packets is set to 512 bytes. The duration of each simulation is 1800 seconds. The values of γ_1 and γ_2 are considered 0.5 in our simulations.

Simulated Attacks

In our simulation, we have implemented and used the following attacks:

- Black-hole attack: In this attack, a misbehaving node uses the routing protocol to advertise itself as having the shortest path to the node whose packets it wants to intercept. The attacker will then receive the traffic which is destined for other nodes, and then it can drop or modify the packets.
- Denial of Service: A node prevents itself from receiving and forwarding data packets to their destinations.
- Malicious Flooding: In this attack, the misbehaving node pumps a great deal of useless and garbage packets to the network. In this way, it corrodes the resources of the network such as bandwidth and energy.
- Packet dropping: A node conditionally or randomly drops data packets which are supposed to be forward.

Simulation Results

The results of simulation in figure 14 show the percentage of detection rate with variation of misbehaving nodes' percentage. In this simulation, the number of nodes is 100 and the number of clusters is 10. Obviously, at first, the percentage of detection rate in all attacks has decreased, and afterwards with increase of misbehaving nodes' percentage the detection rate has increased either. The important reason for this behavior is the application of ICLA. In voting process, gathered information of neighbor nodes is increased which have participated in voting. In fact, the system learns abnormal behavior by increase of gathered information of learning automata from its environment. Therefore, the misbehaving nodes will be detected accurately. Because of using the energy and behavior factors for detecting the malicious nodes in black-hole attack, the results for black-hole attack are detected accurately. Consequently these results are better than that of other attacks with higher population of misbehaving nodes.

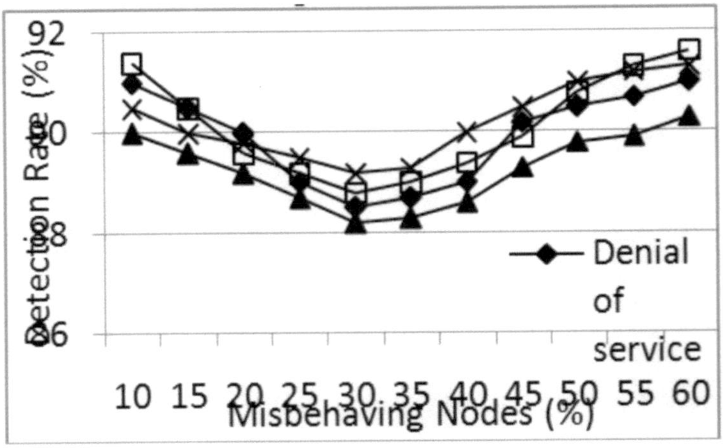

Figure 14. Detection rate vs. percentage of misbehaving nodes

Figure 15 shows the false positive rate with variation in percentage of the misbehaving nodes. In this simulation, the number of nodes is 100 and the number of clusters is 10. In this figure, first, the percentage of false positive rate has increased and then the false positive rate has decreased with increasing the percentage of misbehaving nodes. The learning automaton in each node gathers the information from the environment and this causes detection of misbehaving nodes to be performed properly. So the percentage of false positive rate has decreased after obvious quantity of 40%.

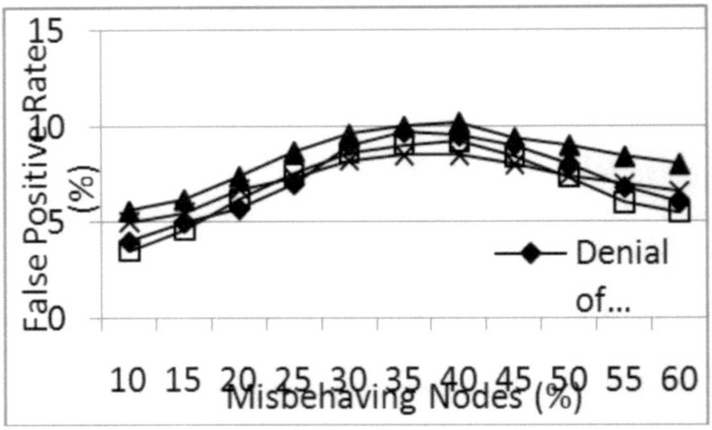

Figure 15. False positive rate vs. percentage of misbehaving nodes

In figure 16, we have shown the results of simulation and have discussed the detection rate with variation in number of clusters. In this simulation, detection rate will be decreased with increasing the number of clusters. Because of the constant total number of nodes in the network and the increase of clusters' number, the number of nodes in each cluster will be decreased. Therefore, the action probability vector in each cluster-head will be decreased, and this causes the detection rate to decrease in each cluster. As it is shown in this figure, after a specific number of clusters (10), the learning rate has increased, and, thus the detection rate has increased too. In this state, ICLA performs very well.

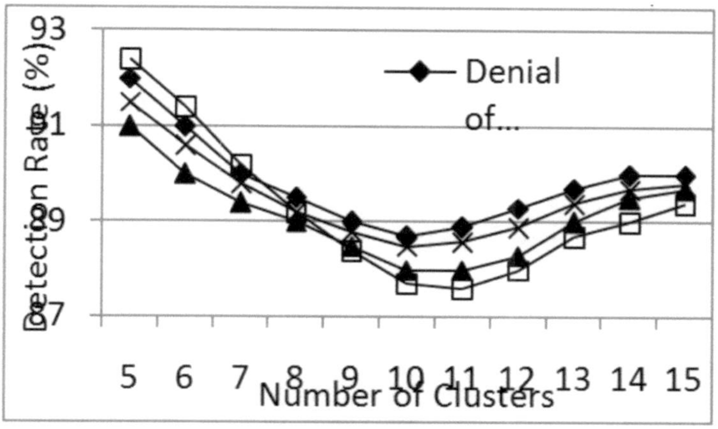

Figure 16. Detection rate vs. number of cluster

In figure 17, the simulation results of false positive rate in variation with number of clusters are illustrated. At first, false positive rate increases with increase of clusters' number, because as number of clusters increases, number of nodes inside each clusters decreases. Therefore, the length of action probability vector in cluster-heads' learning automata decreases, but after specific number of clusters (10) the false positive rate decreases due to increasing of learning rate increases. This decrease for denial of service attack has been more noticeable than the other attacks because of ICLA application in detecting attacks and nodal behavior.

In the next simulation, we have evaluated the effects of mentioned attacks on energy consumption of network in our method. Figure 18 shows the average energy consumption with variation in number of nodes. For all attacks, energy consumption has increased with increase of nodes' number. Moreover, average energy consumption for malicious forwarding attack is lower than black-hole attack, and the average energy consumption of black-hole attack is lower than other attacks. These results were predictable, because the proposed method uses the energy level of each node for detecting malicious flooding and black-hole attacks. In addition, the proposed protocol uses each node's behavior for black-hole attack and this causes the energy consumption to increase.

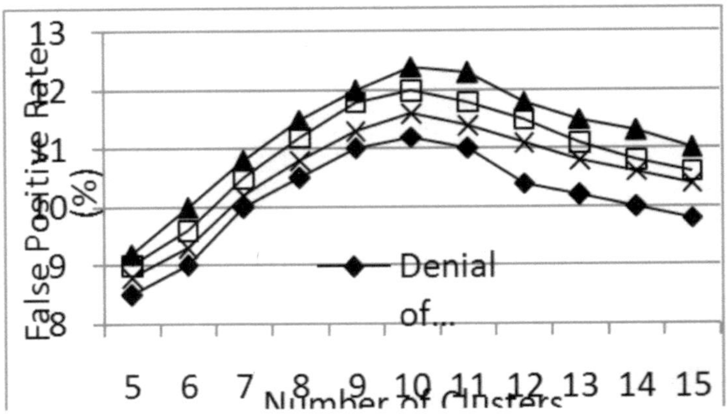

Figure 17. False positive rate vs. number of clusters

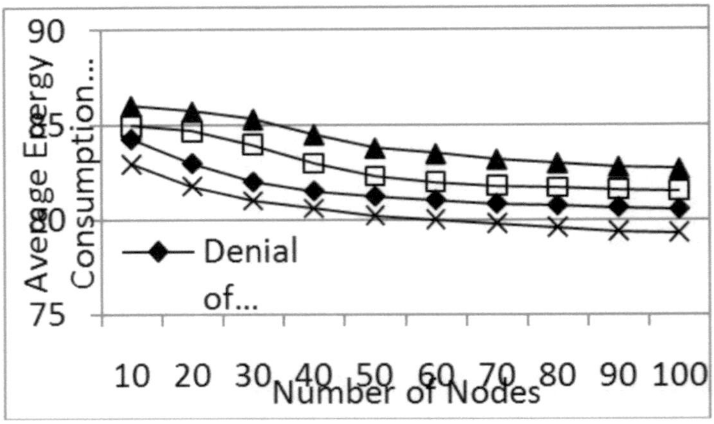

Figure 18. Average energy consumption in the network vs. number of nodes

5. Conclusion

In this Chapter, we have disscussed Cellular Learning Automata which has standard assumption of a rectangular grid structure. Then we have represented Irregular Cellular Learning Automata which are the models cause to develop tools that allow us use both rectangular and even irregular grids within one and the same Cellular Automata modeling framework. Of course, we are aware that the regularity of the grid structure is but one of a number of idealizations used in Cellular Automata modeling. For example, it has been discussed controversially whether and under what conditions a simple influence dynamics similar to our model of spatial collective action can be robust with respect to variation in simultaneous vs.

We applied these tools to intrusion detection protocols which is an application from sensor networks. This is a novel approach which used of Irregular Cellular Learning Automata to detect suspect nodes by using and analyzing nodes' behavior during routing process and nodes' energy level. It also implements Irregular Cellular Learning Automata to detect abnormal behaviors. Afterwards, our method starts its voting process in which it decides to reward or penalize suspect node based on learning automata reports. The simulations show that our proposed method not only has a proper detection rate but also is an energy-aware protocol in detecting malicious nodes.

Author details

Amir Hosein Fathy Navid[1*] and Amir Bagheri Aghababa[2]

*Address all correspondence to: Amir.Fathy.n@qiau.ac.ir

1 Islamic Azad University, Hamedan Beranch, Bahar, Hamedan, Iran

2 Islamic Azad University East Tehran Branch, Tehran, Iran

References

[1] Abolhasani, S. M., Meybodi, M. R., & Esnaashari, M. (2007). LABER: A Learning Automata Based Energy-aware Routing Protocol for Sensor Networks. *IKT conference, Tehran, Iran.*

[2] Al-Karaki, J. N., & Kamal, A. E. Routing techniques in wireless sensor networks: a survey. *IEEE Wireless Communications*, 6-28, 11.

[3] Ankit, M., Arpit, M., Deepak, T. J., Venkateswarlu, R., & Janakiram, D. (2006). TinyLAP: A Scalable learning automata-based energy aware routing protocol for sensor networks. *Communicated to IEEE Wireless and Communications and Networking Conference, Las Vegas, NV USA.*

[4] Beigy, H., & Meybodi, M. R. (2004). A mathematical framework for cellular learning automata. Advances on Complex Systems Nos. 3-4, September/December, New Jersey,., 7, 295-320.

[5] Carvalho, J. P., Carola, M., & Tomé, A. B. (2002). Using Rule-Based Fuzzy Cognitive Maps to Model Dynamic Cell Behavior in Voronoi Based Cellular Automata. *FCT-Portuguese Foundation for Science and Technology, Lisboa, Portugal.*

[6] Chang, J. H., & Tassiulas, L. (2004). Maximum lifetime routing in wireless sensor networks. IEEE/ACM Trans. on Networking August., 12(4), 609-619.

[7] Esnaashari, M., & Meybodi, M. R. (2007). Irregular Cellular Learning Automata and Its Application to Clustering in Sensor Networks. Proceedings of 15th Conference on Electrical Engineering (15th ICEE), Tehran, Iran May., 15-17.

[8] Fathy Navid, A. H. (2010). SELARP: Scalable and Energy-aware Learning Automata-based Routing Protocols for Wireless Sensor Networks. *Proceedings of SENSORCOMM2010, IEEE, Venis, Italy.*

[9] Fathy, Navid. A. H., & Seyyed, Javadi. S. H. (2009). Energy Aware Routing Protocol for WSN Using Irregular Cellular Learning Automata. IEEE Symposium on Industrial Electronics and Applications (ISIEA2009), Kuala Lumpur, Malaysia, October , 4-6.

[10] Flache, A., & Hegselmann, R. (2002). Do Irregular Grids make a Difference? Relaxing the Spatial Regularity Assumption in Cellular Models of Social Dynamics. JASSS, Journal of Artificial Societies and Social Simulation of 26), 11/4/2002., 4(4)

[11] James, C., & Kingsbery Jr, . (2006). Excluded Blocks in Cellular Automata. *WILLIAMS COLLEGE Williamstown, Massachusetts.*

[12] Klein, R., & Aurenhammer, F. (2001). Voronoi diagrams. D. Forschungsgemein schaft Editor.

[13] Papadimitriou, I., & Georgiadis, L. (2005). Energy-aware routing to maximize lifetime in wireless sensor networks with mobile sink. 13th International Conference on Software, Telecommunications and Computer Networks, SoftCOM2005 September., 120-126.

[14] Schiff, J.L. (2005). Introduction to cellular automata. http://psoup.math.wise.edu/491October2008.

[15] Shah, R., & Rabaey, J. (2002). Energy aware routing for low energy ad hoc sensor networks. Proceedings of the IEEE Wireless Communications and Networking Conference (WCNC) Orlando, FL, March., 143-150.

[16] Souvaine, D., Horn, M., & Weber, J. (2005). Voronoi diagrams, Computational Geometry. *Tufts University Editor, Spring.*

[17] Narendra, K. S., & Thathachar, M. A. L. (1989). Learning automata: an introduction. *Prentice Hall.*

[18] Thathachar, M. A. L., & Sastry, P. S. (2002). Varieties of learning automata: an overview. *IEEE Transaction on Systems, Man, and Cybernetics-Part B: Cybernetics,* 32(6).

[19] Zeng, X., Bagrodia, R., & Gerla, M. (1998). GloMoSim: a library for parallel simulation of large-scale wireless networks. *in: PADS.*

[20] Esnaashari, M., Meybodi, M. R., & Sabaei, M. (2007). A novel method for QoS support in sensor networks. CSICC2007, Tehran, I. R. Iran,., 740-747.

[21] Mitrokotsa, A., Mavropodi, R., & Douligeris, C. (2006). Intrusion Detection of Packet Dropping Attacks in Mobile Ad Hoc Networks. *Proceedings of the International Conference on Intelligent Systems And Computing: Theory And Applications, Ayia Napa, Cyprus,* 111-118.

[22] Otrok, H., Debbabi, M., Assi, C., & Bhattacharya, P. (2007). A Cooperative Approach for Analyzing Intrusions in Mobile Ad hoc Networks. *Proceedings of the 27th International Conference on Distributed Computing Systems Workshops, (ICDCSW2007).*

[23] Mishra, A., Nadkarni, K., & Patcha, A. (2004). Intrusion Detection in Wireless Ad Hoc Networks. *IEEE Wireless Communications, IEEE press.*, 48-60.

[24] Sterne, D., Balasubramanyam, P., et al. (2005). A General Cooperative Intrusion Detection Architecture for MANETs. *Proceedings of the 3rd IEEE International Workshop on Information Assurance (IWIA2005)*, 57-70.

[25] Sumalatha, V., & Reddy, P. C. (2009). A Novel Approach for Misbehavior Detection in Ad hoc Networks. International Journal of Cryptography and Security January, 17-24., 2(1)

[26] Kachirski, O., & Guha, R. (2002). Intrusion Detection Using Mobile agents in wireless Ad hoc Networks. *Proceedings of the IEEE workshop on Knowledge Media Networking,* 153-158.

[27] Misra, S., Krishna, P. V., & Abraham, K. I. (2011). A simple learning automata-based solution for intrusion detection in wireless sensor networks. *Wireless Communication and Mobile Computing* [11], 426-441.

[28] Misra, S., Abraham, K. I., et al. (2009). LAID: a learning automata-based approach for intrusion detection in wireless sensor networks. *Security and Communication Networks,* 2(2), 105-115.

[29] Kari, J. (2004). Theory of cellular automata: a survey. FIN-20014, Turku, Finland. Elsevier, 1 October.

Chapter 6

Interactive Maps on Variant Phase Spaces – From Measurements - Micro Ensembles to Ensemble Matrices on Statistical Mechanics of Particle Models

Jeffrey Zheng, Christian Zheng and Tosiyasu Kunii

Additional information is available at the end of the chapter

http://dx.doi.org/10.5772/51635

1. Introduction

1.1. Fundamental models of cellular automata and phase space

1.1.1. White and Black Box Models

Input, output and functions are fundamental elements of the wider applications of dynamic systems [3, 5, 21] such applications include: mathematics, probability, physics, statistics, classical logic, and cellular automata.

For a pair of N bit vectors $X, Y \in B_2^N$ with states, for a given 0-1 function f, the pair of 0-1 vectors are linked by an equation where the function may be expressed by $Y = f(X)$ thus:

$$\text{Input } X \rightarrow \boxed{\begin{array}{c}\text{- White Box -}\\ \text{Given function } f\end{array}} \rightarrow \text{Output } Y. \tag{1}$$

This is called *a white box model* [3, 15, 28]. Using the white box model, a pair (X, Y) can be explicitly calculated by a function f.

If there is no explicit expression for a unknown function U, a pair of vectors (X, Y) could be collected for their correspondences on the pair of input-output relationships. Equation $Y = U(X)$ is still satisfied. This is called *a black box model*. i.e. A pair of (X, Y) can be measured by a unknown function U, or expressed as

$$\text{Input } X \rightarrow \boxed{\begin{array}{c}\text{- Black Box -}\\ \text{Unknow function } U\end{array}} \rightarrow \text{Output } Y. \quad (2)$$

In science and engineering [13, 28, 29], a *black box* is a device, system, or object which can be viewed solely in terms of its input, output and transfer characteristics without any knowledge of its internal works.

From a cellular automata viewpoint, the black box approach is useful in describing a situation where both input and output are in the form of two bit vectors for an unknown function of a digital system.

1.1.2. Characteristic Point and Phase Space

In mathematics and physics [3, 14, 18, 20, 21, 29], the concept of *a phase space* as introduced by W. Gibbs in 1901 is a space in which all possible states of a system are represented. Here, each possible state of the system corresponds to one unique point in the phase space. For cellular automata, the phase space usually consists of all possible values of pairs of input and output vectors in multiple dimensions.

For either a known function f or for an unknown function U, when the states of X, Y reside in the same finite region, it is entirely feasible in principle to undertake an exhaustive procedure to list all pairs of $\{(X, Y)\}$. For a given N bit vector X, the vector generates a *point* with a unique spatial position to indicate the characteristics of the function and by listing all such possible points, a *phase space* for the function is established.

1.2. Historical review on phase spaces of statistical mechanics

Top-down and bottom-up are two distinct strategies of intelligent processing and knowledge ordering used in humanistic and scientific theories [4, 13, 15, 25, 28]. In practice, they can be seen as alternative styles of thinking and problem solving. *Top-down* may be taken to mean an approach based on an analysis or decomposition to identify key components within a global target that has been identified for study and from which there may be constructed a hierarchy of local features. *Bottom-up* may be taken to describe a process of synthesis via integration working from local features towards a global target.

1.2.1. Bottom-up Approaches

Isaac Newton (1642-1727) and Gottfried Wilhelm Leibniz (1646-1716) gave calculus to the world of mathematics during the decade 1670-1680. This established a systematic methodology for the efficient analysis of local variables in order to reveal global features.

Joseph-Louis Lagrange (1736-1813) took the conservation of energy as the foundation for his system of mechanics where he combined the principle of virtual velocities with the principle of least action. Along these lines, W. R. Hamilton (1805-65) established his approach to dynamics in 1834-1835 with the first description of functions on phase space with pairs of conjugate parameters, together with position and momentum. J. Liouville (1809-82) proposed a theorem on the conservation of volume in phase space in 1838. C. G. Jacobi

(1804-51) recognized that Liouville's works could be used to describe mechanical systems and so placed Liouville's mathematical theorem into a mechanical context. Pücker working in Germany and Cayley and Sylvester in the UK, extended projective geometry beyond the ordinary three dimensions in the 1840s and Grassmann developed an n dimensional vector space in 1844.

Riemannn's work in 1868 developed the geometric properties of multi-dimensional manifolds. This was followed by further developments in the 1870s by E. Betti, F. Klein, and C. Jordan then more recently by [23, 24, 31, 33].

As it was Lagrange who took the first steps, a bottom-up approach is now often described as *a Lagrange expression*. Hamiltonian dynamics is a typical representative under this expression as it is founded on *a pair of conjugate parameters* [31, 33].

1.2.2. Top-down Approaches

Robert Boyle (1627-91) developed new physio-mechanical experiments. Boyle's law states that at a constant temperature, the volume of a fixed mass of gas is inversely proportional to its pressure using a set of measures characterizing the global properties of a gas. Anders Celsius (1701-1744) proposed a thermometer scale calibrated to the freezing point and boiling point of water. Benjamin Thompson (later known as Count Rumford) (1753-1814) explored cannon barrel-boring experiments and demonstrated the conversion of work into heat via friction in the absence of any additional weight of the object due to such heating being detected. Leonhard Euler (1707-1783) developed a Kinetic Heat Theory based on his description of a calculus of variations to introduce the concept of moving axes in astronomy. Daniel Bernoulli (1700-1782) and Pierre-Simon Laplace (1749-1827) refined Newton's work to represent gas properties through repulsive interactions. Jean Baptiste Joseph Fourier (1768-1830) developed an understanding of the conduction of heat to represent a periodic function as a Fourier series. Poisson (1781-1840) further developed the theories of heat using Fourier series. Thomas Young (1773-1829) expressed the modern formulation of energy, mathematically associated with mv^2. Sadi Carnot (1796-1832) introduced the concept of ideal gas cycle analysis. William Thomson (later known as Lord Kelvin) (1824-1907) developed a wave theory of heat in homogeneous solid bodies. James Prescott Joule (1818-1889) established the relationship between heat and mechanical work through a series of experiments. John James Waterston (1811-1883) explored a kinetic theory of gases and mean free path. Von Helmholtz (1821-94) further developed the principle of conservation of energy extending Carnot's principle of kinetic energy into a mathematical formulation. Rudolf Clausius (1822-88) explored an expression of the second law for which the only function is the transfer of heat to propose the function dQ/T to compare heat flows with heat conversions using Carnot's techniques to derive *entropy* and show the two laws of thermodynamics were the equivalent of the older caloric theory. Gustav Robert Kirchhoff (1824-1887) derived from the second law of thermodynamics that objects cannot be distinguished by thermal radiation at a uniform temperature to formulate a black body [23, 24, 31, 33].

Leonhard Euler (1707-1783) provided key methodologies in this direction with a top-down approach known as *a Euler expression*. A Fourier series of a periodic function is a typical representative under this expression founded on *a periodic function composed of a set of simple harmonic components* [31, 33].

1.2.3. Formal Expression of Phase Space in Statistical Mechanics

Following methodologies established by Hamilton, Lagrange, and Euler, [26] and L. Boltzmann (1844-1906) went on to lay the foundations of statistical mechanics from 1871. They introduced the term *phase* to describe the analogy they saw between the physical trajectories of particles in two dimensional space and Lissajous figures expressed as interactive maps. When two harmonic frequencies exist as rational fractions, period 4 circular patterns occur. However, when the frequency ratio is irrational, the system trajectories visit all points on the plane bounded by the signal amplitude. J. C. Maxwell (1831-79) adopted Boltzmann's expression of phase to describe the state of systems in 1879. William Thomson (Lord Kelvin) was the first to use the word *demon* for Maxwell's Thermodynamics concept in 1874. H. Poincarè (1854-1912) in 1885 took a geometric approach to visualize a saddle point where stable and unstable trajectories intersected in phase space. Various mapping techniques are relevant to such explorations. These include Poincarè sections (maps), fixed-point classifications, and the conservation of phase space as an integrated invariant. Influenced by the work of Maxwell and Boltzmann together with other wider contributions, J. W. Gibbs (1939-1903) proposed his Elementary Principles in Statistical Mechanics in 1902 to describe a phase as represented by a point of $2n$ dimensions.

From a terminological viewpoint, Gibbs brought us such expressions as *statistical mechanics, micro ensemble, canonical ensemble, and grand ensemble.* He facilitated the establishment of a hierarchy in Statistical Mechanics. However, Gibbs did not use the term *phase space*. The first formal expression of the term *phase space* appeared in the context of ergodic theory in a 1913 publication by A. Rosenthal and M. Plancherel [26, 31, 33].

From 1919 to 1922, Sir Charles Galton Darwin (1887-1962) worked with Sir Ralph Howard Fowler (1889-1944) on statistical mechanics and established the Darwin-Fowler method.

1.2.4. Key Properties in Statistical Mechanics

[23, 24, 31, 33] noted the usefulness of listing key properties in classical statistical mechanics. A typical comparison is presented below in Table 1.

In general, both Maxwell-Boltzmann and Gibbs follow black-box models without involving explicit local functions. However, the Darwin-Fowler method uses a complex function to describe its unit cell so making it a white box model. Both Maxwell-Boltzmann and Darwin-Fowler schemes use Lagrange expressions to calculate cell unit and to form their fundamentals using a bottom-up strategy. Meanwhile, Gibbs applies Euler expressions for analysis using a top-down strategy without involving explicit cell units.

Table 1 uses abbreviations as follows: TM for Time Measurement, PSM for Phase Space Measurement, PS for Phase Space, EPV for Equal Phase Volume, MPD for Most Probable Distribution, MCE for Micro Canonical Ensemble, CE for Canonical Ensemble, and GCE for Grand Canonical Ensemble.

1.2.5. Common Interpretations of Quantum Mechanics

Quantum mechanics is a modern legacy with its roots in classical statistical mechanics [11, 12, 17]. Meanwhile, Bose-Einstein, Fermi-Dirac statistics, and Planck's quantum are deeply connected with the statistical mechanics of Boltzmann and Gibbs [17, 19].

Key Issue	Maxwell-Boltzmann Most probable theory	Darwin-Fowler Average Theory	Gibbs Ensemble Theory
Assumption	Ergodic Average: TM = PSM	Ergodic Average: TM = PSM	Equality of PS: EPV in same probability
Phase Space N	State combination	State combination	Density functions Liouville equation
Cell Unit n	Local cell in n particles Stirling Approximation	Complex function non restriction to n	Ensemble based non-cell required
Balanced States	MPD with maximal entropy	MPD with maximal entropy	MPD with maximal entropy
Expression	Lagrange	Lagrange	Euler
Interaction	No	No	Yes
Prefer System	Isolated system for { MCE, CE} not for GCE	Isolated system for { MCE, CE} not for GCE	MCE: isolated system; CE : closed system; GCE : open system
Model	Black-box non function Bottom-up	White-box explicit function Bottom-up	Black-box non function Top-down

Table 1. Key Methods in Statistical Mechanics

In the context of the pursuit of an interpretation of quantum mechanics, the state vector or wave function has been widely discussed as a model for describing the individual components of a system (e.g. an electron).

The most comprehensive descriptions of an individual physical system are to be found in the various versions of *the Copenhagen interpretation* [8], or in subsequent versions incorporating minor modifications as in *the hidden variable interpretations* [19, 31].

An interpretation according to the state vector based not on an individual system but on an ensemble of identically prepared systems is known as *a statistical ensemble interpretation* or more briefly just as *a statistical interpretation* [19, 31].

The two alternative strategies of top-down and bottom-up strongly influence the direction of various explorations in the field of quantum mechanism. *The Lagrange expression* emphasizes single particles in a bottom-up strategy. In contrast, *the Euler expression* emphasizes complex objects treated as ensembles in a top-down strategy.

From as early as the turn of the 20th century when Plank started his quantum revolution, various interpretations of quantum behaviors have been explored. Following the Heisenberg matrix approach and the Schrödinger wave function equation, the intellectually absorbing anomalies of quantum mechanics have been linked to intrinsic behaviors associated with particle and wave duality.

To address the various paradoxes encountered in the development of quantum mechanics during the course of 20th century, a number of different interpretations may be listed [19, 31].

Probabilistic interpretation Max Born 1926 [19]]

Copenhagen interpretation N. Bohr and Heisenberg 1927 [8]

Double-solution interpretation de Broglie 1927, 1953 [9]

de Broglie-Bohm Theory de Broglie 1927, David Bohm 1952 [9]

Standard interpretation von Neumann 1932 Wigner, Wheeler [32]

Quantum Logic G. Birkhoff and von Neumann 1936 [19]

Ensemble interpretation D. Blokhintsev 1949 [6]

Many-world interpretation H. Everett 1957 [19]

Time-symmetric theory Y. Aharonov 1964

Stochastic interpretation E.Nelson 1966

Many-minds interpretation H. Zeh 1970 [34]

Consistent histories R. Griffiths 1984

Objective collapse theories Ghirardi-Rimini-Weber 1986

Transitional interpretation J. Cramer 1986

Rational interpretation C. Rovelli 1994

In general, the seven key interpretations (Copenhagen, Double-solution, de Broglie-Bohm, Standard, Ensemble, Many-world, and Stochastic) of the first four decades of the 20th century can be separated as follows into the following two general categories [9, 31]:

1) **Lagrange Expression:** comprising the Copenhagen Interpretation (N. Bohr and Heisenberg), the Double-solution (de Broglie), the Standard Interpretation (von Neumann), the Many-world interpretation (H. Everett), and the de Broglie-Bohm Theory (de Broglie & David Bohm)
2) **Euler Expression:** comprising the Double-solution (de Broglie), the Ensemble interpretation (D. Blokhintsev), and the Stochastic interpretation (E. Nelson)

In general, a Lagrange expression is preferred for representing a single quanta while a Euler expression can better describe certain group activities. It is interesting to note that *de Broglie's Double-solution* with a special interpretation can to be involved in both cases [9, 31].

According to Einstein's criteria for quantum mechanics [10], an interpretation of quantum mechanics can be characterized by its treatment of:

- Realism
- Completeness
- Local realism
- Determinism

Here, an interpretation is taken to mean a correspondence between the elements of the mathematical formalism **M** and the elements of an interpreting structure **I**, where:

The Mathematical formalism M consists of the Hilbert space machinery of ket-vectors, self-adjoint operations on the space of ket-vectors, unitary time dependence of the ket-vectors and measurement operations: and ...

The interpreting structure I includes states, transitions between states, measurement operations and possible information about spatial extension of these elements.

Applying Einstein's criteria to this set of interpretations, the ensemble interpretation (statistical interpretation) is a minimalist interpretation. It claims to make the fewest assumptions associated with the standard mathematics. The most notable supporter of such statistical interpretation was Einstein himself [19, 22, 31].

1.2.6. *Statistical Interpretation of Quantum Mechanics*

At the 1927 Solvay Congress, Einstein proposed a statistical interpretation in order to avoid conceptual difficulties if the reduction of a wave packet led to the association of wave functions with individual systems. He hoped that someday a complete theory of microphysics would become available to establish a conceptual base as a (preferred) alternative to modern quantum mechanics [9, 31].

In 1932, von Neumann established *mathematical foundations for quantum mechanics* as a standard interpretation on Hilbert space to provide a proof rejecting any hidden variable approach [32].

Influenced by K.V. Nikolskii and V.A. Fock, D. I. Blokhintsev developed a statistical interpretation in the 1940s. He expressed the view that modern quantum mechanics is not a theory of micro-processes but rather a means of studying their properties by the application of statistical ensembles. Menawhile, the approach taken in the publication was borrowed from classical macro physics [6, 19, 22].

Landé's 1951 book sought to reconcile the contradictions between the two classical concepts of the particle and the wave by providing something equivalent to the descriptions of physical phenomena in either terms. He emphasized that in diffraction experiments, particles exhibit both maximum and minimum intensities of diffraction through a perfectly normal mechanical process that can be described in terms of a wave explanation. Using transition probability, these experimentally-determinable transition probabilities can be shown to map a matrix [19].

1.2.7. *Main weaknesses in key interpretations*

Compared to continuous approaches, Heisenberg's matrix offers several advances in handling the case of a single particle. In July 1926, the first question Heisenberg asked Schrödinger was, "Can you use your continuous wave equation to explain black body radiation or quantum effects in photoelectric actions?"

Due to the inherent differences between the two strategies it is difficult to find a direct answer to the question under the Copenhagen interpretation, "Is the Schrödinger equation a single particle description or an equation for a group of particles?" [16, 19, 31].

Through statistical interpretation is a minimalist interpretation, it too is not a complete interpretation. During the development of statistical interpretation there were various debates between Blokhintsev and Heisenberg during the 1940s [19, 22].

Heisenberg questioned as *self contradictory*, Blokhintsev's basic contention that quantum mechanics eliminates the observer and becomes objectively significant due to the fact that the wave function does not describe the state of a particle but rather identifies that the particle belongs to a particular ensemble. In this, Heisenberg argued that in order to assign a particle to a particular ensemble, some knowledge of the particle is required on the part of the observer [19], p445.

The main weakness of Blokhintsev's ensemble interpretation is that though its mathematical formula can express wave distributions well it fails to describe particle structure properly. This is a common weakness of similar mathematical constructions based on periodic components of a Fourier series [19, 27, 31].

Similar to difficulties faced by the Schrödinger equation, ensemble construction is suitable for wave representations but is weak in particle description. On the other hand, the Copenhagen interpretation is preferred for a single particle but comes with inherent limitations of expression with respect to wave behaviours which require further reliance on Born's probabilistic interpretation of the wave-function.

1.2.8. Other Challenges on Statistical Mechanics

Statistical mechanics presents us with several fundemental difficulties [20, 23, 24, 31, 33]:

Ergodic property: a time sequence average over a large set of local measurements be replaced by space (phase)-average

Analytic apparatus the construction of asymptotic formulas.

Computational Efficiency: use of modern computing power in tackling complexity.

Discrete via continuous: relationships between irregular discrete systems and regular continuous systems.

Logic foundation: solid logic foundation for statistical mechanics.

1.3. Chapter organization

In this chapter, *variant construction* comprising *variant logic, variant measurement and variant phase space* is explored with a view to addressing the main challenges and difficulties associated with statistical interpretations and statistical mechanics. The focus is on a unified model to illustrate a path leading from local measurements to global matrices on phase space via variant construction.

This chapter is organized into 12 sections addressing the following:

1. general introduction (above)
2. system architecture
3. creating micro ensemble
4. canonical ensemble and interactive maps
5. global ensemble and interactive map matrices
6. representation models
7. symbolic representation on selected cases

http://dx.doi.org/10.5772/51635

8. sample results
9. analysis of visual distributions
10. global symmetry properties
11. main results
12. conclusions

2. System architecture

In this section, system architecture and its core components are discussed with the use of diagrams.

2.1. Architecture

The three components of *a Variant Phase Space System* are *the Creating Micro Ensemble (CME), the Canonical Ensemble (CEIM)* together with *the Interactive Map and the Global Ensemble Matrix (GEM)* as shown in Figure 1. The architecture is shown in Figure 1(a) with the key modules of the three core components being shown in Figures 1(b) through 1(d) respectively.

In the first part of the system, a micro ensemble and its eight projections are created for a given vector and function by the CME component. Next, in order to exhaust all possible 2^N vectors, a CE and eight IMs are established by the CEIM component. Then, in order to exhaust all possible 2^{2^n} functions, a CE matrix and eight IM matrices are generated by the GEM component.

With eight parameters in an input group, there are four parameters in the intermediate group and two parameters in the output group.

The three groups of parameters may be listed as follows.

Input group:

N an integer indicates a 0-1 vector with N elements

n an integer indicates n variables for a function

X a 0-1 vector with N elements, $X \in B_2^N$

$\forall X$ exhaustive set of all states of N bit vectors with 2^N elements

J a function with n variables, $J \in B_2^{2^n}$

$\forall J$ exhaustive set of all functions of n variables with 2^{2^n} elements

SM a selection on a pair of measurements

FC A given configuration for variant logic functions: a $2^{2^{n-1}} \times 2^{2^{n-1}}$ matrix

Intermediate group:

$ME(J, X)$ a micro ensemble under either multiple or conditional probability measurements

$IP(J, X)$ a set of eight interactive projections related to $ME(J, X)$

$CE(J)$ a canonical ensemble for an N bit vector under an n variable function J

$IM(J)$ a set of eight interactive maps associated with one $CE(J)$

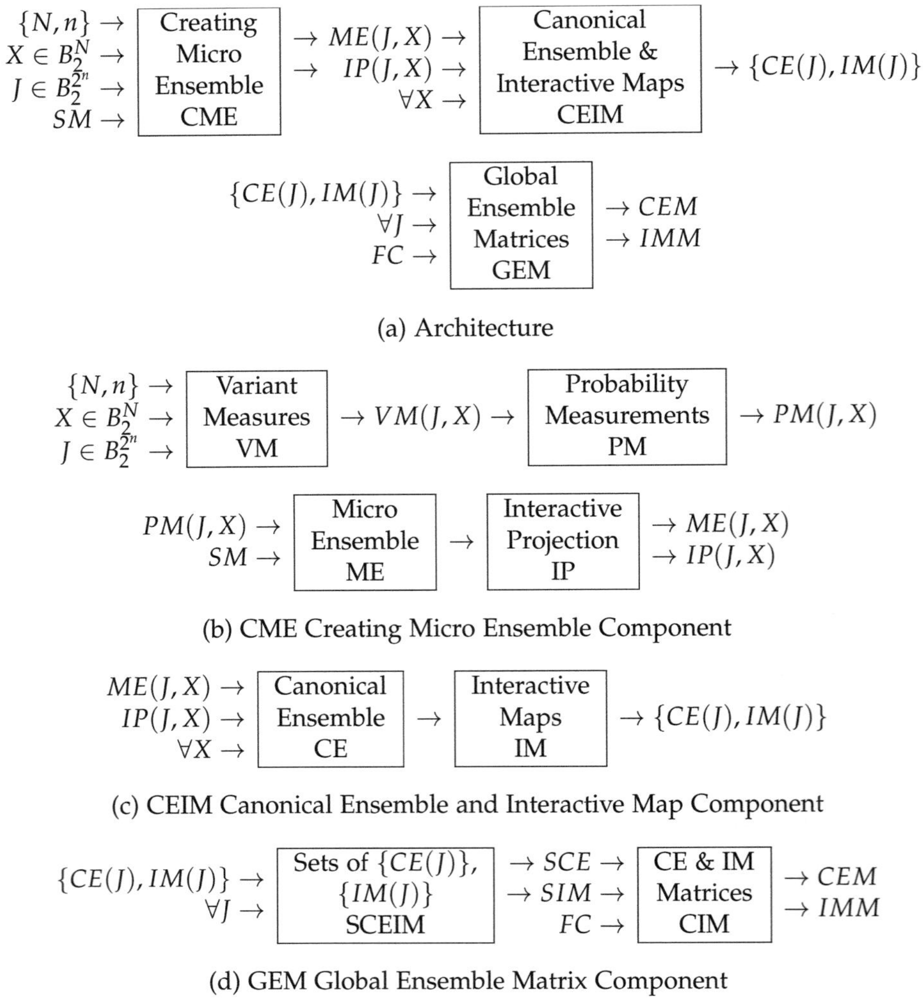

Figure 1. (a-d) Variant Phase Space System; (a) Architecture; (b) CME Creating Micro Ensemble; (c) CEIM Canonical Ensemble and Interactive Map; (d) GEM Global Ensemble Matrix

Output group:

CEM one CE matrix under FC condition

IMM a set of eight IM matrices under FC condition

2.2. CME creating micro ensemble

The CME component as shown in Figure 1(b) is composed of four modules: *VM Variant Measures, PM Probability Measurements, ME Micro Ensemble and IP Interactive Projection.* Five distinct parameters are shown as input signals $\{N, n, X, J, SM\}$ and two groups of vector measurements are performed as a group of output signals $\{ME(J, X), IP(J, X)\}$ respectively.

The various parameter can be described as follows:

http://dx.doi.org/10.5772/51635

Input:

N an integer indicating a 0-1 vector with N elements

n an integer indicating n variables for a function

X a 0-1 vector with N elements, $X \in B_2^N$

J a function with n variables, $J \in B_2^{2^n}$

SM a selection on a pair of measurements

Output:

$ME(J,X)$ a micro ensemble under either multiple or conditional probability measurements

$IP(J,X)$ a set of eight interactive projections under the SM condition

A point in variant phase space can be determined under a set of conditions. A set of relevant projections can be associated with an interactive environment. The operation of this module transfers each set of input parameters to one micro ensemble signal and its distinct interactive projections subject to certain restrictions.

2.3. CEIM canonical ensemble and interactive map

The CEIM component as shown in Figure 1(c) is composed of two modules: *CE Canonical Ensemble and IP Interactive Projection.* This component inputs three groups of parameters $\{ME(J,X), IP(J,X), \forall X\}$ from the CME component and outputs two sets of canonical ensembles together with its interactive maps $\{CE(J), IM(J)\}$ as distinct distributions under certain environments. One additional input and two output parameters are described as follows:

Adding Input:

$\forall X$ exhaustive set of all states of N bit vectors with 2^N elements

Output:

$CE(J)$ a canonical ensemble for an N bit vector under an n variable function J

$IM(J)$ a set of eight interactive maps associated with $CE(J)$

The CEIM component collects all possible micro ensembles for a given function to form a canonical ensemble on variant phase space. Meanwhile, different interactive maps associated with this CE can be calculated to output as a set of $IM(J)$ as distinct distributions under certain environment.

2.4. GIM global ensemble and interactive map matrix

The GIM component as shown in Figure 1(d) is composed of two modules: one for the *SCEIM Set of Cannonical Ensembles together with Interactive Maps, and the other for the CIM CE & IM Matrices.*

Two outputs $\{CE(J), IM(J)\}$ from CEIM are taken as inputs, while another two parameters $\{\forall J, FC\}$ and two outputs can be described as follows:

Adding Input:

$\forall J$ exhaustive set of all functions of n variables with 2^{2^n} elements

FC a given configuration for variant logic functions: a $2^{2^{n-1}} \times 2^{2^{n-1}}$ matrix

Output:

CEM a CE matrix under FC condition

IMM a set of IM matrices under FC condition

The SCEIM module processes an exhaustive operation on all possible values of function J to generate sets of $\{\{CE(J)\}, \{IM(J)\}\}_{\forall J}$ as the output. The CIM module further organizes the data to arrange each set as a $2^{2^{n-1}} \times 2^{2^{n-1}}$ matrix with 2^{2^n} elements and with the specific arrangement determined by FC condition.

After two exhaustive processes through CEIM and GIM activities, a CE matrix and the relevant IM Matrices are generated. Each matrix contains 2^{2^n} elements as distributions. Further symmetry properties can be identified from each specific configuration.

Since specific components and modules are relevant to the detail of the complex mechanisms, further explanations on each component are presented in Sections 3 through 5.

3. Creating micro ensemble

The first part of the system is the CME component composed of four modules: VM Variant Measures, PM Probability Measurements, ME Micro Ensemble and IP Interactive Projection respectively.

It is necessary to clearly describe these four modules in order to understand the measurement properties of variant construction [35]-[44]. Relevant information and supporting materials on fundamental levels of variant construction are briefly descried in Section 3.1 and the four modules are investigated in Sections 3.2 through 3.5.

3.1. Initial preparation on variant measurements

The variant measurement construction is based on n-variable logic functions and N bit vectors taken as input and output results [40, 43, 44].

3.1.1. Two sets of states

For n-variables where $x = x_{n-1}...x_i...x_0$, $0 \leq i < n, x_i \in \{0,1\} = B_2$, let a position j be the selected variable $0 \leq j < n$, x_j be the selected variable. Let output variable y and n-variable function $f, y = f(x)$, $y \in B_2, x \in B_2^n$. For all states of x, a set $S(n)$ composed of the 2^n states can be divided into two sets: $S_0(n)$ and $S_1(n)$.

$$\begin{cases} S_0(n) = \{x | x_j = 0, \forall x \in B_2^n\} \\ S_1(n) = \{x | x_j = 1, \forall x \in B_2^n\} \\ S(n) = \{S_0(n), S_1(n)\} \end{cases} \tag{3}$$

http://dx.doi.org/10.5772/51635

3.1.2. Four variant functions

For a given logic function f, input and output pair relationships define four variant logic functions $\{f_\perp, f_+, f_-, f_\top\}$.

$$\begin{cases} f_\perp(x) = \{f(x)|x \in S_0(n), y = 0\} \\ f_+(x) = \{f(x)|x \in S_0(n), y = 1\} \\ f_-(x) = \{f(x)|x \in S_1(n), y = 0\} \\ f_\top(x) = \{f(x)|x \in S_1(n), y = 1\} \end{cases} \quad (4)$$

3.1.3. Two polarized functions

Considering two standard logic canonical expressions: AND-OR form is selected from $\{f_+(x), f_\top(x)\}$ as $y = 1$ items, and OR-AND form is selected from $\{f_-(x), f_\perp(x)\}$ as $y = 0$ items. Considering $\{f_\top(x), f_\perp(x)\}$, $x_j = y$ items, they are invariant themselves.

To select $\{f_+(x), f_-(x)\}, x_j \neq y$ in forming a variant logic expression. Let $f(x) = \langle f_+|x|f_-\rangle$ be the variant logic expression. Any logic function can be expressed as a variant logic form. In $\langle f_+|x|f_-\rangle$ structure, f_+ selected 1 items in $S_0(n)$ as same as the AND-OR standard expression, and f_- selected 0 items in $S_1(n)$ as same as OR-AND expression.

3.1.4. $n = 2$ representation

For a convenient understanding of the variant representation, 2-variable logic structures are illustrated in Table 2 for its 16 functions in four variant functions as follows.

Let $x^v = \begin{cases} \perp, x = 0, y = 0; \\ +, x = 0, y = 1; \\ -, x = 1, y = 0; \\ \top, x = 1, y = 1. \end{cases}$ and $x^\delta = \begin{cases} x, \delta = 1; \\ \bar{x}, \delta = 0. \end{cases}$

For a pair of $\{f_+, f_-\}$ functions selected from the structure, relevant representations are illustrated in Table 3 to show the variant capacity on the full expression of all logic functions.

Checking two functions $f = 3$ and $f = 6$ respectively.
$\{f = 3 := \{1, 0\}, f_+ = 11 := \langle 0|\varnothing\rangle, f_- = 2 := \langle\varnothing|3\rangle\}$;
$\{f = 6 := \{2, 1\}, f_+ = 14 := \langle 2|\varnothing\rangle, f_- = 2 := \langle\varnothing|3\rangle\}$.

3.1.5. Variant measure functions

Let Δ be the variant measure function [1, 35]-[42]

$$\begin{aligned} \Delta &= \langle \Delta_\perp, \Delta_+, \Delta_-, \Delta_\top \rangle \\ \Delta J(x) &= \langle \Delta_\perp J(x), \Delta_+ J(x), \Delta_- J(x), \Delta_\top J(x) \rangle \\ \Delta_\alpha J(x) &= \begin{cases} 1, \ J(x) \in J_\alpha(x), \alpha \in \{\perp, +, -, \top\} \\ 0, \ \text{others} \end{cases} \end{aligned} \quad (7)$$

For any given n-variable state there is one position in $\Delta J(x)$ to be 1 and other 3 positions are 0.

f No.	$f \in S(n)$	3 11	2 10	1 01	0 00	3^v 11^v	2^v 10^v	1^v 01^v	0^v 00^v	$f_\perp \in S_0(n)$	$f_+ \in S_0(n)$	$f_- \in S_1(n)$	$f_\top \in S_1(n)$
0	$\{\emptyset\}$	0	0	0	0	$-$	$\perp$	$-$	$\perp$	$\{2,0\}$	$\{\emptyset\}$	$\{3,1\}$	$\{\emptyset\}$
1	$\{0\}$	0	0	0	1	$-$	$\perp$	$-$	$+$	$\{2\}$	$\{0\}$	$\{3,1\}$	$\{\emptyset\}$
2	$\{1\}$	0	0	1	0	$-$	$\perp$	$\top$	$\perp$	$\{2.0\}$	$\{\emptyset\}$	$\{3\}$	$\{1\}$
3	$\{1,0\}$	0	0	1	1	$-$	$\perp$	$\top$	$+$	$\{2\}$	$\{0\}$	$\{3\}$	$\{1\}$
4	$\{2\}$	0	1	0	0	$-$	$+$	$-$	$\perp$	$\{0\}$	$\{2\}$	$\{3,1\}$	$\{\emptyset\}$
5	$\{2,0\}$	0	1	0	1	$-$	$+$	$-$	$+$	$\{\emptyset\}$	$\{2,0\}$	$\{3,1\}$	$\{\emptyset\}$
6	$\{2,1\}$	0	1	1	0	$-$	$+$	$\top$	$\perp$	$\{0\}$	$\{2\}$	$\{3\}$	$\{1\}$
7	$\{2,1,0\}$	0	1	1	1	$-$	$+$	$\top$	$+$	$\{\emptyset\}$	$\{2,0\}$	$\{3\}$	$\{1\}$
8	$\{3\}$	1	0	0	0	$\top$	$\perp$	$-$	$\perp$	$\{2,0\}$	$\{\emptyset\}$	$\{1\}$	$\{3\}$
9	$\{3,0\}$	1	0	0	1	$\top$	$\perp$	$-$	$+$	$\{2\}$	$\{0\}$	$\{1\}$	$\{3\}$
10	$\{3,1\}$	1	0	1	0	$\top$	$\perp$	$\top$	$\perp$	$\{2,0\}$	$\{\emptyset\}$	$\{\emptyset\}$	$\{3,1\}$
11	$\{3,1,0\}$	1	0	1	1	$\top$	$\perp$	$\top$	$+$	$\{2\}$	$\{0\}$	$\{\emptyset\}$	$\{3,1\}$
12	$\{3,2\}$	1	1	0	0	$\top$	$+$	$-$	$\perp$	$\{0\}$	$\{2\}$	$\{1\}$	$\{3\}$
13	$\{3,2,0\}$	1	1	0	1	$\top$	$+$	$-$	$+$	$\{\emptyset\}$	$\{2,0\}$	$\{1\}$	$\{3\}$
14	$\{3,2,1\}$	1	1	1	0	$\top$	$+$	$\top$	$\perp$	$\{0\}$	$\{2\}$	$\{\emptyset\}$	$\{3,1\}$
15	$\{3,2,1,0\}$	1	1	1	1	$\top$	$+$	$\top$	$+$	$\{\emptyset\}$	$\{2,0\}$	$\{\emptyset\}$	$\{3,1\}$

(5)

Table 2. Four Variant Functions in 2-variable logic

f No.	$f \in S(n)$	3 11	2 10	1 01	0 00	$f_+ \in S_0(n)$	3^0 11^0	2^1 10^1	1^0 01^0	0^1 00^1	$f_- \in S_1(n)$
0	$\{\emptyset\}$	0	0	0	0	$\langle\emptyset\vert$	1	0	1	0	$\vert 3,1\rangle$
1	$\{0\}$	0	0	0	1	$\langle 0\vert$	1	0	1	1	$\vert 3,1\rangle$
2	$\{1\}$	0	0	1	0	$\langle\emptyset\vert$	1	0	0	0	$\vert 3\rangle$
3	$\{1,0\}$	0	0	1	1	$\langle 0\vert$	1	0	0	1	$\vert 3\rangle$
4	$\{2\}$	0	1	0	0	$\langle 2\vert$	1	1	1	0	$\vert 3,1\rangle$
5	$\{2,0\}$	0	1	0	1	$\langle 2,0\vert$	1	1	1	1	$\vert 3,1\rangle$
6	$\{2,1\}$	0	1	1	0	$\langle 2\vert$	1	1	0	0	$\vert 3\rangle$
7	$\{2,1,0\}$	0	1	1	1	$\langle 2,0\vert$	1	1	0	1	$\vert 3\rangle$
8	$\{3\}$	1	0	0	0	$\langle\emptyset\vert$	0	0	1	0	$\vert 1\rangle$
9	$\{3,0\}$	1	0	0	1	$\langle 0\vert$	0	0	1	1	$\vert 1\rangle$
10	$\{3,1\}$	1	0	1	0	$\langle\emptyset\vert$	0	0	0	0	$\vert\emptyset\rangle$
11	$\{3,1,0\}$	1	0	1	1	$\langle 0\vert$	0	0	0	1	$\vert\emptyset\rangle$
12	$\{3,2\}$	1	1	0	0	$\langle 2\vert$	0	1	1	0	$\vert 1\rangle$
13	$\{3,2,0\}$	1	1	0	1	$\langle 2,0\vert$	0	1	1	1	$\vert 1\rangle$
14	$\{3,2,1\}$	1	1	1	0	$\langle 2\vert$	0	1	0	0	$\vert\emptyset\rangle$
15	$\{3,2,1,0\}$	1	1	1	1	$\langle 2,0\vert$	0	1	0	1	$\vert\emptyset\rangle$

(6)

Table 3. A pair of selected functions and their full expression

3.1.6. Variant measures on vector

For any N bit 0-1 vector $X, X = X_{N-1}...X_j...X_0$, $0 \leq j < N, X_j \in B_2, X \in B_2^N$ under n-variable function J, n bit 0-1 output vector Y, $Y = J(X) = \langle J_+|X|J_-\rangle$, $Y = Y_{N-1}...Y_j...Y_0, 0 \leq j < N, Y_j \in B_2, Y \in B_2^N$. For the j-th position $x^j = [...X_j...] \in B_2^n$ to form $Y_j = J(x^j) = \langle J_+|x^j|J_-\rangle$. Let N bit positions be cyclic linked. Variant measures of $J(X)$ can be decomposed as a quaternion

$$\Delta(X:Y) = \Delta J(X) = \sum_{j=0}^{N-1} \Delta J(x^j) = \langle N_\perp, N_+, N_-, N_\top \rangle \tag{8}$$

$\langle N_\perp, N_+, N_-, N_\top \rangle$, $N = N_\perp + N_+ + N_- + N_\top$.

3.1.7. Example

E.g. $N = 12$, given $J, Y = J(X)$.

$$\begin{aligned} X &= 1\ 0\ 1\ 1\ 1\ 0\ 1\ 1\ 1\ 0\ 0\ 1 \\ Y &= 0\ 0\ 1\ 0\ 1\ 0\ 1\ 0\ 1\ 1\ 0\ 0 \\ \Delta(X:Y) &= -\ \perp\ \top\ -\ \top\ \perp\ \top\ -\ \top\ +\ \perp\ - \end{aligned}$$

$\Delta J(X) = \langle N_\perp, N_+, N_-, N_\top \rangle = \langle 3, 1, 4, 4 \rangle, N = 12$.

Input and output pairs are 0-1 variables for only four combinations. For any given function J, the quantitative relationship of $\{\perp, +, -, \top\}$ is directly derived from the input/output sequences. Four meta measures are determined.

3.1.8. Basic Properties of Variant Logic

For given n 0-1 variables, a given function J and an N bit vector X, the following corollaries can be described [35]-[44].

Corollary 3.1: For n 0-1 variables, the state set contains a total of 2^n states.

Corollary 3.2: For n 0-1 variables, the function set contains a total of 2^{2^n} functions.

Corollary 3.3: For an N bit vector X, the phase space is composed of a total of 2^N vectors.

Corollary 3.4: A logic function f can be partitioned as four variant functions as $f = (f_\perp, f_+, f_-, f_\top)$ respectively.

Corollary 3.5: For a given vector X and a given function J, a measure vector of four meta measures for variant measures can be determined as a quaternion $\Delta J(X) = \langle N_\perp, N_+, N_-, N_\top \rangle$.

3.2. VM variant measures

Using defined variant functions, it is possible to describe the VM module in Fig. 1(b) as follows.

Under variant construction, N bits of 0-1 vector X under a function J produce seven Meta measures composed of a measure vector $VM(J,X)$.

$$\begin{array}{r}
(X:J(X)) \rightarrow (N_\perp, N_+, N_-, N_\top),\\
N_0 = N_\perp + N_+,\\
N_1 = N_- + N_\top,\\
N = N_0 + N_1.
\end{array} \tag{9}$$

From a measuring viewpoint, there are seven measures identified in this set of parameters. They can be expressed in three levels.

$$\begin{array}{ccccccc}
 & & & N & & & \\
 & N_0 & & & & N_1 & \\
N_\perp & & N_+ & & N_- & & N_\top
\end{array} \tag{10}$$

In the current system, the output of the VM module is expressed as $VM(J,X) = \{N_\perp, N_+, N_-, N_\top, N_0, N_1, N\}$.

3.3. PM probability measurements

Measures of $VM(J,X)$ are input as numeric vectors into the PM module. Using variant quaternion and other three core measures, local measurements of probability signals are calculated as eight meta measurements in two groups by following the given equations. For any N bit 0-1 vector X, function J, under Δ measurement: $\Delta J(X) = \langle N_\perp, N_+, N_-, N_\top \rangle$, $N_0 = N_\perp + N_+, N_1 = N_- + N_\top, N = N_0 + N_1$

The first group of probability signal vectors ρ and $\{\rho_0, \rho_1\}$ are defined by

$$\begin{cases}
\rho = \frac{\Delta J(X)}{N} = (\rho_\perp, \rho_+, \rho_-, \rho_\top,)\\
\rho_\alpha = \frac{N_\alpha}{N}, \alpha \in \{\perp, +, -, \top\};\\
\rho_0 = N_0/N,\\
\rho_1 = N_1/N.
\end{cases} \tag{11}$$

The second group of probability signal vectors $\tilde{\rho}$ and $\{\tilde{\rho}_0, \tilde{\rho}_1\}$ is defined by

$$\begin{cases}
\tilde{\rho} = \frac{\Delta J(X)}{N_0|N_1} = (\tilde{\rho}_\perp, \tilde{\rho}_+, \tilde{\rho}_-, \tilde{\rho}_\top),\\
\tilde{\rho}_\perp = \frac{N_\perp}{N_0},\\
\tilde{\rho}_+ = \frac{N_+}{N_0},\\
\tilde{\rho}_- = \frac{N_-}{N_1},\\
\tilde{\rho}_\top = \frac{N_\top}{N_1};\\
\tilde{\rho}_0 = N_0/N,\\
\tilde{\rho}_1 = N_1/N.
\end{cases} \tag{12}$$

The two groups of probability measurements are key components in variant measurement. The first group corresponds to multiple probability measurements and the second group corresponds to conditional probability measurements. In this Chapter, only two quaternion measurements are used in order to focus attention on the simplest interactive combinations without further measurements of $\{\rho_0, \rho_1\}$ and $\{\tilde{\rho}_0, \tilde{\rho}_1\}$ involved.

Under such condition, the output signals of the PM module can be expressed as a pair of probability vectors in quaternion forms $PM(J, X) = \{\rho, \tilde{\rho}\}$.

3.4. ME micro ensemble

The ME module has two inputs. $PM(J, X)$ provides probability measurement vectors to provide the basis of the measurement. The input parameter SM indicates Selected Measurements from $PM(J, X)$.

In this paper, two cases for a pair of measurement selections are restricted to permit an investigation of possible configurations of interactive distributions in their variant phase spaces under simple conditions.

Case A: (p_i, p_j) or $(p_+, p_-) \in P \subset \rho$ with two measurements from ρ;

Case B: $(\tilde{p}_i, \tilde{p}_j)$ or $(\tilde{p}_+, \tilde{p}_-) \in \tilde{P} \subset \tilde{\rho}$ with two measurements from $\tilde{\rho}$.

Under these conditions, each $(p_i(J, X), p_j(J, X))$ or $(\tilde{p}_i(J, X), \tilde{p}_j(J, X))$ determines a fixed position on variant phase space as a Micro Ensemble. The output of the ME module can be expressed as $ME(J, X) = (p_i(J, X), p_j(J, X))|(\tilde{p}_i(J, X), \tilde{p}_j(J, X))$ under a given function J, an N bit vector X and SM conditions.

3.4.1. Variant Phase Space

Since each ME must be located on a certain position in a square area on variant phase space, it is convenient to show the restrictions and specific properties according to the following propositions.

Proposition 3.1: In the Case A condition, a total of six configurations can be identified in different P selections. For each configuration, its pair of probability measurements can be restricted in a triangle area of a $[0, 1]^2$ region.

Proof: Any selection of two elements $(p_i(J, X), p_j(J, X))$ from P, it satisfies $0 \leq p_i(J, X) + p_j(J, X) \leq 1$, there are six distinct selections. ■

Proposition 3.2: In the Case B condition, a total of six configurations can be identified into two groups in different $\tilde{P}$ selections, four configurations in the first group are restricted in a square area and two configurations of the second group are restricted on a diagonal line.

Proof: Since two equations in $\tilde{\rho}$ quaternion are in the conditions of $\tilde{\rho_\perp} + \tilde{\rho_+} = \tilde{\rho_-} + \tilde{\rho_\top} = 1$. For the first group, two selected components can satisfy $0 \leq \tilde{p}_i, \tilde{p}_j \leq 1$, four distinct selections are identified in a $[0, 1]^2$ restricted region. For the second group, two selected components can satisfy $0 \leq \tilde{p}_i, \tilde{p}_j \leq 1$ and $\tilde{p}_i + \tilde{p}_j = 1$, only two distinct selections are identified on a diagonal line distributed in a $[0, 1]^2$ region. ■

Under this arrangement, all measurements are relevant to variant construction. Now, let this type of phase spaces be *Variant Phase Space VPS*. For an N bit vector X, a pair of probability measurements determines a micro ensemble to be a specific position in VPS.

In order to distinguish between the two types of VPS, let us name a subset of VPS under Case A conditions as *a Multiple Phase Space MPS* while we name a subset of VPS under Case B conditions as *a Conditional Phase Space CPS*. Samples of canonical ensembles of the six combinations under a given SM condition under a function in both MPS & CPS are shown in Figure 2(I,II) respectively.

3.5. IP interactive projections

Using a micro ensemble $ME(J,X)$, different projections can be identified in an IP module under various interactive conditions. Based on the input micro ensemble for each Case, two groups of eight interactive projections can be distinguished by symmetry/anti-symmetry and synchronous/asynchronous conditions.

3.5.1. Synchronous and Asynchronous Operations

Each $ME(J,X)$ is a pair of probability measurements and it is essential to establish corresponding rules to place their interactive projection in the same probability region i.e. $[0,1]$ segment.

We can distinguish between Synchronous and Asynchronous time-related operations.

Under a synchronous operation $\{+,-,\times,/,\}$, only one merged measurement is located in $[0,1]$ region to express one activity from a ME.

However, under an asynchronous operation $\oplus$, two input measurements $p_+ \neq p_-$, generate an output result as a vector that has two positions of p_+ and p_- with a weighted value 1 on each position; when $p = p_+ = p_-$ there is a weighted value of 2 on the position p.

Under asynchronous operations, merged results may be distinguished by their position or overlap each other with a cumulative weight value of 2. However, under synchronous operations, two measurements are merged as a unit weight to shift interactive measurements to one position in the $[0,1]$ region.

From an integrative viewpoint, the two types of operations may be considered capable of either merging two particles (asynchronous) on two positions or integrating two waves (synchronous) on a position.

3.5.2. Case A: Multiple Probability Interactive Projections

For each $ME(J,P) = (p_i(J,X), p_j(J,X))$ has a position on a unit square $[0,1]^2$.

Let $P = \{p_+, p_-\}$ (or $\{p_x, p_y\}$) locate a pair of measurements, the IP module projects two measurements and its weight into four conditions in different symmetric properties to form two groups of eight weight vectors as interactive projections.

Using $P = \{p_+, p_-\}$, a pair of measurement vectors $\{u, v\}$ are formulated:

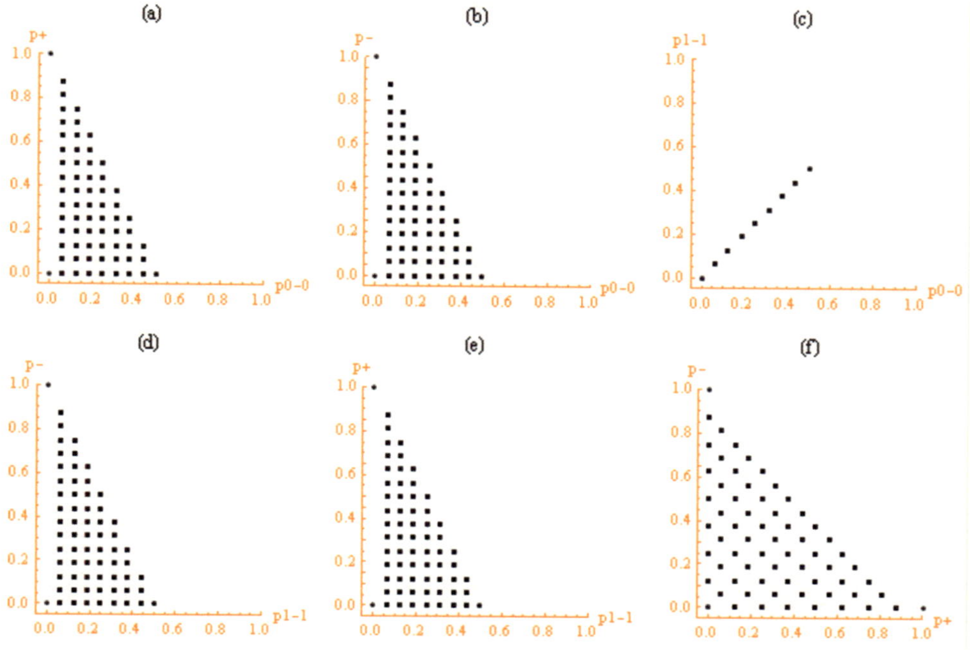

(I) Type A

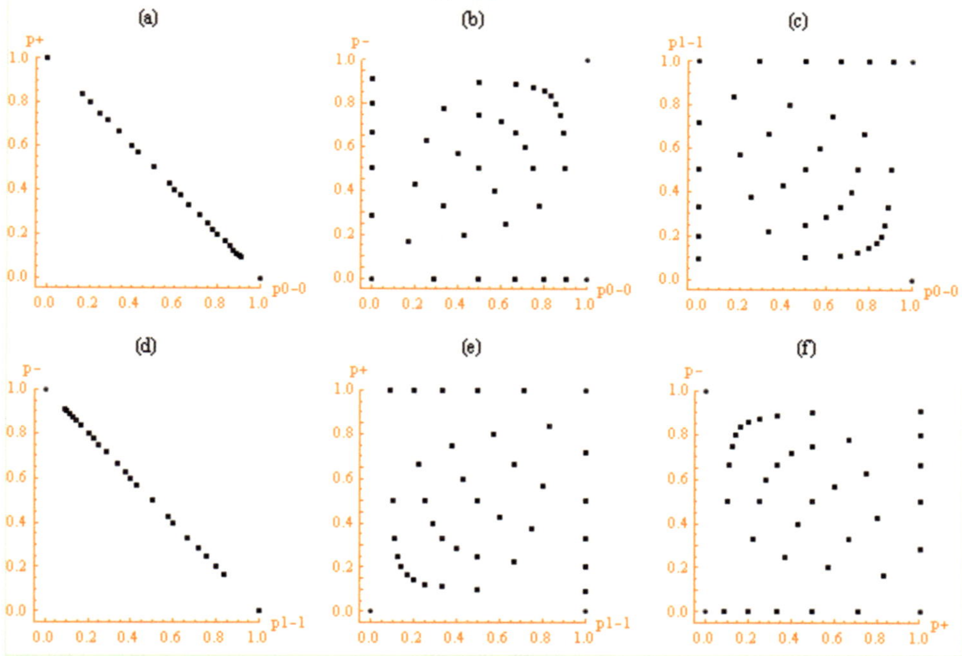

(II) Type B

Figure 2. (I-II) Six combinations of two selected measurements for a function on VPS of two probability models (I) Type A:(a-f) Six combinations in MPS; (II) Type B:(a-f) Six combinations in CPS

$$\begin{cases} u = (u_+, u_-, u_0, u_1) = \{u_\beta\} \\ v = (v_+, v_-, v_0, v_1) = \{v_\beta\} \\ \quad \beta \in \{+, -, 0, 1\} \end{cases} \tag{13}$$

$$\begin{cases} u_+ = p_+ \\ u_- = p_- \\ u_0 = u_+ \oplus u_- \\ u_1 = u_+ + u_- \\ v_+ = \frac{1+p_+}{2} \\ v_- = \frac{1-p_-}{2} \\ v_0 = v_+ \oplus v_- \\ v_1 = v_+ + v_- - 0.5 \end{cases} \tag{14}$$

where $0 \leq u_\beta, v_\beta \leq 1, \beta \in \{+, -, 0, 1\}$, $\oplus$: Asynchronous addition, $+$: Synchronous addition.

3.5.3. Case B: Conditional Probability Interactive Projections

For each $ME(J, \tilde{P}) = (\tilde{p}_i(J, X), \tilde{p}_j(J, X))$ we can note that it has a position on a unit square $[0, 1]^2$.

Let $\tilde{P} = \{\tilde{p}_+, \tilde{p}_-\}$ locate a pair of measurements, the IP module projects two measurements and its weight into four conditions in different symmetric properties to form two groups of eight weights as interactive projections.

Using $\tilde{P} = \{\tilde{p}_+, \tilde{p}_-\}$, a pair of vectors $\{\tilde{u}, \tilde{v}\}$ are formulated:

$$\begin{cases} \tilde{u} = (\tilde{u}_+, \tilde{u}_-, \tilde{u}_0, \tilde{u}_1) = \{\tilde{u}_\beta\} \\ \tilde{v} = (\tilde{v}_+, \tilde{v}_-, \tilde{v}_0, \tilde{v}_1) = \{\tilde{v}_\beta\} \\ \quad \beta \in \{+, -, 0, 1\} \end{cases} \tag{15}$$

For the four projections in a square area, the following equations are required.

$$\begin{cases} \tilde{u}_+ = \tilde{p}_+ \\ \tilde{u}_- = \tilde{p}_- \\ \tilde{u}_0 = \tilde{u}_+ \oplus \tilde{u}_- \\ \tilde{u}_1 = \frac{\tilde{u}_+ + \tilde{u}_-}{2} \\ \tilde{v}_+ = \frac{1+\tilde{p}_+}{2} \\ \tilde{v}_- = \frac{1-\tilde{p}_-}{2} \\ \tilde{v}_0 = \tilde{v}_+ \oplus \tilde{v}_- \\ \tilde{v}_1 = \tilde{v}_+ + \tilde{v}_- - 0.5 \end{cases} \tag{16}$$

http://dx.doi.org/10.5772/51635

For the two projections in a diagonal line, the following equations are satisfied.

$$\begin{cases} \tilde{u}_+ = \tilde{p}_i \\ \tilde{u}_- = \tilde{p}_j \\ \tilde{u}_0 = \tilde{u}_+ \oplus \tilde{u}_- \\ \tilde{u}_1 = \tilde{u}_+ + \tilde{u}_- \\ \tilde{v}_+ = \frac{1+\tilde{p}_i}{2} \\ \tilde{v}_- = \frac{1-\tilde{p}_j}{2} \\ \tilde{v}_0 = \tilde{v}_+ \oplus \tilde{v}_- \\ \tilde{v}_1 = \tilde{v}_+ + \tilde{v}_- - 0.5 \end{cases} \tag{17}$$

where $0 \leq \tilde{u}_\beta, \tilde{v}_\beta \leq 1, \beta \in \{+,-,0,1\}$, $\oplus$: Asynchronous addition, $+$: Synchronous addition.

3.5.4. Key Properties in IP Module

Under Symmetry/Anti-symmetry and Synchronous/Asynchronous conditions, one ME corresponds to eight interactive projections to express their selected characteristics.

Proposition 3.3: Two types of distinguished projections can be identified under symmetry/anti-symmetry conditions for each ME.

Proof: For two projection vectors $\{u, v\}$, we can note that u represents a symmetry condition and v represents an anti-symmetry condition. ■

Proposition 3.4: Synchronous and Asynchronous conditions lead to significant different output results.

Proof: In a synchronous operation, only one unit weight is output as $\{u_1, v_1\}$. However, in an asynchronous operation, two positions may be seen to have a combined weight $\{u_0, v_0\}$. ■

Proposition 3.5: Other projections are simple ones corresponding to relevant measurement projections.

Proof: Other output results are $\{u_+, u_-, v_+, v_-\}$, each parameter is only dependent on one measurement to get a similar distribution from a projection viewpoint. There is no real interactive activity involved. ■

Proposition 3.6: If two probability measurements are required to satisfy $p_i + p_j \leq 1$, then their symmetry interactive projection result is equal to $p_i + p_j$.

Proof: Merged result is in the $[0, 1]$ region. ■

Proposition 3.7: If two probability measurements independently have $0 \leq p_i, p_j \leq 1$, then their symmetry interactive projection is $(p_i + p_j)/2$.

Proof: Under this condition, merged results are in the $[0, 1]$ region. ■

Proposition 3.8 From a selected ME, eight interactive projections can be formulated.

Proof: By Propositions 3.3-3.7. ■

Under different conditions, one pair of probability measurements can be interactively projected into eight distinct results. However, from a variant viewpoint, it is not sufficient for a serious analysis to use only a single set of measurements from a ME, further extensions are required.

To distinguish among different measurements in interactive projections, four types of measurements are defined as *Left, Right, D-P and D-W* , where $\{u_+, v_+, \tilde{u}_+, \tilde{v}_+\}$ are *Left* measurements, $\{u_-, v_-, \tilde{u}_-, \tilde{v}_-\}$ are *Right* measurements, $\{u_0, v_0, \tilde{u}_0, \tilde{v}_0\}$ are *D-P* measurements and $\{u_1, v_1, \tilde{u}_1, \tilde{v}_1\}$ are *D-W* measurements respectively.

4. CEIM canonical ensemble and interactive maps

It is a basic step to generate a micro ensemble and eight interactive projections on variant phase space. For a given function J, it is necessary to determine the specific positions of all possible vectors of $\forall X$ to form a canonical ensemble on variant phase space.

The CEIM component is composed of two modules: the CE Canonical Ensemble and the IM Interactive Map.

The CE module collects all possible MEs into a canonical ensemble. In addition, the IM module makes relevant interactive projections via IP's outputs to generate a list of interactive distributions in the relevant maps as output results.

4.1. CE canonical ensemble

In the CE module, all the MEs are collected to form a CE in variant phase space according to the following equations.

For a function J and all 2^N vectors of $\forall X$, let $CEL(J, X)$ be a point of $CEL(J)$ on a plane lattice

$$CEL(J, X) = \begin{cases} T, ME(J, X) = P|\tilde{P} \\ F, \text{Otherwise} \end{cases} \tag{18}$$

$$CEL(J) = \bigcup_{\forall X} CEL(J, X) \tag{19}$$

Applying the equation for $CEL(J)$, a canonical lattice CEL can be established to indicate a specific distribution from a logic viewpoint.

Since different $CEL(J, X)$ may have the same position, let $CE(J, X)$ be a point of $CE(J)$ in a canonical ensemble

$$CE(J, X) = \begin{cases} 1, CEL(J, X) = T \\ 0, \text{Otherwise} \end{cases} \tag{20}$$

$$CE(J) = \sum_{\forall X} CE(J, X) \tag{21}$$

Using equation $CE(J)$, a canonical ensemble of variant phase space is produced. Each non-zero position has a numeric weight as a value to indicate numbers of MEs collected in a position.

4.1.1. Key Properties in CE

Proposition 4.1: Under Case A conditions, $O(N^2/2)$ points may be identified on a $CEL(J)$ lattice.

Proof: For each probability measurement, $N+1$ values may be distinguished; points are located in a triangular area and a total of $(N+1)N/2$ points may be distinguished. ■

Proposition 4.2: Under Case B conditions, $O(N) - O(N^2)$ points may be distinguished on a $CEL(J)$ lattice.

Proof: For each probability measurement, $N+1$ values may be distinguished; points are located in a square area and $(N+1)^2$ points may be distinguished for four square distributions and $N+1$ points may be distinguished for two diagonal line distributions. ■

Proposition 4.3: In Case A or Case B, values of all possible points of $CE(J)$ collected are equal to 2^N.

Proof: This is the total number of vectors that may be distinguished for $\forall X$. ■

Proposition 4.4: For a given SM condition, $CE(J)$ is a statistical canonical ensemble on variant phase space.

Proof: For a given SM condition, a $CE(J)$ distribution is independent of special sequences of collection. Its detailed configuration is relevant to $\{n, N\}$ and SM respectively. All valid positions can be statistically generated. ■

Under this organization, each $CE(J)$ has a fixed plane lattice with a distinct distribution. This invariant property is useful for our further explorations.

4.2. IM interactive map

In an IM module, all possible IP projections of either $\{u, v\}$ or $\{\tilde{u}, \tilde{v}\}$ are collected. Each projection corresponds to a specific IM distribution.

The IM module provides a statistical means to accumulate all possible vectors of N bits for a selected signal and generate a histogram. Eight signals correspond to eight histograms respectively. Among these, four histograms exhibit properties of symmetry and another four histograms exhibit properties of anti-symmetry.

4.2.1. Statistical distributions

For a function J, all measurement signals are collected from the IP and the relevant histogram represents a complete statistical distribution as an IP map.

Using u and v signals, each u_β or v_β determines a fixed position in the relevant histogram to make vector X on a position. After completing 2^N data sequences, eight symmetry/anti-symmetry histograms of $\{H(u_\beta|J)\},\{H(v_\beta|J)\}|\{H(\tilde{u}_\beta|J)\},\{H(\tilde{v}_\beta|J)\}$ are generated.

Under the multiple probability condition, $\beta \in \{+,-,0,1\}$

$$\begin{cases} H(u_\beta|J) = \sum_{\forall X \in B_2^N} H(u_\beta|J(X)) \\ H(v_\beta|J) = \sum_{\forall X \in B_2^N} H(v_\beta|J(X)), J \in B_2^{2^n} \end{cases} \tag{22}$$

Under the conditional probability condition, $\beta \in \{+,-,0,1\}$

$$\begin{cases} H(\tilde{u}_\beta|J) = \sum_{\forall X \in B_2^N} H(\tilde{u}_\beta|J(X)) \\ H(\tilde{v}_\beta|J) = \sum_{\forall X \in B_2^N} H(\tilde{v}_\beta|J(X)), J \in B_2^{2^n} \end{cases} \tag{23}$$

4.2.2. Normalized probability histograms

Let $|H(..)|$ denote the total number in the histogram $H(..)$, a normalized probability histogram ($P_H(..)$) can be expressed as

$$\begin{cases} P_H(u_\beta|J) = \frac{H(u_\beta|J)}{|H(u_\beta|J)|} \\ P_H(v_\beta|J) = \frac{H(v_\beta|J)}{|H(v_\beta|J)|}, J \in B_2^{2^n} \\ P_H(\tilde{u}_\beta|J) = \frac{H(\tilde{u}_\beta|J)}{|H(\tilde{u}_\beta|J)|} \\ P_H(\tilde{v}_\beta|J) = \frac{H(\tilde{v}_\beta|J)}{|H(\tilde{v}_\beta|J)|}, J \in B_2^{2^n} \end{cases} \tag{24}$$

Here, all interactive maps are also restricted in $[0,1]^2$ areas respectively.

Distributions are dependant on the data set as a whole and are not sensitive to varying under special sequences. Under this condition, when the data set has been exhaustively listed, then the same distributions are always linked to the given signal set.

Let $IM(J) = \{P_H(u|J), P_H(v|J)\}$ or $\{P_H(\tilde{u}|J), P_H(\tilde{v}|J)\}$ be the output results of an IM module. Then the eight histogram distributions provide invariant spectrums to represent properties among different interactive conditions.

Using such descriptions, the output results of the CEIM component are $\{CE(J), IM(J)\}$.

From a given function, a set of histograms can be generated as a group of eight probability histograms in variant phase space. Two groups of sixteen histograms are required. Sample cases are shown in Figures 3-4(I-II).

http://dx.doi.org/10.5772/51635

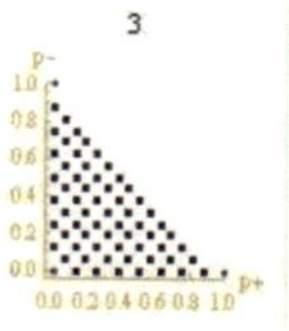

⇒

$P_H(u_+\|J)$ (a) Left	$P_H(u_-\|J)$ (b) Right
$P_H(u_0\|J)$ (c) D-P	$P_H(u_1\|J)$ (d) D-W
$P_H(v_+\|J)$ (e) Left	$P_H(v_-\|J)$ (f) Right
$P_H(v_0\|J)$ (g) D-P	$P_H(v_1\|J)$ (h) D-W

CEL $J = 3$ in MPS Eight Interactive Maps

(I) Representative patterns of Histograms for function J (a-d) symmetric cases; (e-h) antisymmetric cases

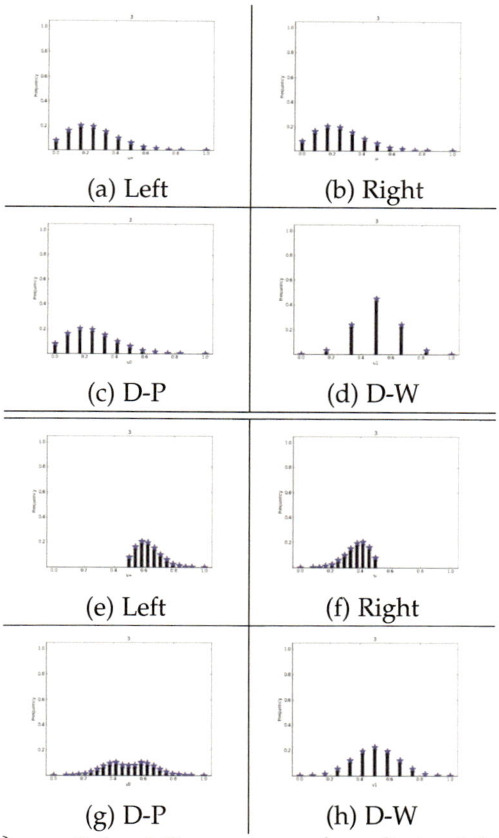

(II) $N = \{12\}, n = 2, J = 3$ Two groups of results in eight histograms

Figure 3. (I-II) $N = \{12\}, n = 2, J = 3$ Simulation results ; (I) Representative Patterns for $P_H(u_+|J) = P_H(u_-|J)$ and $P_H(v_+|J) = P_H(1 - v_-|J)$ conditions; (II) $N = \{12\}, n = 2, J = 3$ Two groups of eight interactive histograms on MPS

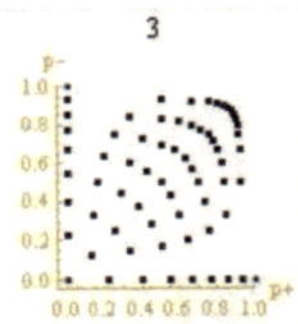

CEL $J = 3$ in CPS

$\Rightarrow$

$P_H(\tilde{u}_+\|J)$ (a) Left	$P_H(\tilde{u}_-\|J)$ (b) Right
$P_H(\tilde{u}_0\|J)$ (c) D-P	$P_H(\tilde{u}_1\|J)$ (d) D-W
$P_H(\tilde{v}_+\|J)$ (e) Left	$P_H(\tilde{v}_-\|J)$ (f) Right
$P_H(\tilde{v}_0\|J)$ (g) D-P	$P_H(\tilde{v}_1\|J)$ (h) D-W

Eight Interactive Maps

(I) Representative patterns of Histograms for function J (a-d) symmetric cases; (e-h) antisymmetric cases

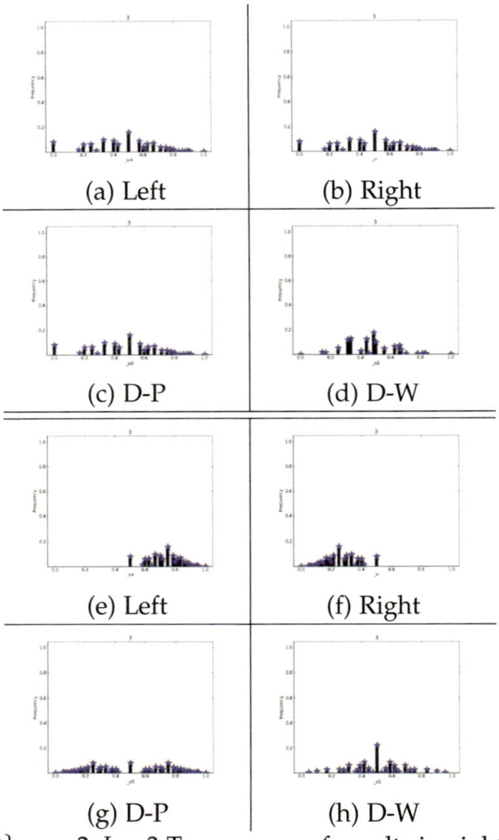

(II) $N = \{12\}, n = 2, J = 3$ Two groups of results in eight histograms

Figure 4. (I-II) $N = \{12,\}, n = 2, J = 3$ Simulation results; (I) Representative Patterns for $P_H(\tilde{u}_+|J) = P_H(\tilde{u}_-|J)$ and $P_H(\tilde{v}_+|J) = P_H(1 - \tilde{v}_-|J)$ conditions; (II) $N = \{12\}, n = 2, J = 3$ Two groups of eight interactive histograms on CPS

http://dx.doi.org/10.5772/51635

5. GEIM global ensemble and interactive map matrices

The GEIM component is composed of two modules: SCEIM Sets of CE&IM, and CIM CE&IM Matrices.

$\{CE(J), IM(J)\}$ and $\forall J$ are put in the SCEIM module to generate sets of CEs and IMs on each given function exhaustively. All generated CEs and IMs are organized by the CIM module under the FC condition in which a special variant coding scheme is applied for a global configuration of output matrices.

5.1. SCEIM sets of canonical ensembles and interactive maps

The SCEIM module produces $\{SCE, SIM\}$ composed of all possible CE and IM sets of $\forall J$ under exhaustive conditions.

$$\begin{aligned} SCE &= \{\forall J, CE(J) | J \in B_2^{2^n}\} \\ SIM &= \{\forall J, \{P_H(u|J), P_H(v|J)\} \text{ or } \{P_H(\tilde{u}|J), P_H(\tilde{v}|J)\} | J \in B_2^{2^n}\} \end{aligned} \tag{25}$$

Meanwhile, the SCE and the SIM provide output results to the CIM module.

5.2. CIM canonical ensemble and interactive map matrices

In addition to using $\{SCE, SIM\}$ as inputs, the *FC* also inputs a code scheme to determine a detailed configuration for each matrix.

5.2.1. Global Matrix Representations

In the CIM module, $\{SCE, SIM\}$ inputs have nine sets of CEs and IMs. Each set is composed of 2^{2^n} elements and each element is a histogram or a plane lattice. The CIM module arranges all 2^{2^n} elements generated as a matrix by a given FC code scheme.

5.2.2. The Matrix and Its elements

For a given FC scheme, let $FC(J) = \langle J^1 | J^0 \rangle$, each element

$$\begin{cases} M_{\langle J^1|J^0\rangle}(u_\beta|J) = P_H(u_\beta|J) \\ M_{\langle J^1|J^0\rangle}(v_\beta|J) = P_H(v_\beta|J) \\ \qquad J \in B_2^{2^n};\ J^1, J^0 \in B_2^{2^{n-1}} \end{cases} \tag{26}$$

5.2.3. Representative patterns of matrices

Four cases of FC codes are selected for illustrations in this Chapter. Further discussion on the details of variant coding scheme has been previously published in [40, 44].

For example, four sample cases are shown in Figure 5 under relevant conditions.

0	1	2	3
4	5	6	7
8	9	10	11
12	13	14	15

(a) SL code

0	8	1	9
2	10	3	11
4	12	5	13
6	14	7	15

(b) W code

0	2	1	3
4	6	5	7
8	10	9	11
12	14	13	15

(c) F code

0	4	1	5
2	6	3	7
8	12	9	13
10	14	11	15

(d) C code

Figure 5. (a-c) Four Cases of Matrix configurations for $n = 2$ on FC (a) Case 1. SL code (b) Case 2. W code (c) Case 3. F code (d) Case 4. C code

Case 1: $FC = \{n = 2, P = (3210)\}$ a SL code;

Case 2: $FC = \{n = 2, P = (2103)\}$ a W code;

Case 3: $FC = \{n = 2, P = (3201)\}$ a F code;

Case 4: $FC = \{n = 2, P = (3102)\}$ a C code.

Under each condition, each FC code is a special configuration to make sixteen elements arranged as a 4×4 matrix.

For the matrices in this chapter, four configurations are applied to construct sample matrices with elements arranged for illustration purposes.

6. Representation model

Figure 6 presents a graphical summary of the above. Further representations are offered in Figure 7 to show the main steps in creating a CE in the MPS or CPS and IMs relevant to global CEM and IMM procedures.

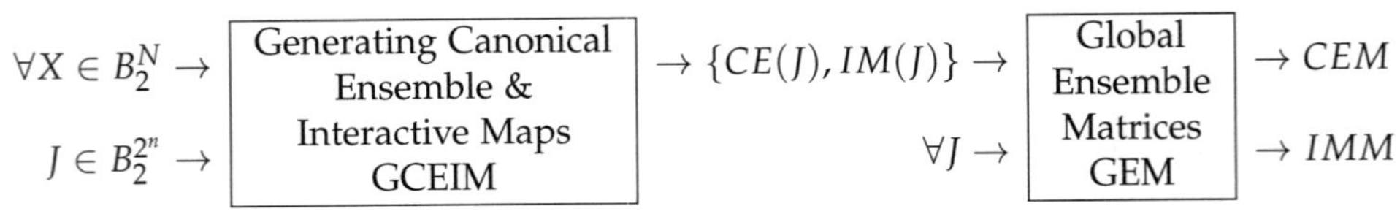

Figure 6. Diagrammatical Representation of VPS Model

7. Symbolic representations on selected cases

Using a representational model, for a given condition, there are two sets of CEM in both MPS and CPS. Each set contains a CEM and eight IMMs. Since each matrix contains 2^{2^n} elements, the existence of so many possible configurations adds to the difficulties in reaching a satisfactory understanding of the data sets. In this section, symbolic representations are applied to show more clearly the essential symmetric properties of various matrices. Using variant logic, the following equations can be established for an $n = 2$ condition to apply $(a, b, c, d) = (10, 8, 2, 0)$ and $(\tilde{a}, \tilde{b}, \tilde{c}, \tilde{d}) = (10, 14, 11, 15)$ for each meta function.

http://dx.doi.org/10.5772/51635

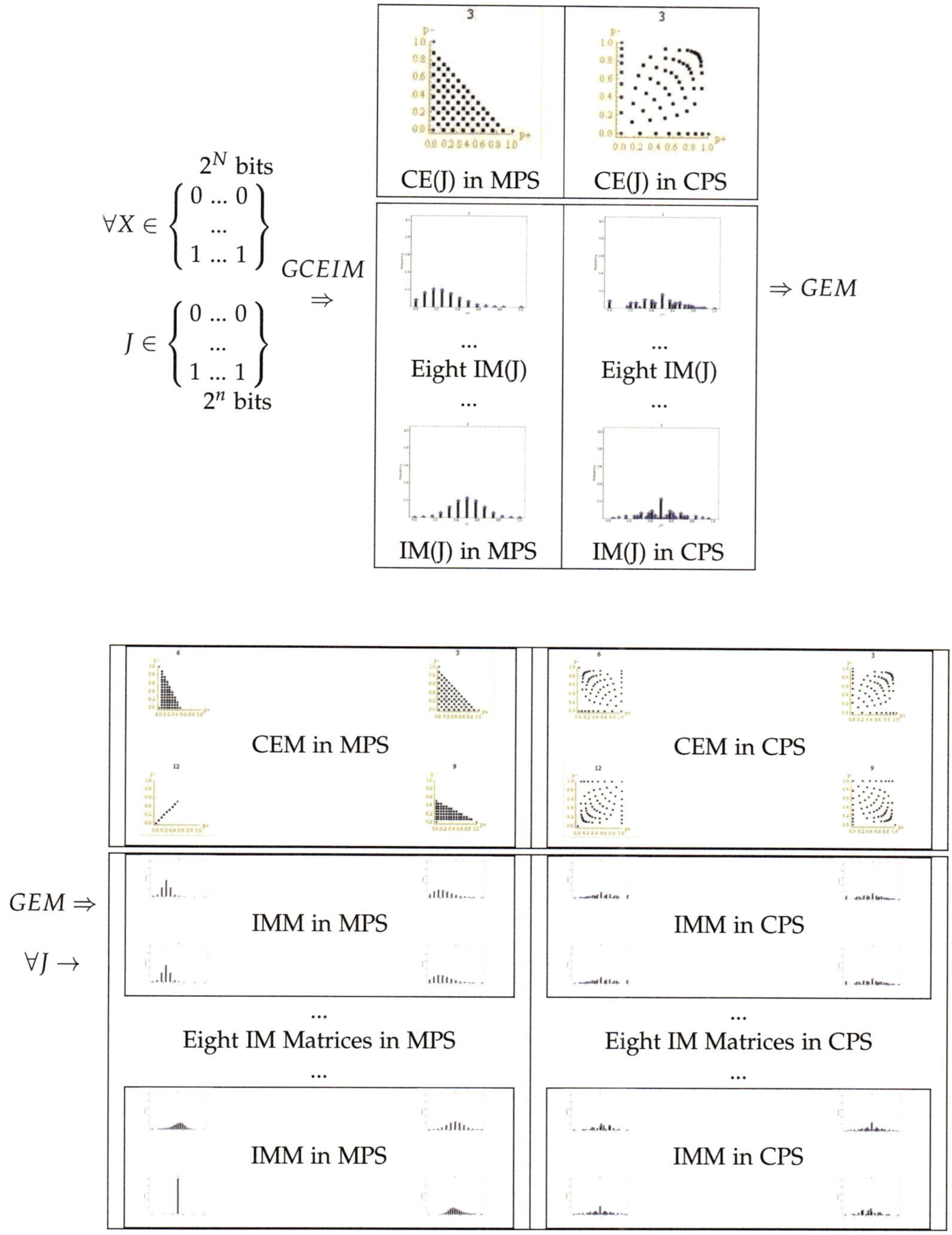

Figure 7. Illustrations of Representative Model of the VPS for GCEIM and GEM results

$$\begin{cases} 0 = \langle 0|10\rangle = \langle d|\tilde{a}\rangle = d; & 1 = \langle 0|11\rangle = \langle d|\tilde{c}\rangle; \\ 2 = \langle 2|10\rangle = \langle c|\tilde{a}\rangle = c; & 3 = \langle 2|11\rangle = \langle c|\tilde{c}\rangle; \\ 4 = \langle 0|14\rangle = \langle d|\tilde{b}\rangle; & 5 = \langle 0|15\rangle = \langle d|\tilde{d}\rangle; \\ 6 = \langle 2|14\rangle = \langle c|\tilde{b}\rangle; & 7 = \langle 2|15\rangle = \langle c|\tilde{d}\rangle; \\ 8 = \langle 8|10\rangle = \langle b|\tilde{a}\rangle = b; & 9 = \langle 8|11\rangle = \langle b|\tilde{c}\rangle; \\ 10 = \langle 10|10\rangle = \langle a|\tilde{a}\rangle = a = \tilde{a}; & 11 = \langle 10|11\rangle = \langle a|\tilde{c}\rangle = \tilde{c}; \\ 12 = \langle 8|14\rangle = \langle b|\tilde{b}\rangle; & 13 = \langle 8|15\rangle = \langle b|\tilde{d}\rangle; \\ 14 = \langle 10|14\rangle = \langle a|\tilde{b}\rangle = \tilde{b}; & 15 = \langle 10|15\rangle = \langle a|\tilde{d}\rangle = \tilde{d}. \end{cases} \tag{27}$$

Using this symbolic style, four cases of configurations and their polarized decompositions are represented as follows.

Case 1: SL code $P = (3210)$

$$\begin{aligned} \begin{pmatrix} 0 & 1 & 2 & 3 \\ 4 & 5 & 6 & 7 \\ 8 & 9 & 10 & 11 \\ 12 & 13 & 14 & 15 \end{pmatrix} &= \left\langle \begin{pmatrix} 0 & 0 & 2 & 2 \\ 0 & 0 & 2 & 2 \\ 8 & 8 & 10 & 10 \\ 8 & 8 & 10 & 10 \end{pmatrix} \middle| \begin{pmatrix} 10 & 11 & 10 & 11 \\ 14 & 15 & 14 & 15 \\ 10 & 11 & 10 & 11 \\ 14 & 15 & 14 & 15 \end{pmatrix} \right\rangle \\ &= \left\langle \begin{pmatrix} d & d & c & c \\ d & d & c & c \\ b & b & a & a \\ b & b & a & a \end{pmatrix} \middle| \begin{pmatrix} \tilde{a} & \tilde{c} & \tilde{a} & \tilde{c} \\ \tilde{b} & \tilde{d} & \tilde{b} & \tilde{d} \\ \tilde{a} & \tilde{c} & \tilde{a} & \tilde{c} \\ \tilde{b} & \tilde{d} & \tilde{b} & \tilde{d} \end{pmatrix} \right\rangle \\ &= \begin{pmatrix} \langle d|\tilde{a}\rangle & \langle d|\tilde{c}\rangle & \langle c|\tilde{a}\rangle & \langle c|\tilde{c}\rangle \\ \langle d|\tilde{b}\rangle & \langle d|\tilde{d}\rangle & \langle c|\tilde{b}\rangle & \langle c|\tilde{d}\rangle \\ \langle b|\tilde{a}\rangle & \langle b|\tilde{c}\rangle & \langle a|\tilde{a}\rangle & \langle a|\tilde{c}\rangle \\ \langle b|\tilde{b}\rangle & \langle b|\tilde{d}\rangle & \langle a|\tilde{b}\rangle & \langle a|\tilde{d}\rangle \end{pmatrix} \\ &= \langle \text{2x2Block}|\text{Cross}\rangle; \end{aligned} \tag{28}$$

Case 2: W code $P = (2103)$

$$\begin{aligned} \begin{pmatrix} 0 & 8 & 1 & 9 \\ 2 & 10 & 3 & 11 \\ 4 & 12 & 5 & 13 \\ 6 & 14 & 7 & 15 \end{pmatrix} &= \left\langle \begin{pmatrix} 0 & 8 & 0 & 8 \\ 2 & 10 & 2 & 10 \\ 0 & 8 & 0 & 8 \\ 2 & 10 & 2 & 10 \end{pmatrix} \middle| \begin{pmatrix} 10 & 10 & 11 & 11 \\ 10 & 10 & 11 & 11 \\ 14 & 14 & 15 & 15 \\ 14 & 14 & 15 & 15 \end{pmatrix} \right\rangle \\ &= \left\langle \begin{pmatrix} d & b & d & b \\ c & a & c & a \\ d & b & d & b \\ c & a & c & a \end{pmatrix} \middle| \begin{pmatrix} \tilde{a} & \tilde{a} & \tilde{c} & \tilde{c} \\ \tilde{b} & \tilde{b} & \tilde{d} & \tilde{d} \\ \tilde{a} & \tilde{a} & \tilde{c} & \tilde{c} \\ \tilde{b} & \tilde{b} & \tilde{d} & \tilde{d} \end{pmatrix} \right\rangle \\ &= \begin{pmatrix} \langle d|\tilde{a}\rangle & \langle b|\tilde{a}\rangle & \langle d|\tilde{c}\rangle & \langle b|\tilde{c}\rangle \\ \langle c|\tilde{b}\rangle & \langle a|\tilde{b}\rangle & \langle c|\tilde{d}\rangle & \langle a|\tilde{d}\rangle \\ \langle d|\tilde{a}\rangle & \langle b|\tilde{a}\rangle & \langle d|\tilde{c}\rangle & \langle b|\tilde{c}\rangle \\ \langle c|\tilde{b}\rangle & \langle a|\tilde{b}\rangle & \langle c|\tilde{d}\rangle & \langle a|\tilde{d}\rangle \end{pmatrix} \\ &= \langle \text{Cross}|\text{2x2Block}\rangle; \end{aligned} \tag{29}$$

Case 3: F code $P = (3201)$

$$\begin{aligned}
\begin{pmatrix} 0 & 2 & 1 & 3 \\ 4 & 6 & 5 & 7 \\ 8 & 10 & 9 & 11 \\ 12 & 14 & 13 & 15 \end{pmatrix} &= \left\langle \begin{pmatrix} 0 & 2 & 0 & 2 \\ 0 & 2 & 0 & 2 \\ 8 & 10 & 8 & 10 \\ 8 & 10 & 8 & 10 \end{pmatrix} \middle| \begin{pmatrix} 10 & 10 & 11 & 11 \\ 14 & 14 & 15 & 15 \\ 10 & 10 & 11 & 11 \\ 14 & 14 & 15 & 15 \end{pmatrix} \right\rangle \\
&= \left\langle \begin{pmatrix} d & c & d & c \\ d & c & d & c \\ b & a & b & a \\ b & a & b & a \end{pmatrix} \middle| \begin{pmatrix} \tilde{a} & \tilde{a} & \tilde{c} & \tilde{c} \\ \tilde{b} & \tilde{b} & \tilde{d} & \tilde{d} \\ \tilde{a} & \tilde{a} & \tilde{c} & \tilde{c} \\ \tilde{b} & \tilde{b} & \tilde{d} & \tilde{d} \end{pmatrix} \right\rangle \\
&= \begin{pmatrix} \langle d|\tilde{a}\rangle & \langle c|\tilde{a}\rangle & \langle d|\tilde{c}\rangle & \langle c|\tilde{c}\rangle \\ \langle d|\tilde{b}\rangle & \langle c|\tilde{b}\rangle & \langle d|\tilde{d}\rangle & \langle c|\tilde{d}\rangle \\ \langle b|\tilde{a}\rangle & \langle a|\tilde{a}\rangle & \langle b|\tilde{c}\rangle & \langle a|\tilde{c}\rangle \\ \langle b|\tilde{b}\rangle & \langle a|\tilde{b}\rangle & \langle b|\tilde{d}\rangle & \langle a|\tilde{d}\rangle \end{pmatrix} \\
&= \langle \text{V-2Run} | \text{H-2Run} \rangle;
\end{aligned} \tag{30}$$

Case 4: C code $P = (3102)$

$$\begin{aligned}
\begin{pmatrix} 0 & 4 & 1 & 5 \\ 2 & 6 & 3 & 7 \\ 8 & 12 & 9 & 13 \\ 10 & 14 & 11 & 15 \end{pmatrix} &= \left\langle \begin{pmatrix} 0 & 0 & 0 & 0 \\ 2 & 2 & 2 & 2 \\ 8 & 8 & 8 & 8 \\ 10 & 10 & 10 & 10 \end{pmatrix} \middle| \begin{pmatrix} 10 & 14 & 11 & 15 \\ 10 & 14 & 11 & 15 \\ 10 & 14 & 11 & 15 \\ 10 & 14 & 11 & 15 \end{pmatrix} \right\rangle \\
&= \left\langle \begin{pmatrix} d & d & d & d \\ c & c & c & c \\ b & b & b & b \\ a & a & a & a \end{pmatrix} \middle| \begin{pmatrix} \tilde{a} & \tilde{b} & \tilde{c} & \tilde{d} \\ \tilde{a} & \tilde{b} & \tilde{c} & \tilde{d} \\ \tilde{a} & \tilde{b} & \tilde{c} & \tilde{d} \\ \tilde{a} & \tilde{b} & \tilde{c} & \tilde{d} \end{pmatrix} \right\rangle \\
&= \begin{pmatrix} \langle d|\tilde{a}\rangle & \langle d|\tilde{b}\rangle & \langle d|\tilde{c}\rangle & \langle d|\tilde{d}\rangle \\ \langle c|\tilde{a}\rangle & \langle c|\tilde{b}\rangle & \langle c|\tilde{c}\rangle & \langle c|\tilde{d}\rangle \\ \langle b|\tilde{a}\rangle & \langle b|\tilde{b}\rangle & \langle b|\tilde{c}\rangle & \langle b|\tilde{d}\rangle \\ \langle a|\tilde{a}\rangle & \langle a|\tilde{b}\rangle & \langle a|\tilde{c}\rangle & \langle a|\tilde{d}\rangle \end{pmatrix} \\
&= \langle \text{H-4Run} | \text{V-4Run} \rangle.
\end{aligned} \tag{31}$$

Six pairs $\{0:15, 1:7, 2:11, 4:13, 6:9, 8:14\}$ of distributions may have symmetry properties

$$\begin{aligned}
0:15 &= \langle d|\tilde{a}\rangle : \langle a|\tilde{d}\rangle; \\
1:7 &= \langle d|\tilde{c}\rangle : \langle c|\tilde{d}\rangle; \\
2:11 &= \langle c|\tilde{a}\rangle : \langle a|\tilde{c}\rangle; \\
4:13 &= \langle d|\tilde{b}\rangle : \langle b|\tilde{d}\rangle; \\
6:9 &= \langle c|\tilde{b}\rangle : \langle b|\tilde{c}\rangle; \\
8:14 &= \langle b|\tilde{a}\rangle : \langle a|\tilde{b}\rangle.
\end{aligned} \tag{32}$$

Six pairs $\{1:8, 2:4, 3:12, 5:10, 7:14, 11:13\}$ of distributions may have anti-symmetry properties

$$\begin{aligned}1:8 &= \langle d|\tilde{c}\rangle : \langle b|\tilde{a}\rangle;\\ 2:4 &= \langle c|\tilde{a}\rangle : \langle d|\tilde{b}\rangle;\\ 3:12 &= \langle c|\tilde{c}\rangle : \langle b|\tilde{b}\rangle;\\ 5:10 &= \langle d|\tilde{d}\rangle : \langle a|\tilde{a}\rangle;\\ 7:14 &= \langle c|\tilde{d}\rangle : \langle a|\tilde{b}\rangle;\\ 11:13 &= \langle a|\tilde{c}\rangle : \langle b|\tilde{d}\rangle.\end{aligned} \tag{33}$$

Two pairs $\{3:12, 5:10\}$ of distributions may have self-conjugate properties with both symmetry and anti-symmetry properties.

$$\begin{aligned}3:12 &= \langle c|\tilde{c}\rangle : \langle b|\tilde{b}\rangle;\\ 5:10 &= \langle d|\tilde{d}\rangle : \langle a|\tilde{a}\rangle.\end{aligned} \tag{34}$$

Four pairs $\{0:15, 3:12, 5:10, 6:9\}$ of distributions may have special properties.

$$\begin{aligned}0:15 &= \langle d|\tilde{a}\rangle : \langle a|\tilde{d}\rangle;\\ 3:12 &= \langle c|\tilde{c}\rangle : \langle b|\tilde{b}\rangle;\\ 5:10 &= \langle d|\tilde{d}\rangle : \langle a|\tilde{a}\rangle;\\ 6:9 &= \langle c|\tilde{b}\rangle : \langle b|\tilde{c}\rangle.\end{aligned} \tag{35}$$

Regions of Measurements in MPS can be illustrated as

$$MPS: \begin{pmatrix} 0 & & 5 \\ & \cdots & \\ & & \cdots \\ 10 & & 15 \end{pmatrix} \Rightarrow \begin{pmatrix} [1,0] & (-,-) & \ldots & [1/2,1/2] \\ (-,0) & \ldots & & \ldots \\ \ldots & & \ldots & (-,-) \\ (0,0) & \ldots & (0,-) & [0,1] \end{pmatrix} \tag{36}$$

Regions of Measurements in CPS can be illustrated as

$$CPS: \begin{pmatrix} 0 & & 5 \\ & \cdots & \\ & & \cdots \\ 10 & & 15 \end{pmatrix} \Rightarrow \begin{pmatrix} [1,0] & (1,-) & \ldots & [1,1] \\ (-,0) & \ldots & & \ldots \\ \ldots & & \ldots & (-,1) \\ (0,0) & \ldots & (0,-) & [0,1] \end{pmatrix} \tag{37}$$

8. Sample results

8.1. CEM groups

Using $n = 2$ configurations, relevant CEMs on either MPS or CPS are shown in Figure 8(a-h).

http://dx.doi.org/10.5772/51635

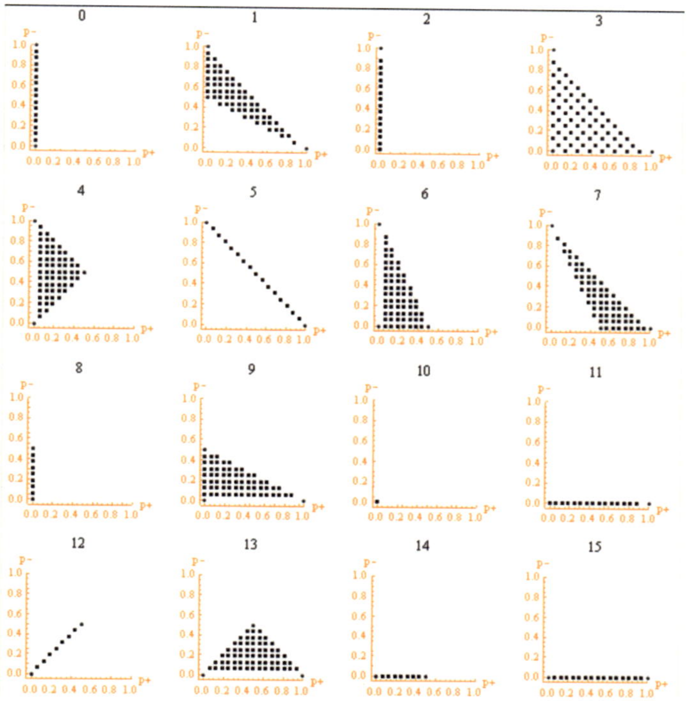

(a) SL in MPS

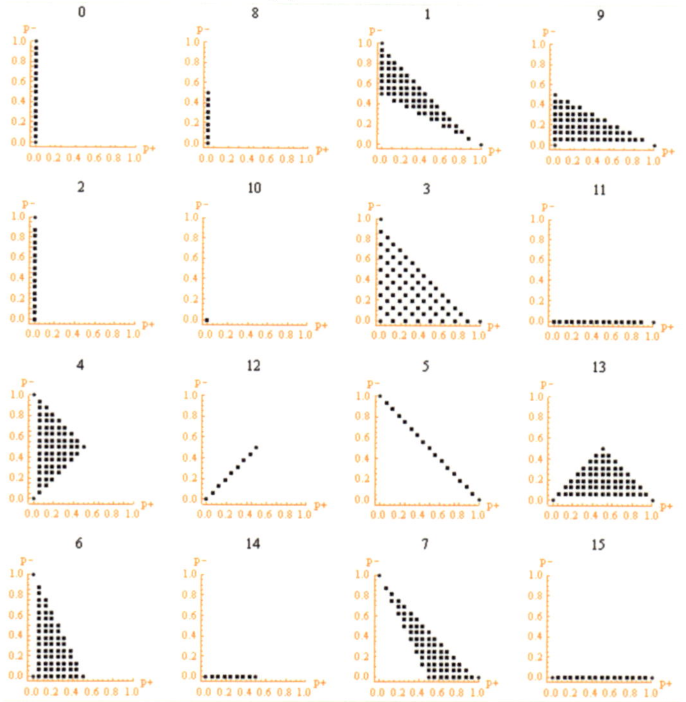

(b) W in MPS

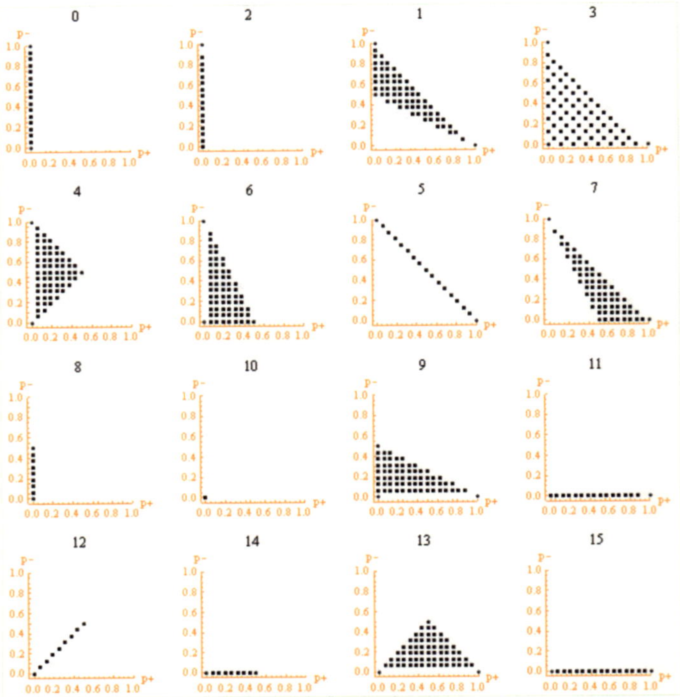

(c) F in MPS

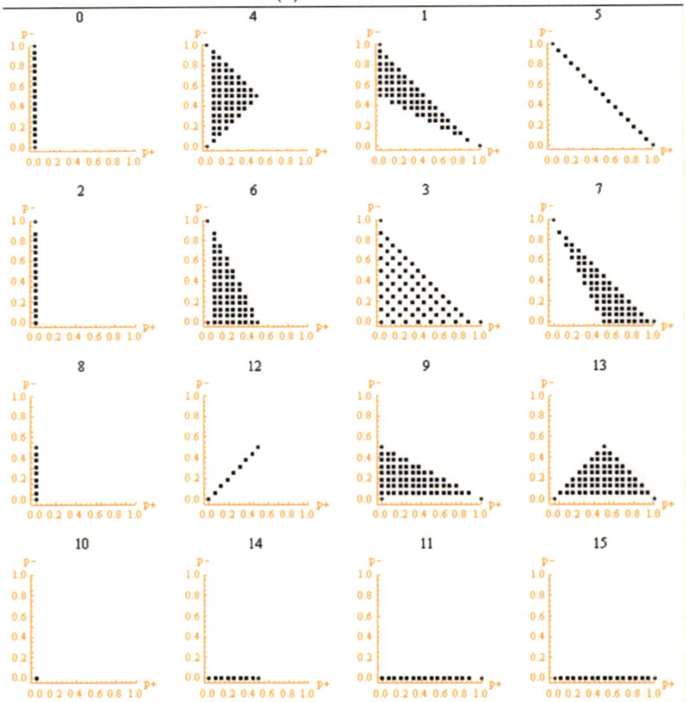

(d) C in MPS

http://dx.doi.org/10.5772/51635

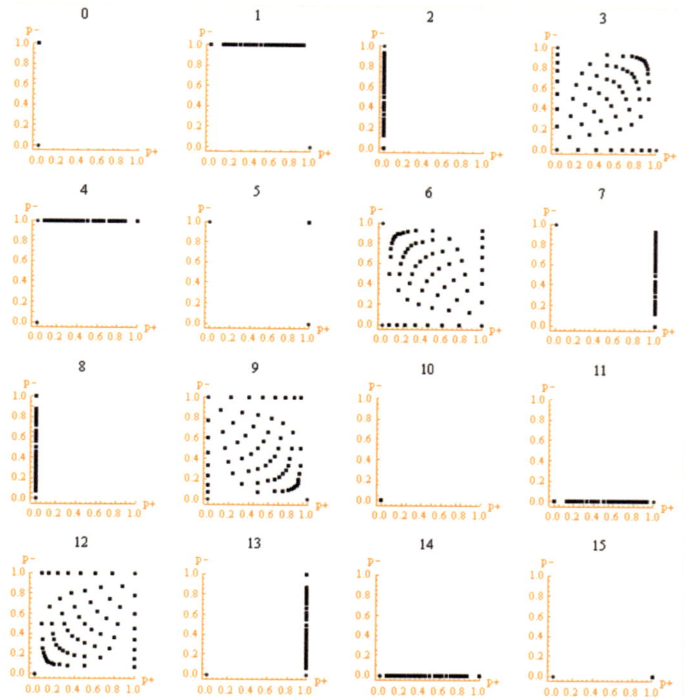

(e) SL in CPS

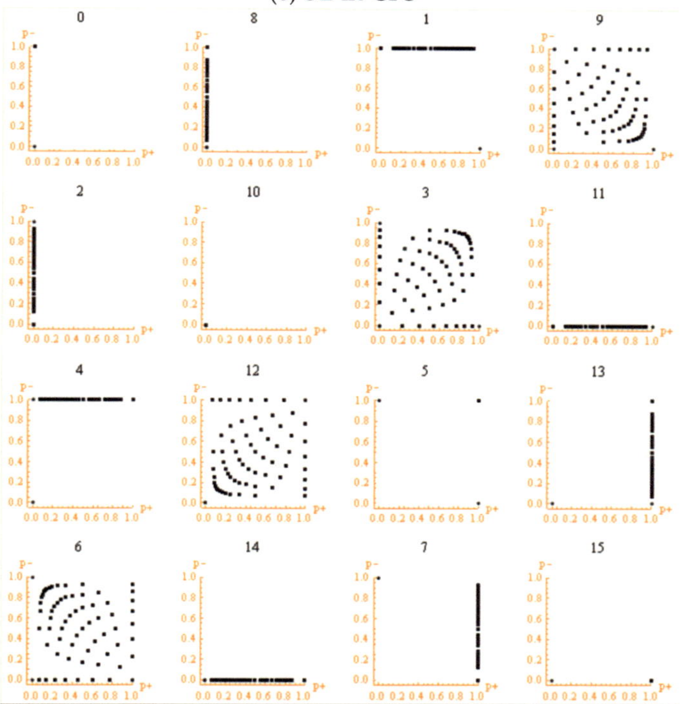

(f) W in CPS

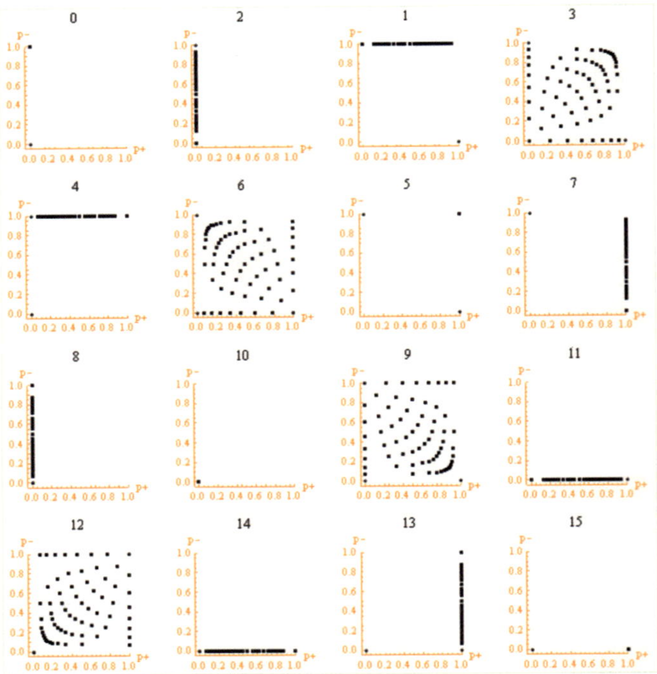

(g) F in CPS

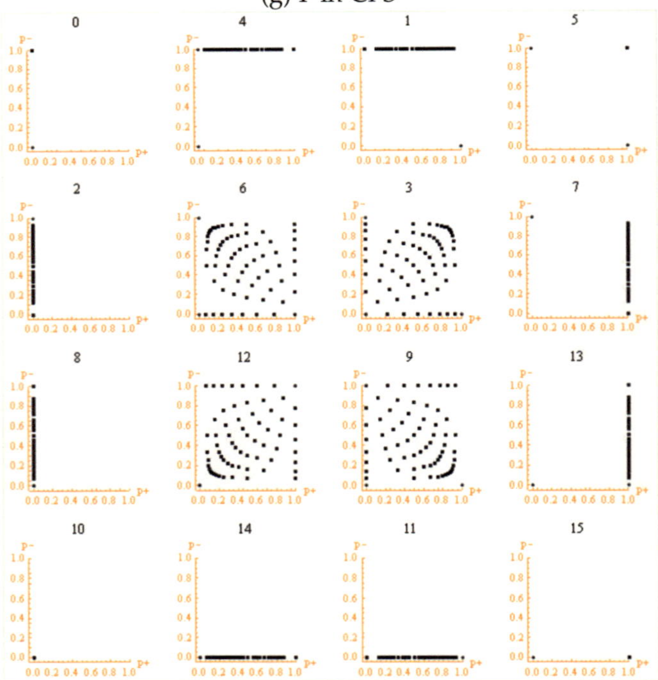

(h) C in CPS

Figure 8. (a-f) Matrices of Plane Lattices of VPS for MPS and CPS in $\{SL, W, F, C\}$ codes, (a-d) MPS, (e-h) CPS; (a,e) SL code, (b,f) W code,(c,g) F code, (d,h) C code.

8.2. IMM groups

IM Matrices under MPS are shown in Figures 9(M1-M32) and IM Matrices under CPS are shown in Figures 10(C1-C32).

9. Analysis of visual distributions

9.1. VPS organization

Two groups of matrices are shown in Figure 8. The four matrices shown as 8 (a-d) illustrate MPS conditions and the four matrices shown as 8 (e-h) illustrate CPS conditions. Considering various CEs exhibiting conjugate symmetry properties, such arrangements may be noted to have similar distributions along the diagonal and anti-diagonal directions so that it is possible to find a pair of CEs with each CE pair-matched by a geometric transformation to another CE through either rotation or reflection.

9.1.1. MPS Structures

The four CE matrices in the MPS group as shown in Figure 8(a-d) can be analyzed as follows.

SL in MPS

For the matrix in Figure 8(a) showing SL in MPS, 16 CEs are arranged in linear order from 0-15 in the 4×4 matrix. Only two pairs of {0:15, 6:9} CEs have conjugate symmetry properties.

W in MPS

For the matrix in Figure 8(b) showing W in MPS, 16 CEs are not arranged in linear order in {0,...,15} in the 4×4 matrix. Only two pairs of {0:15, 6:9} CEs have conjugate symmetry properties.

F in MPS

However, for the matrix in Figure 8(c) showing F in MPS, 16 CEs exhibit more conjugate pairs in the 4×4 matrix. Here, six pairs of CEs {0:15, 1:7, 2:11, 4:13, 6:9, 8:14} show conjugate symmetry properties.

C in MPS

Also, for the matrix in Figure 8(d) showing C in MPS, we find the same number of conjugate pairs as with the F condition. Moreover, not only do six pairs of CEs {0:15, 1:7, 2:11, 4:13, 6:9, 8:14} exhibit conjugate symmetry properties, but also four CEs {10,8,2,0} are polarized on the vertical as per the left column and four CEs {10,14,11,15} are polarized on the horizontal direction as per the bottom row. In addition, nine CEs showing interactive properties are evident top-right in a 3×3 matrix.

9.1.2. CPS Structures

The four CE matrices shown in Figure 8(e-h) in the CPS group can be analyzed as follows.

SL in CPS

For the matrix in Figure 8(e) showing SL in CPS, 16 CEs are arranged in linear order from 0-15 as a 4×4 matrix. Four pairs of CEs {0:15, 3:12, 5:10, 6:9} have conjugate symmetry properties.

W in CPS

For the matrix in Figure 8(f) showing W in CPS, 16 CEs are not arranged in linear order. However, four pairs of CEs {0:15, 3:12, 5:10, 6:9} have conjugate symmetry properties.

F in CPS

For the matrix in Figure 8(g) showing F in CPS, we can recognize two CE groups where each group has six pairs of CEs with conjugate symmetry properties {0:15, 1:7, 2:11, 4:13, 6:9, 8:14} and {2:4, 1:8, 3:12, 5:10, 7:14, 11:13}.

C in CPS

For the matrix in Figure 8(h) showing C in CPS, 12 CEs (out of 16) show conjugate pairing. This is the same number of conjugate pairs as is evident with the F condition in CPS. Also, if we look at polarization, the matrix for C in CPS is very different from the other coding matrices. It has significant polarized properties connecting the outer elements of the matrix. Here, four CEs {10,8,2,0} are polarized on the vertical as per the left column, and another four CEs {5,7,13,15} as per the right column. Also, four CEs {0,4,1,8} are polarized on the horizontal as per the top-row and another four CEs {10,14,11,15} as per the bottom-row. Four more CEs {3,6,9,12} exhibit interactive properties in a 2 x 2 central grid. In all, five distinct regions can be identified as significant. It is interesting to note such remarkable symmetry illustrating interactions between and among these meta functions.

9.2. IMM organization

From one matrix in VPS, eight matrices corresponding to the two vectors $\{u,v\} = \{(u_+, u_-, u_0, u_1), (v_+, v_-, v_0, v_1)\}$ can be generated showing interactive properties under symmetry/anti-symmetry, and synchronous/asynchronous conditions respectively. A total of 64 matrices are shown in two groups in Figures 9 (M1-M32) for MPS and in Figures 10 (C1-C32) for CPS, respectively.

9.2.1. MPS Structures

SL group in MPS

For the SL group in Figure 9 (M1-M8), the two matrix vectors $\{u,v\} = \{(u_+, u_-, u_0, u_1), (v_+, v_-, v_0, v_1)\}$ are best considered separately.

M1-M4: Let us first consider elements M1-M4 where the four matrices of (u_+, u_-, u_0, u_1) are in a symmetry group,

In u_+ matrix M1, elements in the columns and rows are arranged in what may be described as a periodic crossing structure.

In u_- matrix M2, four elements with the same IMs are arranged in a 2×2 block with four distinct distributions being observed.

In u_0 matrix M3, each element shows simple additions from elements in u_+ and u_- respectively. It it interesting to note that only two pairs of positions {0:15, 6:9} are similarly distributed in the relevant MPS matrix.

However, in u_1 matrix M4, significant symmetry properties can be observed. Four pairs {0:15, 3:12, 5:10, 6:9} have symmetry or anti-symmetry properties that are different from the u_0 condition.

M4-M8: Let us now consider elements M5-M8 where the four matrices of (v_+, v_-, v_0, v_1) are in an anti-symmetry group,

In v_+ matrix M5, elements in the columns and rows are arranged as periodic crossing structures.

In v_- matrix M6, four elements with the same IMs are arranged in a 2×2 block with four distinct distributions observed.

In v_0 matrix M7, each element shows simple additions from elements in v_+ and v_- respectively. Only two pairs of positions {0:15, 6:9} are similarly distributed in the relevant MPS matrix.

In v_1 matrix M8, significant symmetry properties can be observed. Two pairs {0:15, 6:9} have anti-symmetry properties that are the same as the v_0 condition.

W group in MPS

For the W group in Figure 9 (M9-M16), the two matrix vectors $\{u, v\} = \{(u_+, u_-, u_0, u_1), (v_+, v_-, v_0, v_1)\}$ are best considered separately.

M9-M12: Let us now consider elements M9-M12 where the four matrices (u_+, u_-, u_0, u_1) are in a symmetry group,

In u_+ matrix M9, four elements with the same IMs are arranged in a 2×2 block with four distinct distributions observed.

In u_- matrix M10, elements in the columns and rows are arranged as a periodic crossing structure.

In u_0 matrix M11, each element shows simple additions with elements in u_+ and u_- respectively. It it interesting to note that only two pairs of positions {0:15, 6:9} are similarly distributed in the relevant MPS matrix.

However, in u_1 matrix M12, significant symmetry properties can be observed. Four pairs {0:15, 3:12, 5:10, 6:9} have symmetry or anti-symmetry properties that are different from the u_0 condition.

M13-M16: Let us now consider elements M13-M16 where the four matrices (v_+, v, v_0, v_1) are in an anti-symmetry group,

In v_+ matrix M13, four elements with the same IMs are arranged in a 2×2 block with four distinct distributions observed.

In v_- matrix M14, elements in the columns and rows are arranged as a periodic crossing structure.

In v_0 matrix M15, each element shows simple additions with elements in v_+ and v_- respectively. Only two pairs of positions {0:15, 6:9} are similarly distributed in the relevant MPS matrix.

In v_1 matrix M16, significant symmetry properties can be observed. Two pairs {0:15, 6:9} have anti-symmetry properties the same as under the v_0 condition.

F group in MPS

For the F group in Figure 9 (M17-M24), the two matrix vectors $\{u,v\} = \{(u_+,u_-,u_0,u_1),(v_+,v_-,v_0,v_1)\}$ are best considered separately.

M17-M20: Let us now consider elements M17-M20 where the four matrices (u_+,u_-,u_0,u_1) are in a symmetry group,

In u_+ matrix M17, the horizontal elements are arranged in H-2R patterns and vertical elements are in a periodic crossing structure.

In u_- matrix M18, vertical elements are arranged in V-2R patterns and the horizontal elements as a periodic crossing structure.

In u_0 matrix M19, each element shows simple additions with elements in u_+ and u_- respectively. It it interesting to note that six pairs of positions {0:15, 1:7. 2:11, 4:13, 6:9, 8:14} are similarly distributed.

However, in u_1 matrix M20, significant symmetry properties can be observed. Not only do six pairs {0:15, 1:7. 2:11, 4:13, 6:9, 8:14} have symmetry properties and another six pairs of {1:8, 2:4, 3:12, 5:10, 7:14, 11:13 } with anti-symmetry properties but there are also significantly differences compared with the u_0 condition.

M21-M24: Let us now consider elements M17-M20 where the four matrices of (v_+,v,v_0,v_1) are in an anti-symmetry group,

In v_+ matrix M21, the horizontal elements are arranged in H-2R patterns and the vertical elements as a periodic crossing structure.

In v_- matrix M22, the vertical elements are arranged in V-2R patterns and the horizontal elements as a periodic crossing structure.

In v_0 matrix M23, each element shows simple additions with elements in v_+ and v_- respectively. It it interesting to note that six pairs of positions {0:15, 1:7. 2:11, 4:13, 6:9, 8:14} are in the anti-symmetry distribution.

In v_1 matrix M24, significant symmetry properties can be observed. Six pairs {0:15, 1:7. 2:11, 4:13, 6:9, 8:14} have anti-symmetry properties and two pairs {2:4, 11:13} have symmetry properties.

C group in MPS

For the C group in Figure 9 (M25-M32), two matrix vectors $\{u,v\} = \{(u_+,u_-,u_0,u_1),(v_+,v_-,v_0,v_1)\}$ are best considered separately.

M25-M28: Let us now consider elements M25-M28 where the four matrices of (u_+,u_-,u_0,u_1) are in a symmetry group,

In u_+ matrix M25, the horizontal elements are in a periodic crossing structure and the vertical elements are arranged in V-4R patterns

In u_- matrix M26, the horizontal elements are arranged in H-4R patterns and the vertical elements as a periodic crossing structure.

In u_0 matrix M27, each element shows simple additions with elements in u_+ and u_- respectively. It it interesting to note that six pairs of positions {0:15, 1:7. 2:11, 4:13, 6:9, 8:14} are similarly distributed.

However, in u_1 matrix M28, significant symmetry properties can be observed. Not only do six pairs {0:15, 1:7. 2:11, 4:13, 6:9, 8:14} have symmetry but another six pairs {1:8, 2:4, 3:12, 5:10, 7:14, 11:13 } have anti-symmetry properties, all significantly different from the u_0 condition.

M29-M32: Let us now consider elements M29-M32 where the four matrices of $(v_+, v_, v_0, v_1)$ are in an anti-symmetry group,

In v_+ matrix M29, the horizontal elements are arranged in H-4R patterns and the vertical elements as a periodic crossing structure.

In v_- matrix M30, the horizontal elements are arranged in H-4R patterns and the vertical elements as a periodic crossing structure.

In v_0 matrix M31, each element shows simple additions with elements in v_+ and v_- respectively. The distribution of six pairs of positions {0:15, 1:7. 2:11, 4:13, 6:9, 8:14} exhibit anti-symmetry.

In v_1 matrix M32, significant symmetry properties can be observed. Six pairs {0:15, 1:7. 2:11, 4:13, 6:9, 8:14} have anti-symmetry properties and two pairs {2:4, 11:13} have symmetry properties.

9.2.2. CPS Structures

Four groups of different configurations shown in Figure 10 (C1-C32) are discussed separately as follows.

SL group in CPS

For the SL group in Figure 10 (C1-C8), he two matrix vectors $\{\tilde{u}, \tilde{v}\} = \{(\tilde{u}_+, \tilde{u}_-, \tilde{u}_0, \tilde{u}_1), (\tilde{v}_+, \tilde{v}_-, \tilde{v}_0, \tilde{v}_1)\}$ are best considered separately.

C1-C4: Let us now consider elements C1-C4 where the four matrices of $(\tilde{u}_+, \tilde{u}_-, \tilde{u}_0, \tilde{u}_1)$ are in a symmetry group,

In $\tilde{u}_+$ matrix C1, elements in the columns and rows are in a periodic crossing structure.

In $\tilde{u}_-$ matrix C2, four elements with the same IMs are arranged in a 2×2 block with four distinct distributions observed.

In $\tilde{u}_0$ matrix C3, each element shows simple additions from elements in $\tilde{u}_+$ and $\tilde{u}_-$ respectively. It it interesting to note that four pairs of positions {0:15, 3:12, 5:10, 6:9} are similarly distributed in the relevant CPS matrix.

In $\tilde{u}_1$ matrix C4, similar symmetry properties can be observed. Four pairs {0:15, 3:12, 5:10, 6:9} have symmetry or anti-symmetry properties that are the same as for the $\tilde{u}_0$ condition.

C5-C8: Let us now consider elements C5-C8 where the four matrices of $(\tilde{v}_+,\tilde{v},\tilde{v}_0,\tilde{v}_1)$ are in an anti-symmetry group,

In $\tilde{v}_+$ matrix C5, elements in the columns and rows are arranged in a periodic crossing structure.

In $\tilde{v}_-$ matrix C6, four elements with same IMs are arranged in a 2×2 block and four distinct distributions are observed.

In $\tilde{v}_0$ matrix C7, each element shows simple additions from elements in $\tilde{v}_+$ and $\tilde{v}_-$ respectively. Only two pairs of positions {0:15, 6:9} are in the same distribution in similar arrangements.

In $\tilde{v}_1$ matrix C8, similar symmetry properties can be observed. Four pairs {0:15, 3:12, 5:10, 6:9} have anti-symmetry properties significantly different from those in the $\tilde{v}_0$ condition.

W group in CPS

For the W group in Figure 10 (C9-C16), the two matrix vectors $\{\tilde{u},\tilde{v}\} = \{(\tilde{u}_+,\tilde{u}_-,\tilde{u}_0,\tilde{u}_1),(\tilde{v}_+,\tilde{v}_-,\tilde{v}_0,\tilde{v}_1)\}$ are best considered separately.

C9-C12: Let us now consider elements C9-C12 where the four matrices of $(\tilde{u}_+,\tilde{u}_-,\tilde{u}_0,\tilde{u}_1)$ are in a symmetry group,

In $\tilde{u}_+$ matrix C9, four elements with the same IMs are arranged in a 2×2 block and four distinct distributions are observed.

In $\tilde{u}_-$ matrix C10, elements in the columns and rows are arranged as a periodic crossing structure.

In $\tilde{u}_0$ matrix C11, each element shows simple additions from elements in $\tilde{u}_+$ and $\tilde{u}_-$ respectively. It it interesting to note that four pairs of positions {0:15, 3:12, 5:10, 6:9} are distributed in similar arrangements in the relevant CPS matrix.

In $\tilde{u}_1$ matrix C12, similar symmetry properties can be observed. Four pairs {0:15, 3:12, 5:10, 6:9} have symmetry or anti-symmetry properties that are the same as under the $\tilde{u}_0$ condition.

C13-C16: Let us now consider elements C13-C16 where the four matrices of $(\tilde{v}_+,\tilde{v},\tilde{v}_0,\tilde{v}_1)$ are in an anti-symmetry group,

In $\tilde{v}_+$ matrix C13, four elements with the same IMs are arranged in a 2×2 block and four distinct distributions are observed.

In $\tilde{v}_-$ matrix C14, elements in the columns and rows are arranged as a periodic crossing structure.

In $\tilde{v}_0$ matrix C15, each element shows simple additions from elements in $\tilde{v}_+$ and $\tilde{v}_-$ respectively. Only two pairs of positions {0:15, 6:9} show the same distribution in similar arrangements.

In $\tilde{v}_1$ matrix C16, significant symmetry properties can be observed. Four pairs {0:15, 3:12, 5:10, 6:9} have anti-symmetry properties that are different from those under $\tilde{v}_0$ conditions.

F group in CPS

http://dx.doi.org/10.5772/51635

For the F group in Figure 10 (C17-C24), the two matrix vectors $\{\tilde{u},\tilde{v}\} = \{(\tilde{u}_+,\tilde{u}_-,\tilde{u}_0,\tilde{u}_1),(\tilde{v}_+,\tilde{v}_-,\tilde{v}_0,\tilde{v}_1)\}$ are best considered separately.

C17-C20: Let us now consider elements C17-C20 where the four matrices of $(\tilde{u}_+,\tilde{u}_-,\tilde{u}_0,\tilde{u}_1)$ are in a symmetry group,

In $\tilde{u}_+$ matrix C17, horizontal elements are arranged in H-2R patterns and vertical elements are in a periodic crossing structure.

In $\tilde{u}_-$ matrix C18, vertical elements are arranged in V-2R patterns and horizontal elements as a periodic crossing structure.

In $\tilde{u}_0$ matrix C19, each element shows simple additions from elements in $\tilde{u}_+$ and $\tilde{u}_-$ respectively. It interesting to note that six pairs of positions {0:15, 1:7. 2:11, 4:13, 6:9, 8:14} and {0:15, 1:7. 2:11, 4:13, 6:9, 8:14} are in the similar distributions.

In $\tilde{u}_1$ matrix C20, similar symmetry properties can be observed. Not only do six pairs {0:15, 1:7. 2:11, 4:13, 6:9, 8:14} have symmetry but also another six pairs {1:8, 2:4, 3:12, 5:10, 7:14, 11:13 } exhibit anti-symmetry properties that are the same as under $\tilde{u}_0$ conditions.

C21-C24: Let us now consider elements C21-C24 where the four matrices of $(\tilde{v}_+,\tilde{v},\tilde{v}_0,\tilde{v}_1)$ are in an anti-symmetry group,

In $\tilde{v}_+$ matrix C21, horizontal elements are arranged in H-2R patterns and vertical elements as periodic crossing structures.

In $\tilde{v}_-$ matrix C22, vertical elements are arranged in V-2R patterns and horizontal elements as a periodic crossing structure.

In $\tilde{v}_0$ matrix C23, each element shows simple additions from elements in $\tilde{v}_+$ and $\tilde{v}_-$ respectively. It is interesting to note that only six pairs of positions {0:15, 1:7. 2:11, 4:13, 6:9, 8:14} show anti-symmetry distributions.

In $\tilde{v}_1$ matrix C24, significant symmetry properties can be observed. Six pairs {0:15, 1:7. 2:11, 4:13, 6:9, 8:14} have anti-symmetry properties and six pairs {1:8, 2:4, 3:12, 5:10, 7:14, 11:13 } have symmetry properties.

C group in CPS

For the C group in Figure 10 (C25-C32), the two matrix vectors $\{\tilde{u},\tilde{v}\} = \{(\tilde{u}_+,\tilde{u}_-,\tilde{u}_0,\tilde{u}_1),(\tilde{v}_+,\tilde{v}_-,\tilde{v}_0,\tilde{v}_1)\}$ are best considered separately.

C25-C28: Let us now consider elements C25-C28 where the four matrices of $(\tilde{u}_+,\tilde{u}_-,\tilde{u}_0,\tilde{u}_1)$ are in a symmetry group,

In $\tilde{u}_+$ matrix C25, horizontal elements are arranged as a periodic crossing structure. and vertical elements are arranged in V-4R patterns

In $\tilde{u}_-$ matrix C26, horizontal elements are arranged in H-4R patterns and vertical elements as a periodic crossing structure.

In $\tilde{u}_0$ matrix C27, each element shows simple additions from elements in u_+ and u_- respectively. It is interesting to note that six pairs of positions {0:15, 1:7. 2:11, 4:13, 6:9, 8:14} are similarly distributed and six pairs of positions {1:8, 2:4, 3:12, 5:10, 7:14, 11:13 } show anti-symmetry properties.

Type	Case	CP ∈ MPS	CP ∈ CPS	GP	Notes
SL	P=(3210)	2(a)	4(a,d)	N	Limited conjugate symmetry
W	P=(2103)	2(a)	4(a,d)	N	Limited conjugate symmetry
F	P=(3201)	6(e)	12(e,f)	N	Pairs conjugate symmetry
C	P=(3102)	6(e)	12(e,f)	Y	Global symmetry

Table 4. Global Symmetry Properties on CE Matrices

In $\tilde{u}_1$ matrix C28, significant symmetry properties can be observed. Not only do six pairs {0:15, 1:7. 2:11, 4:13, 6:9, 8:14} show symmetry but also another six pairs {1:8, 2:4, 3:12, 5:10, 7:14, 11:13 } exhibit anti-symmetry properties similar to those under $\tilde{u}_0$ conditions.

C29-C32: Let us now consider elements C29-C32 where the four matrices of $(\tilde{v}_+, \tilde{v}, \tilde{v}_0, \tilde{v}_1)$ are in an anti-symmetry group,

In $\tilde{v}_+$ matrix C29, horizontal elements are arranged in H-4R patterns and vertical elements are arranged as a periodic crossing structure.

In $\tilde{v}_-$ matrix C30, horizontal elements are arranged in H-4R patterns and vertical elements are arranged as a periodic crossing structure.

In $\tilde{v}_0$ matrix C31, each element shows simple additions from elements in $\tilde{v}_+$ and $\tilde{v}_-$ respectively. Two pairs of positions {0:15, 4:13, 6:9, 8:14} exhibit anti-symmetry distributions.

In $\tilde{v}_1$ matrix C32, significant symmetry properties can be observed. Six pairs {0:15, 1:7. 2:11, 4:13, 6:9, 8:14} have anti-symmetry properties and another six pairs {1:8, 2:4, 3:12, 5:10, 7:14, 11:13 } have symmetry properties that are different from those under $\tilde{v}_0$ condition.

10. Global symmetric properties

Working from four sets of CEM and IMM results, key global symmetry properties are presented and summarized in Table 4 for CEMs and in Table 5 for IMMs as follows.

Where CP is a conjugate pair, GP is global polarization and a:(0:15,6:9), d:(3:12,5:10), e:(0:15,1:7,2:11,4:13,6:9,8:14), f:(1:8,2:4,3:12,5:10,7:14,11:13), are pair functions.

It is interesting to note that significant differences in symmetry properties between MPS and CPS can be observed for CEM conjugate pairs.

In general, we find double the number of incidences of symmetry properties with CPS compared with MPS shown in Table 4.

Where SP is a Symmetric Pair, ASP is an Anti-symmetric Pair, GS is Global Symmetry and a:(0:15,6:9), b:(0:15,6:9,3:12), c:(5:10), d:(3:12,5:10), e:(0:15,1:7,2:11,4:13,6:9,8:14), f:(1:8,2:4,3:12,5:10,7:14,11:13), g:(2:4,11:13) are pair functions.

It is interesting to note that symmetry properties evident in IMM groups in Table 5 are more refined than the original configurations under MPS and CPS conditions.

The classification of different projections and polarized properties can be further refined to show their various interactive activities in relevant sub-categories. Further details for conjugate pairs can be distinguished under symmetry/anti-symmetry and synchronous/asynchronous configurations. Conjugate pairs can be further differentiated as being either symmetric or anti-symmetric pairs.

http://dx.doi.org/10.5772/51635

Type	Case	Left	Right	SP(D-P)	ASP(D-P)	SP(D-W)	ASP(D-W)	GS
SL	P=(3210)	Cross	2x2Block					Weak
	u			2 (a)	0	3 (b)	1 (c)	
	v			0	2 (a)	0	2 (a)	
	$\tilde{u}$			2 (a)	2 (d)	2 (a)	2 (d)	
	$\tilde{v}$			0	2 (a)	2 (d)	2 (a)	
W	P=(2103)	2x2Block	Cross					Weak
	u			2 (a)	0	3 (b)	1 (c)	
	v			0	2 (a)	0	2 (a)	
	$\tilde{u}$			2 (a)	2 (d)	2 (a)	2 (d)	
	$\tilde{v}$			0	2 (a)	2 (d)	2 (a)	
F	P=(3201)	V-2R	H-2R					Stronger
	u			6 (e)	0	6 (e)	6 (f)	
	v			0	6 (e)	2 (g)	6 (e)	
	$\tilde{u}$			6 (e)	6 (f)	6 (e)	6 (f)	
	$\tilde{v}$			0	6 (e)	6 (e)	6 (f)	
C	P=(3102)	V-4R	H-4R					Strongest
	u			6 (e)	0	6 (e)	6 (f)	
	v			0	6 (e)	2 (g)	6 (e)	
	$\tilde{u}$			6 (e)	6 (f)	6 (e)	6 (f)	
	$\tilde{v}$			0	6 (e)	6 (e)	6 (f)	

Table 5. Global Symmetry Properties on IM Matrices

10.1. Comparison of variant phase space and statistical mechanics

Both Maxwell-Boltzmann and Darwin-Fowler schemes are considered suitable for processing isolated systems. Meanwhile, a Gibbs scheme can be applied to several different systems namely, an isolated system on a micro canonical ensemble, a closed system on a canonical ensemble, and an open system on a grand canonical ensemble [20, 23, 24, 31, 33]. Such significant differences can offer useful comparisons when considering *Variant Phase Space*.

Using Variant Phase Space (VPS) components and key properties of Classical Statistical Mechanics (CSM), two types of systems are compared in Table 6.

Table 6 shows some key differences that may be distinguished between VPS and CSM. Both approaches use parameters $\{n, N, X\}$ on a selected function. However, there is a distinct difference for ME with a split into non-interactive and interactive activities between Maxwell-Boltzmann on ME(VPS) and Gibbs on IP(VPS), respectively. This difference is further distinguished on CE(VPS) and IM(VPS) levels.

Normally statistical mechanics is not based on all possible functions Instead, one function with the most probable properties is selected. Only the Maxwell demon mechanism provides any possible function for potential applications, under such restriction, modern statistical mechanics has no computational mechanism for GEM capacities.

GEM capacities do not cover a Gibbs grand canonical ensemble. However, using a given configuration of variant logic function to arrange full sets of distributions similar to variation, functional capacities can be associated with a truly large number of configurations: $2^n! \times 2^{2^n}$. This provides an opportunity to exhaust distributions for possible functions on a scale that goes way beyond the conventional framework of modern statistical mechanics.

Component	VPS	Meaning	CSM	Notes
Parameter	n	Variables	Local unit	Cell unit on rule space
	N	Dimension	Dimension	Vector Dimension on value space
	X	Nbit vector $X \in B_2^N$	Random events	I/O vectors
	J	n-function $J \in B_2^{2^n}$	Probable function	Selected function
	$\{p_+, p_-\}$	Probability pairs of measurements	$\{q, p\}$	Conjugate pairs of measurements
CME	VM	Variant Measures	Classes of events	Types of vector elements
	PM	Probability Measurements	Density Probability	Probability on each class
	ME	Micro Ensemble	Phase Point Maxwell-Boltzmann	Unit in Phase Space for non interaction
	IP	Interactive Projections	Micro Canonical Ensemble Gibbs	Unit in Ensemble with interaction
CEIM	CE	Canonical Ensemble	Canonical Ensemble Maxwell-Boltzmann	Non-interactive distribution
	IM	Interactive Maps	Canonical Ensemble Gibbs	Interactive distributions
GEM	SCEIM	Sets of CE&IM	Full set of Maxwell demons	Full set of possible distributions
	CIM	CE&IM Matrices	Global distribution Matrices	Matrices for non-interactive and interactive distributions

Table 6. Comparison between VPS and CSM

Key	Output	Operation	Strategy	Expression
CIM	Matrices for CE&IMs	Global organization of distributions for a configuration	Top	Hilbert space, Dynamic systems, Variation functional
			⇓	Top-down
SCEIM	Sets of CE&IMs	Global Integration on distributions for all functions	Down	Meta distribution, distribution function, periodic distribution
CEIM	CE&IMs	Integration of distributions for a function	UP	Maxwell-Boltzmann, Gibbs, Euler, Canonical ensemble
			⇑	Bottom-up
CME	ME&IPs	From local measures to micro ensemble and projections	Bottom	Hamilton,Lagrange, Uncertainty, Fourier pairs, Phase point

Table 7. Operation, strategy and expression of VPS

10.2. Corresponding structures on variant phase space

Top-down and bottom-up strategies can both be applied to Variant Phase Space. See Table 7.

Top-down and bottom-up strategies can each open a window through which to glimpse the mysteries of Variant Phase Space. Such glimpses do not yet provide a complete picture and further investigation is clearly required.

11. Main results

It is appropriate to present the results as a series of detailed propositions and predictions as follows.

http://dx.doi.org/10.5772/51635

For an n variable function $J \in B_2^{2^n}$ and an N bit vector $X \in B_2^N$, following propositions can be established.

11.1. Propositions

Proposition 11.1: Two types of probability measurements, Multiple and Conditional probabilities determine two distinct phase spaces, MPS and CPS.

Proof: In a PM module, multiple probabilities generates MPS and conditional probabilities create CPS. ■

Proposition 11.2: Two types of operations: symmetry/anti-symmetry and synchronous/asynchronous generate eight interactive projections.

Proof: Two pairs of measurement vectors $\{u, v\}$ or $\{\tilde{u}, \tilde{v}\}$ are involved in projections, where $u = (u_+, u_-, u_0, u_1), v = (v_+, v_-, v_0, v_1)$ and $\tilde{u} = (\tilde{u}_+, \tilde{u}_-, \tilde{u}_0, \tilde{u}_1), \tilde{v} = (\tilde{v}_+, \tilde{v}_-, \tilde{v}_0, \tilde{v}_1)$, each pair has eight interactive projections. ■

Proposition 11.3: Following a bottom-up approach, two CE and 16 IMs can be generated to exhaust all 2^N input vectors for the relevant ME and IP measurements.

Proof: Results may be generated using a CEIM module and Proposition 11.3 is further supported by Propositions 11.1 to 11.2. ■

Proposition 11.4: Each CE is a statistical distribution and each IM corresponds to one of eight IP modes.

Proof: A pair of probability measurements has one fixed CE combination and each IP mode corresponds to one IM distribution. ■

Proposition 11.5: Both Proposition 11.3 and Proposition 11.4 provide a general Maxwell Demon mechanism.

Proof: For any function, CE and IMs can be fully and exhaustively generated without reference to thermodynamic issues. ■

Proposition 11.6: Exhausting $\forall J \in B_2^{2^n}$, two sets of {CE} and 16 sets of {IM} can be generated, each set contains 2^{2^n} elements and each element is a distribution.

Proof: Using the SCEIM module, they are natural outputs. ■

Proposition 11.7: In a variant logic framework, there are $2^n! \times 2^{2^n}$ configurations for arranging a set of {CE} and eight sets of {IM} into a CEM and eight IMMs.

Proof: Since each IMM has the same organization as the CEM, a total of $2^n! \times 2^{2^n}$ configurations can be distinguished and each configuration corresponds to a variant logic matrix. ■

Proposition 11.8: With a top-down approach, either a CEM or an IMM on a proper configuration can be composed of two polarized matrices. Each polarized matrix has periodic structures on its columns and/or rows.

Proof: Since a proper configuration is based on n periodic meta vectors and their combinations, its relative arrangements are invariant under permutation and complementary operations on the vector with 2^{2^n} bits that determine each polarized structure. ■

Proposition 11.9: For MPS on C code conditions, a pair of measurements in a CEM can be arranged in a square with corners having values $\{[0,0],[1,0],[1/2,1/2],[0,1]\}$.

Proof: Under a C code configuration, the possible regions of measurements for a CEM in MPS can be shown in

$$MPS : CEM = \begin{pmatrix} [1,0] & ... & (-,-) & ... & [1/2,1/2] \\ ... & & & & ... \\ (-,0) & & ... & & (-,-) \\ ... & & & & ... \\ (0,0) & ... & (0,-) & ... & [0,1] \end{pmatrix}$$

■

Proposition 11.10: For CPS on C code conditions, a pair of measurements in a CEM can be arranged in a square with corners having values $\{[0,0],[1,0],[1,1],[0,1]\}$.

Proof: Under a C code configuration, the possible regions of measurements for a CEM in CPS can be shown in

$$CPS : CEM = \begin{pmatrix} [1,0] & ... & (1,-) & ... & [1,1] \\ ... & & & & ... \\ (-,0) & & ... & & (-,1) \\ ... & & & & ... \\ (0,0) & ... & (0,-) & ... & [0,1] \end{pmatrix}$$

■

11.2. Predictions

Prediction 11.1: Following a bottom-up strategy, it is not possible to determine CE properties using limited numbers of ME.

This prediction points towards a more general intrinsic restriction on uncertainty effects for incomplete procedures applied to random events.

Prediction 11.2: For a configuration that is not in a variant logic framework, there may be a square integral configuration capable of providing an approximate solution.

Periodic matrices could play a key role as core components of approximation procedures.

Prediction 11.3: A sound statistical interpretation of quantum mechanics can be established using VPS construction.

Since both top-down and bottom-up strategies are included, further exploration is feasible.

Prediction 11.4: VPS construction can provide a foundation based on logic and hierarchies of measurement levels for complex dynamic systems, statistical mechanics, and cellular automata.

Through VPS construction clearly offers significant potential, this prediction needs to be tested by solid experimental and theoretical results backed by evidence.

http://dx.doi.org/10.5772/51635

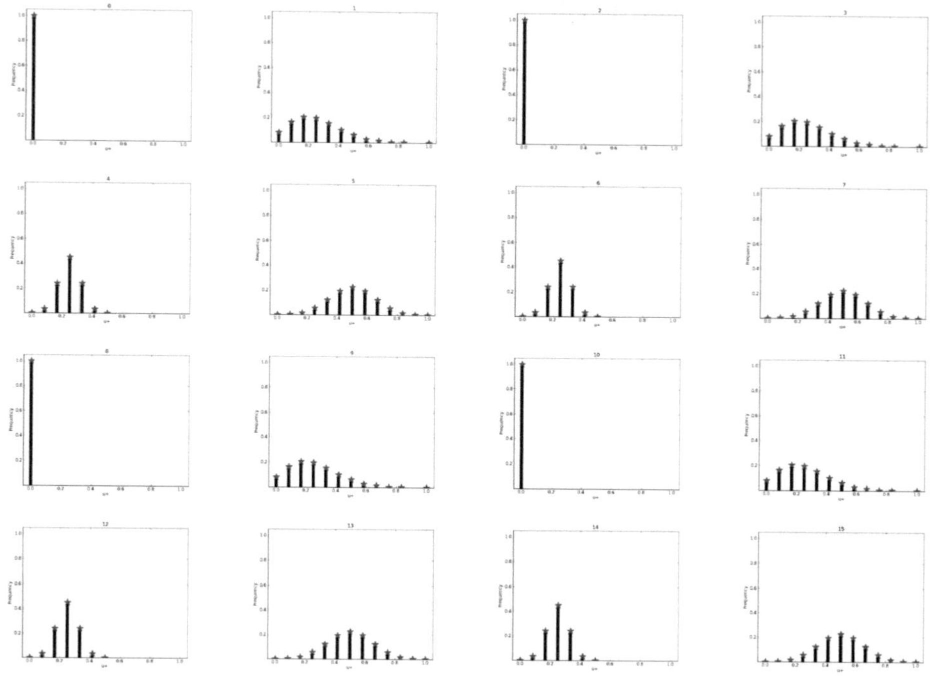

(M1) u_+ SL group

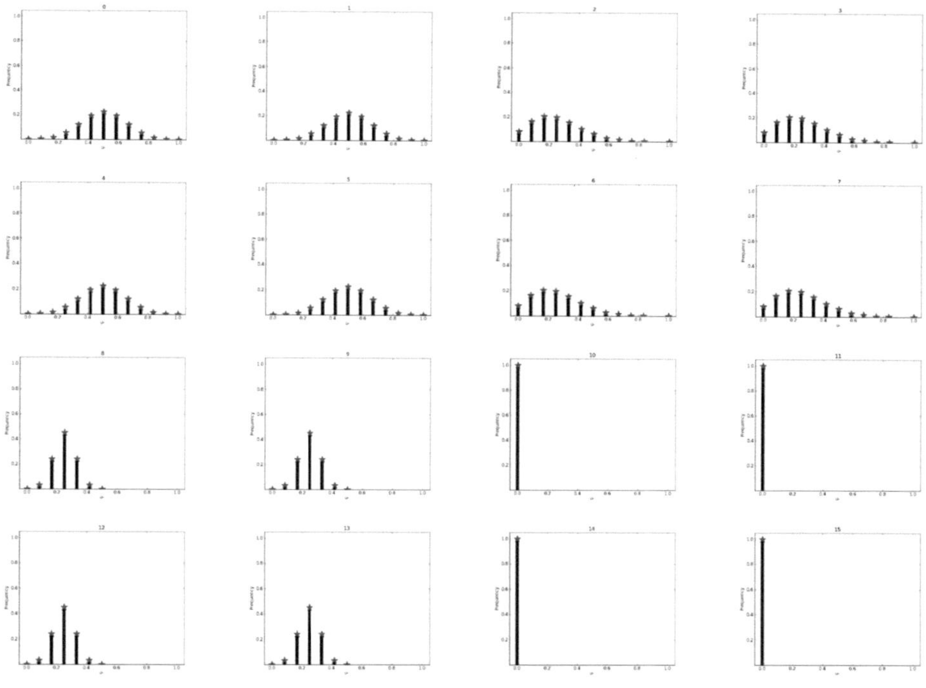

(M2) u_- SL group

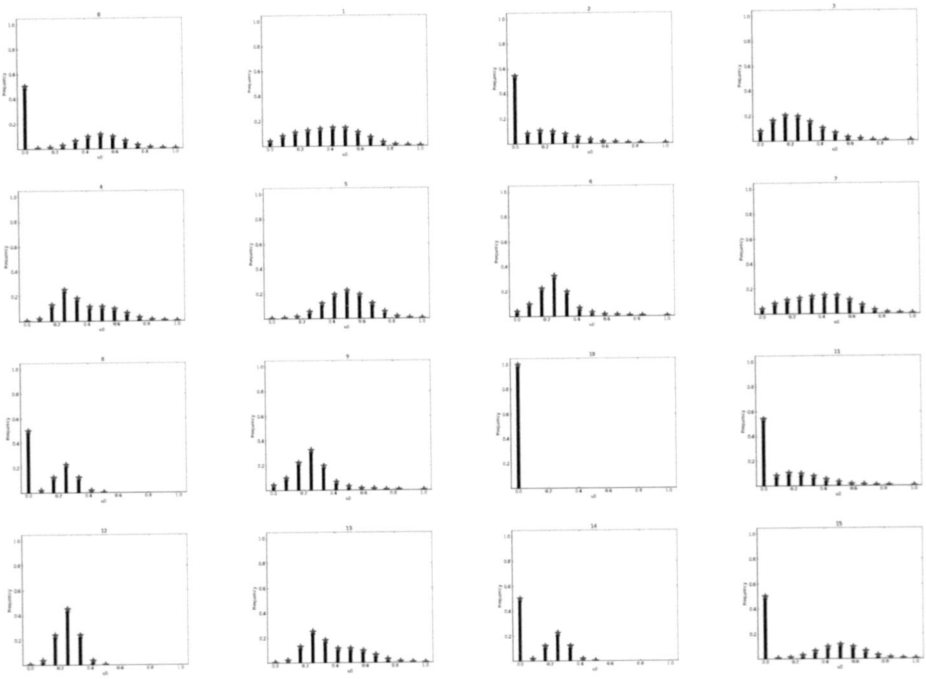

(M3) u_0 SL group

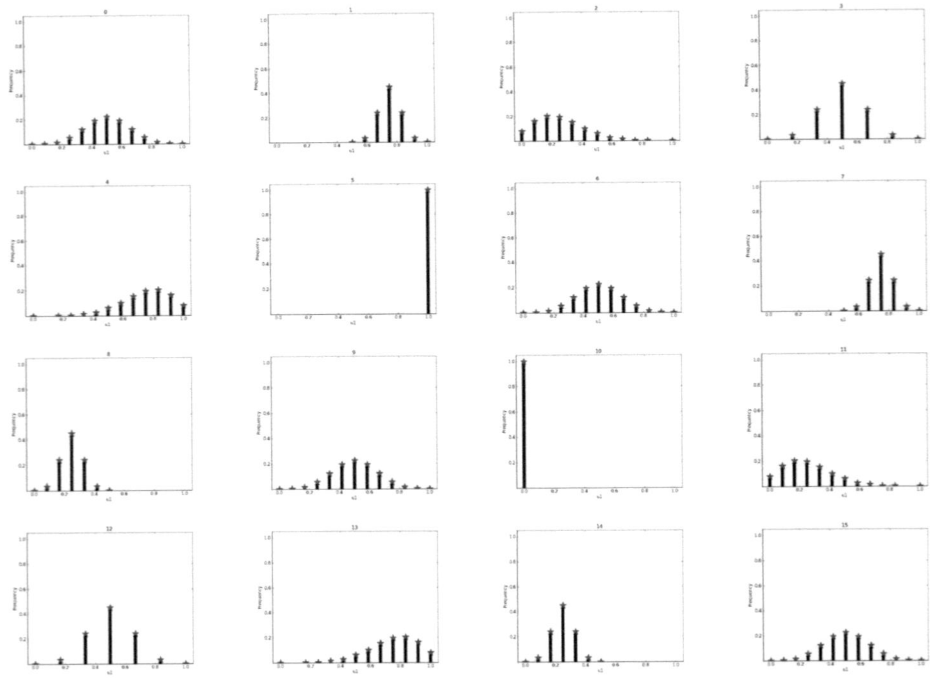

(M4) u_1 SL group

http://dx.doi.org/10.5772/51635

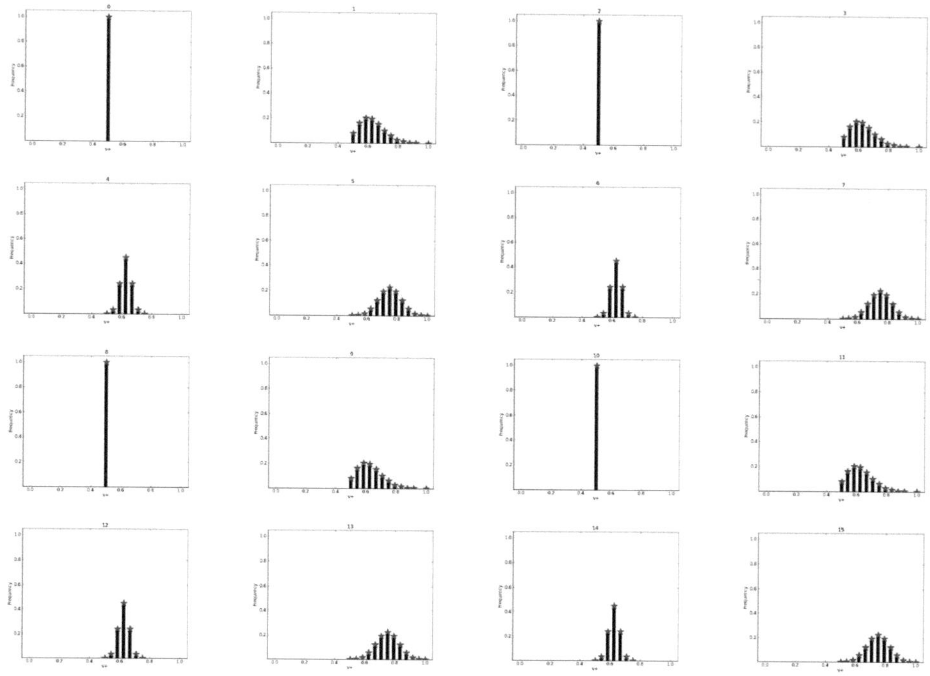

(M5) v_+ SL group

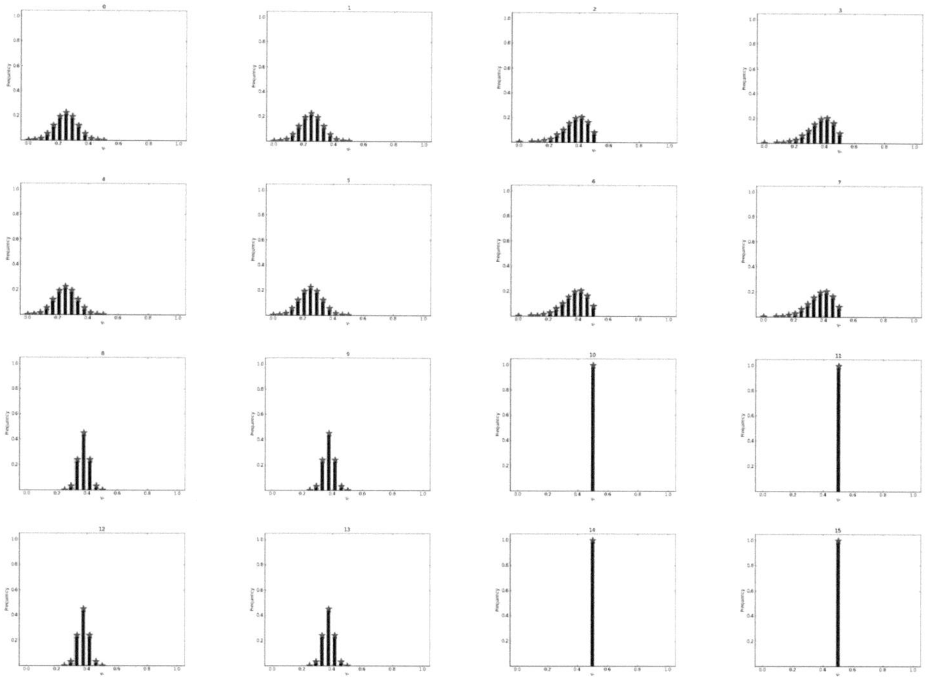

(M6) v_- SL group

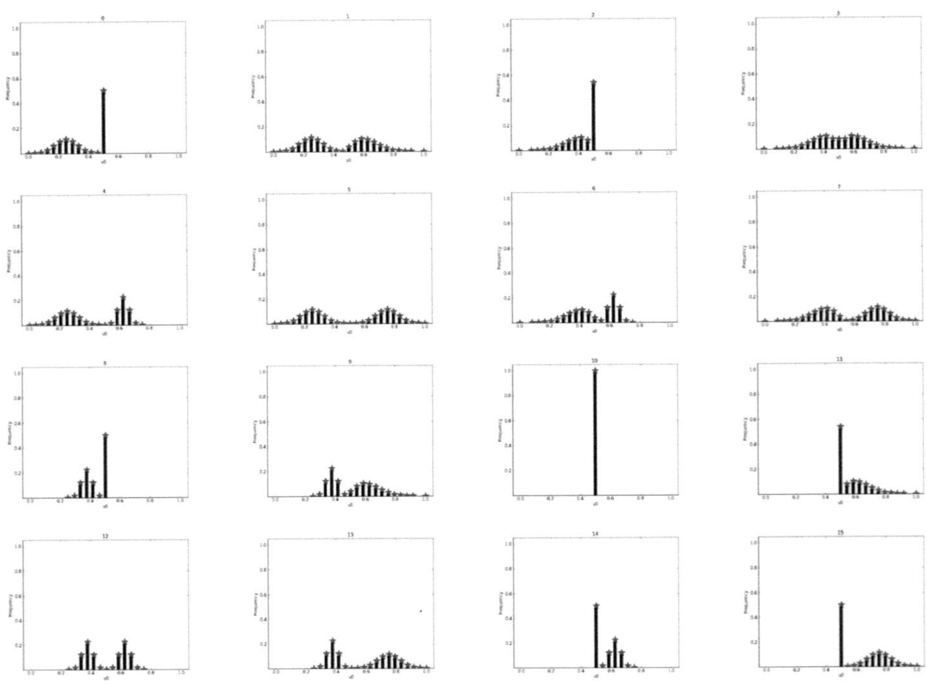

(M7) v_0 SL group

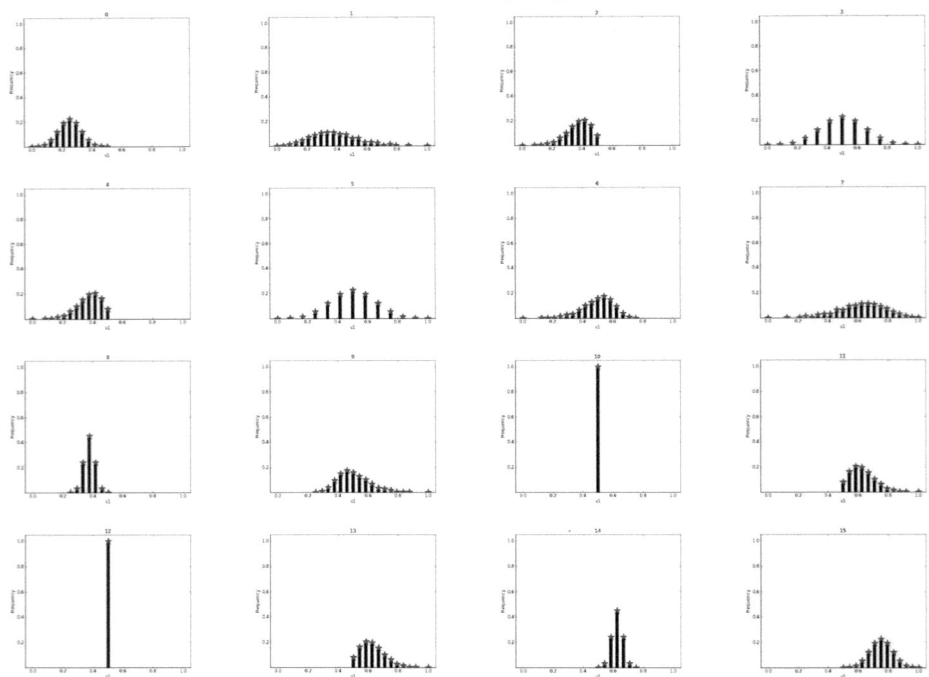

(M8) v_1 SL group

http://dx.doi.org/10.5772/51635

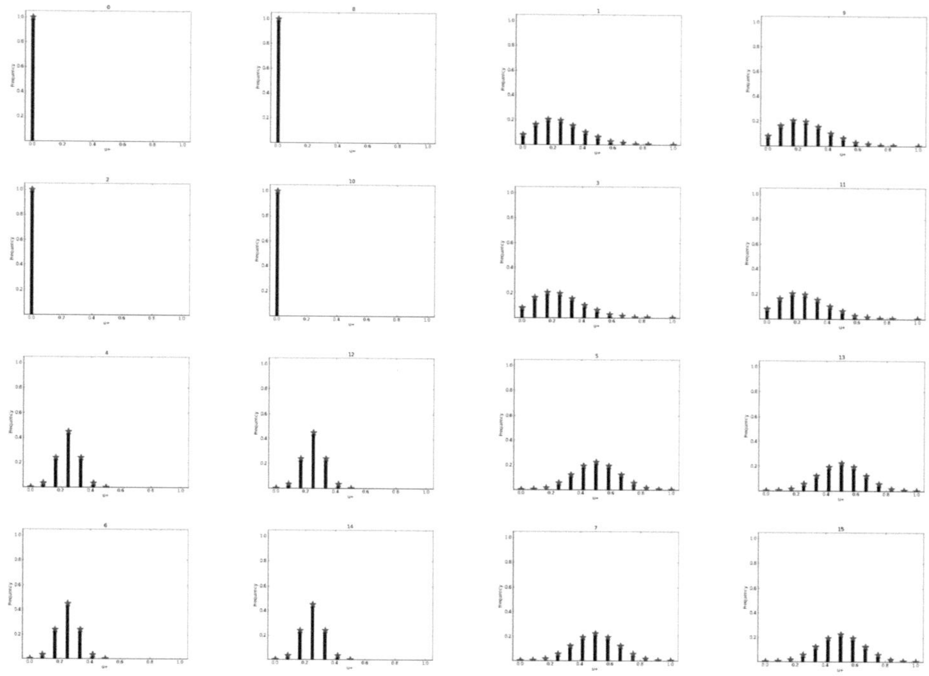

(M9) u_+ W group

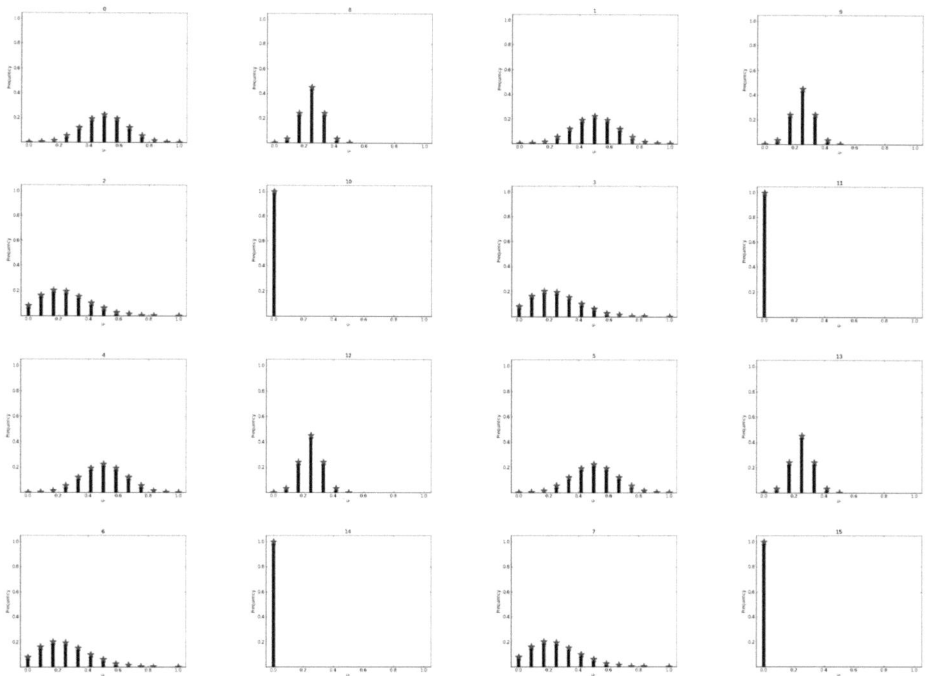

(M10) u_- W group

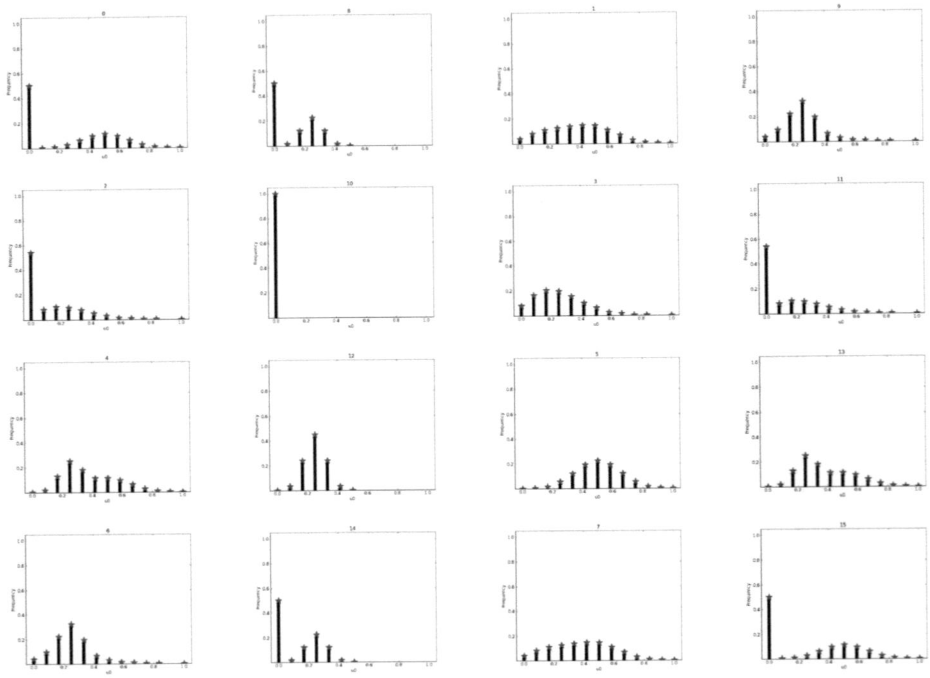

(M11) u_0 W group

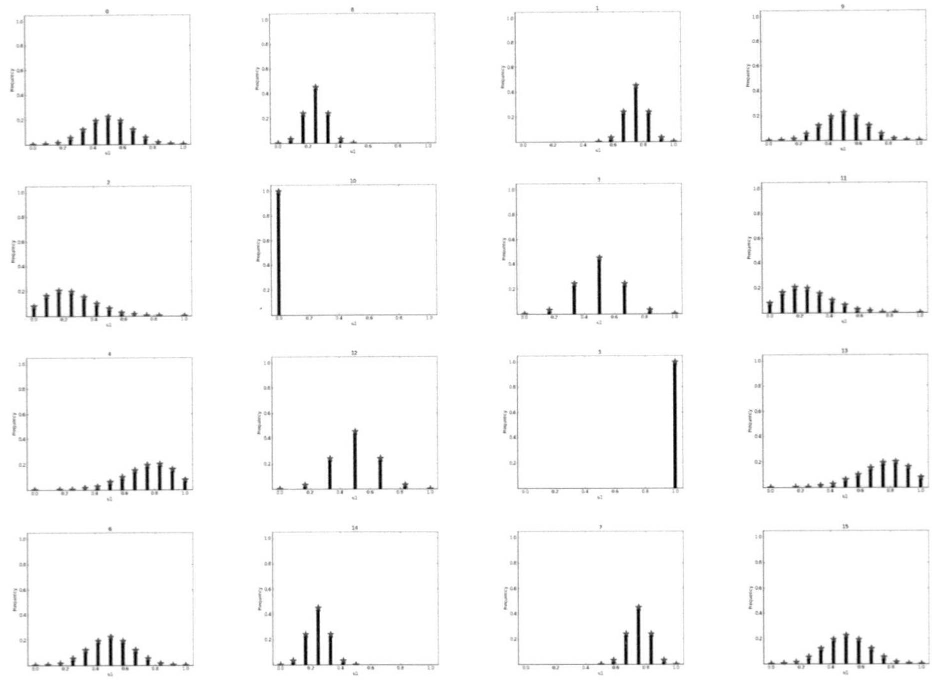

(M12) u_1 W group

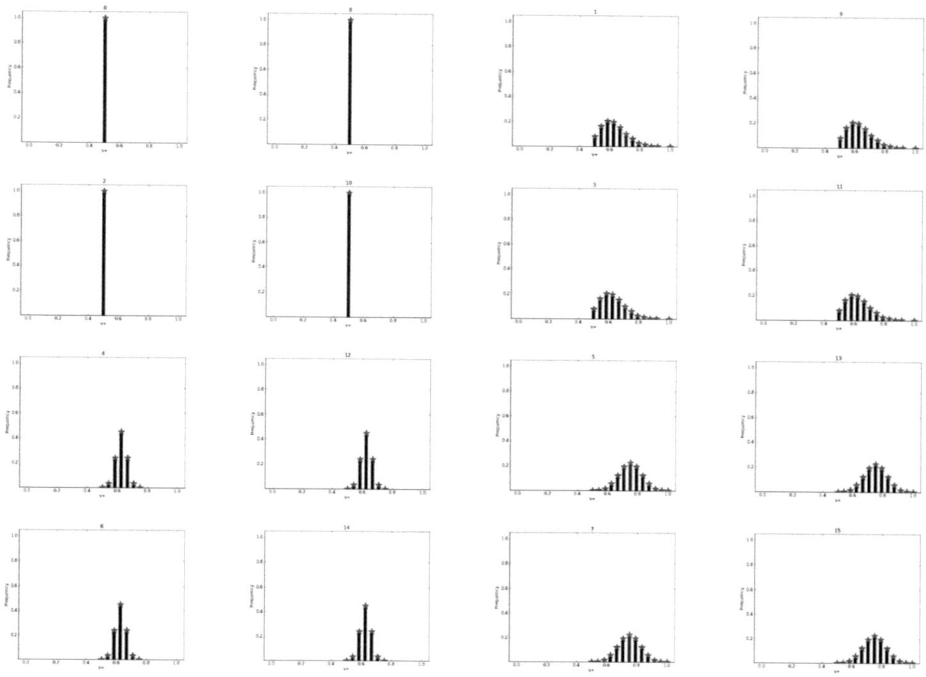

(M13) v_+ W group

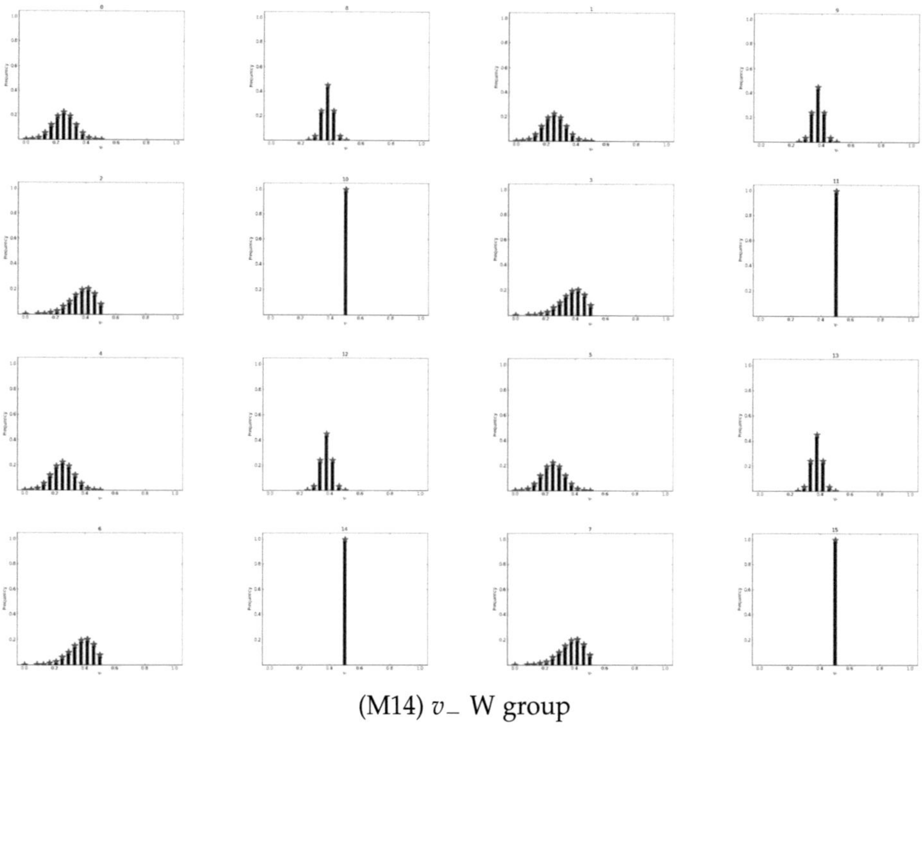

(M14) v_- W group

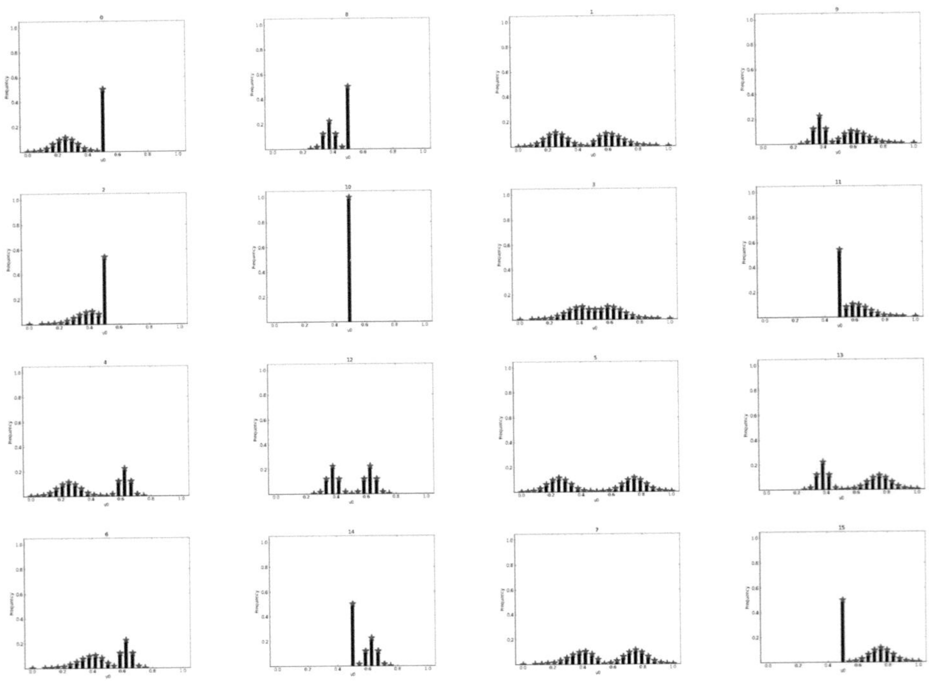

(M15) v_0 W group

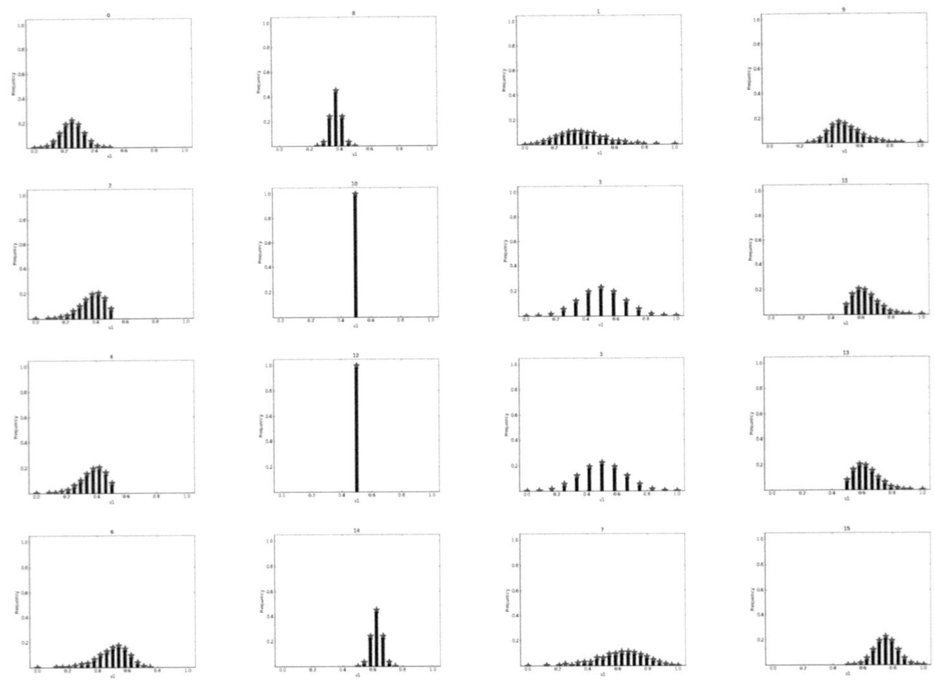

(M16) v_1 W group

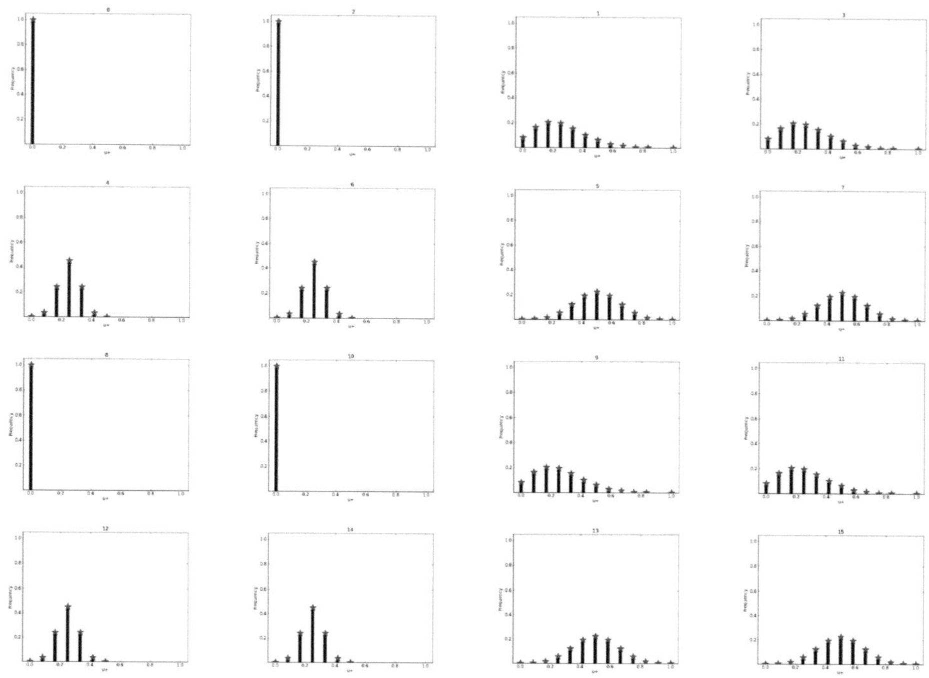

(M17) u_+ F group

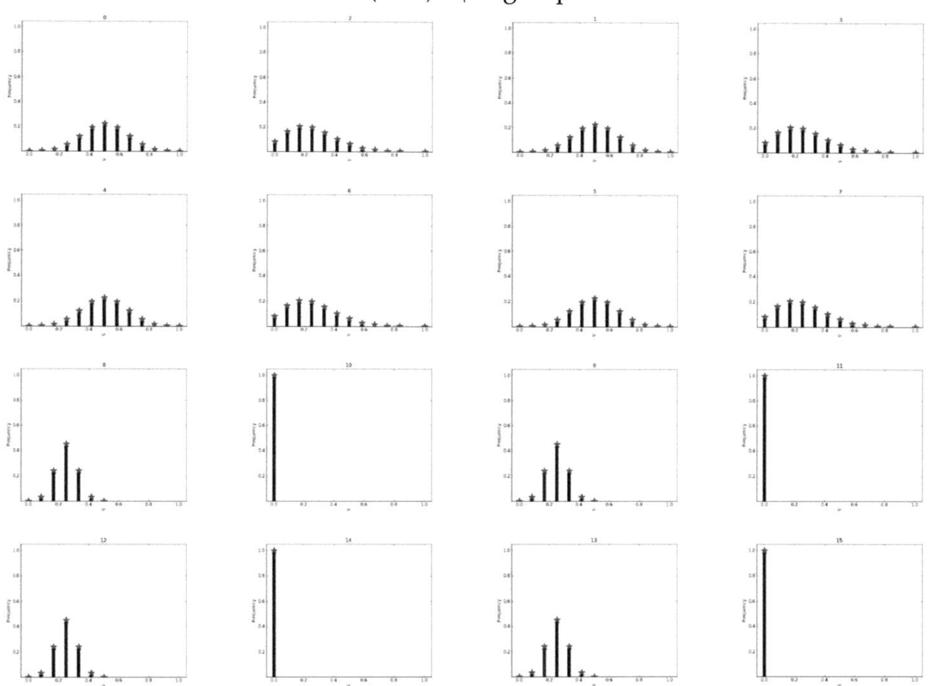

(M18) u_- F group

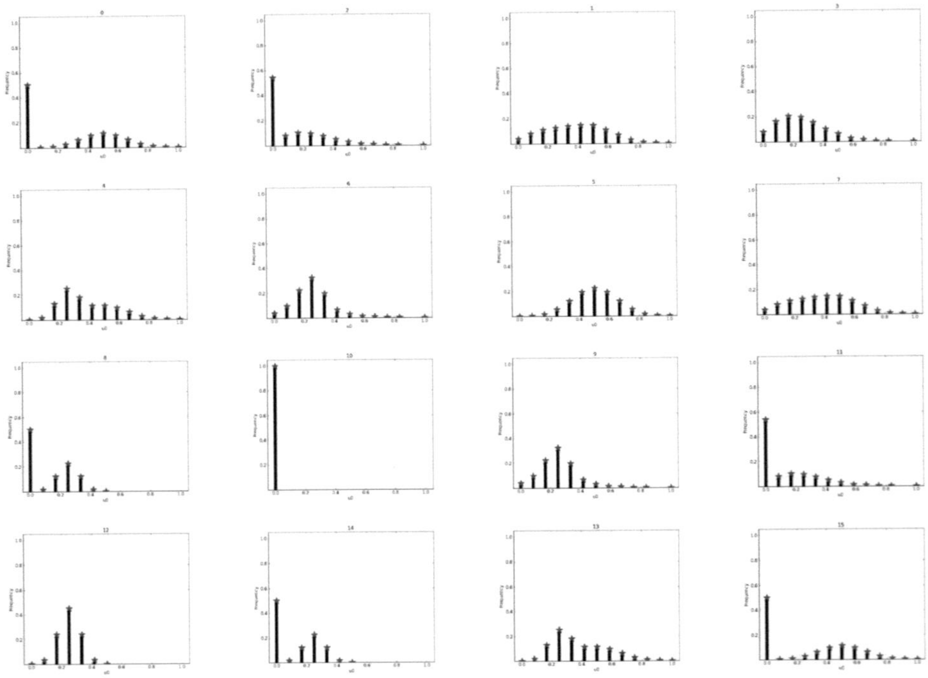

(M19) u_0 F group

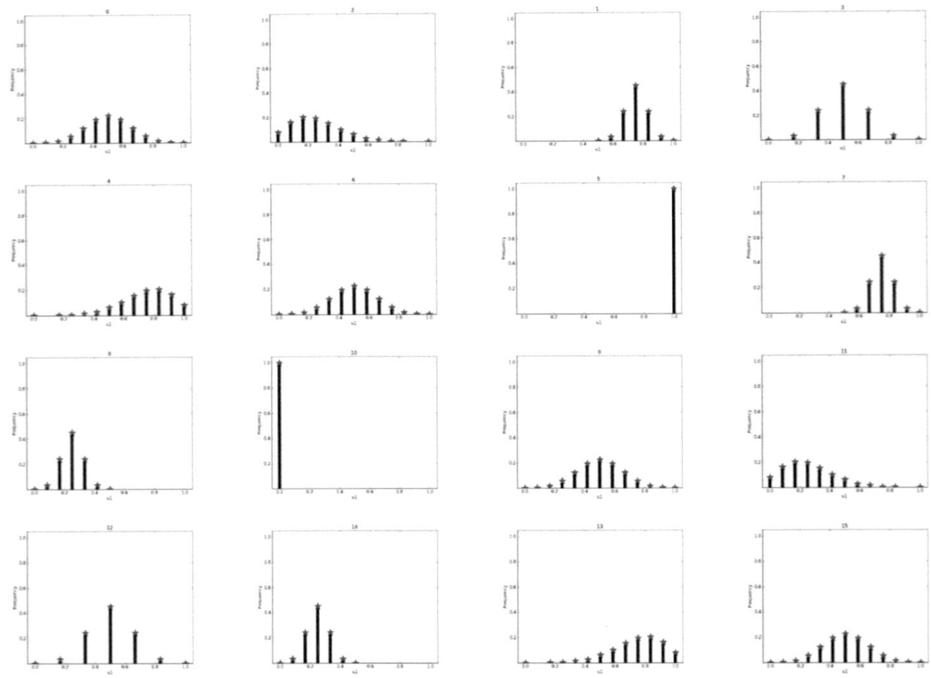

(M20) u_1 F group

http://dx.doi.org/10.5772/51635

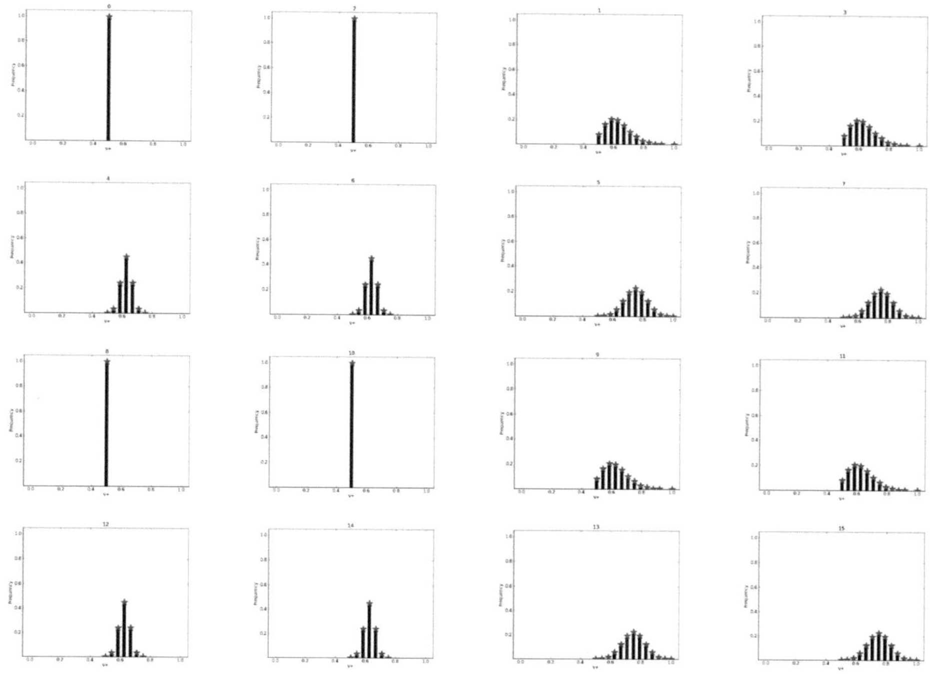

(M21) v_+ F group

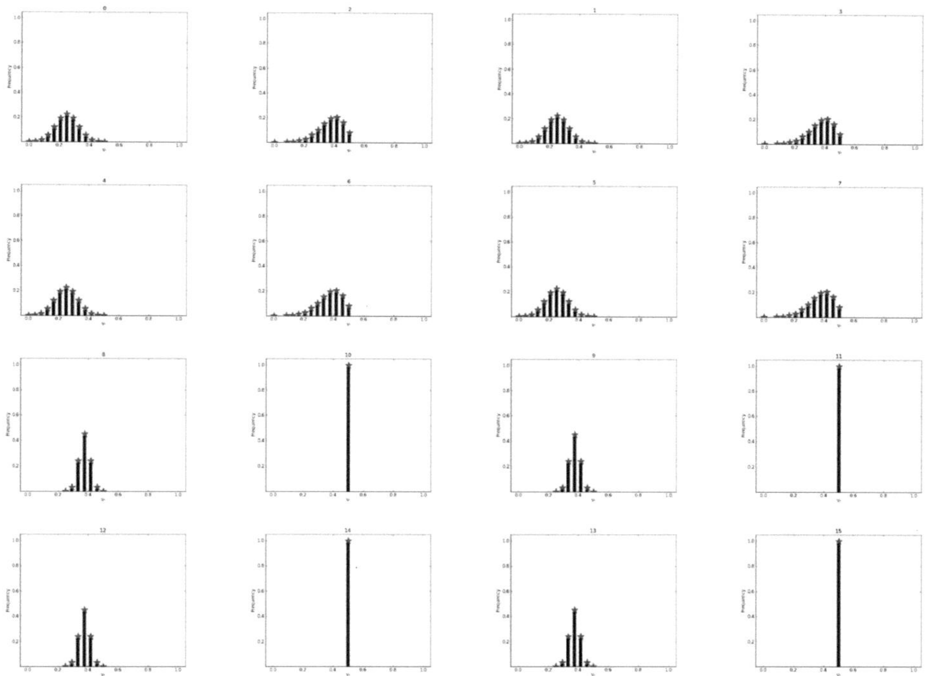

(M22) v_- F group

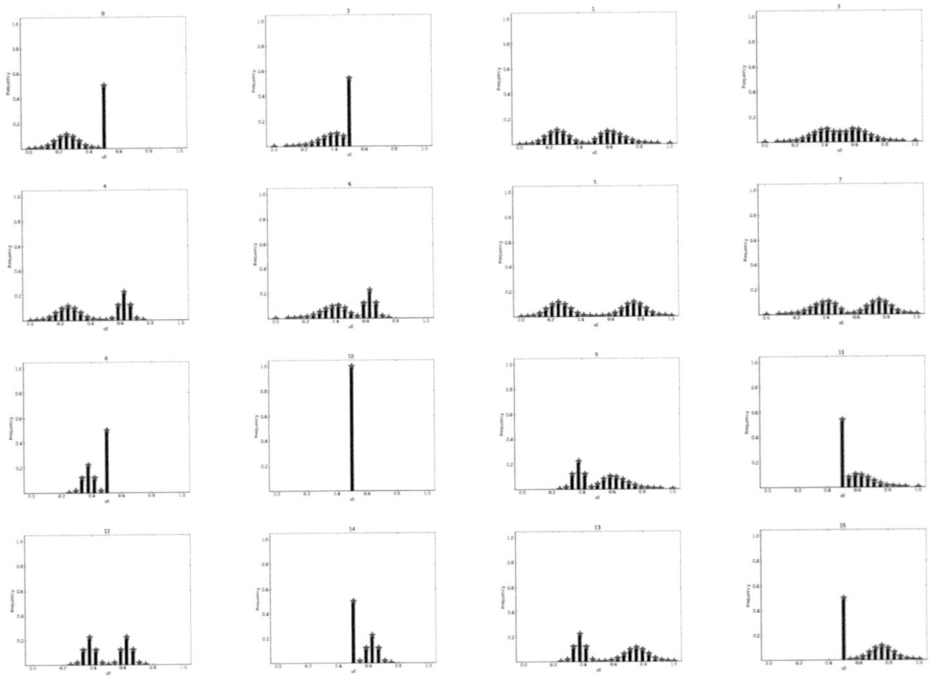

(M23) v_0 F group

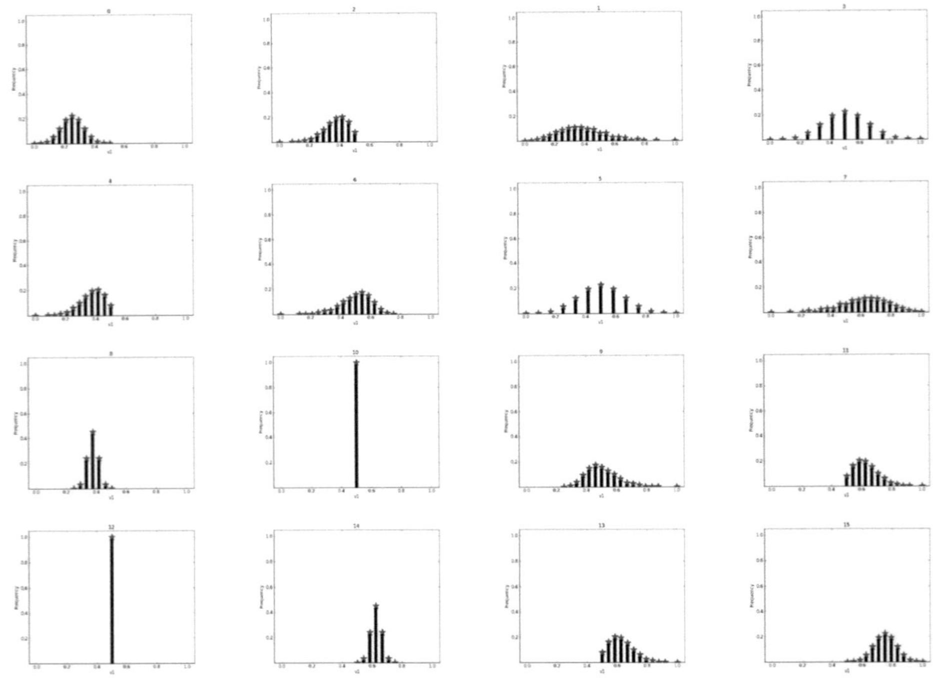

(M24) v_1 F group

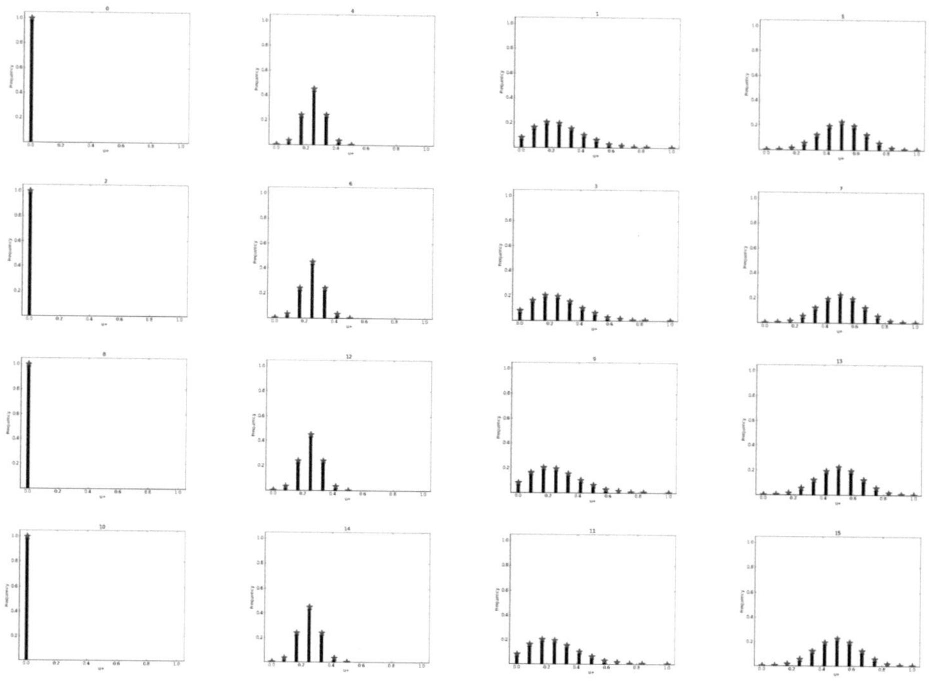

(M25) u_+ C group

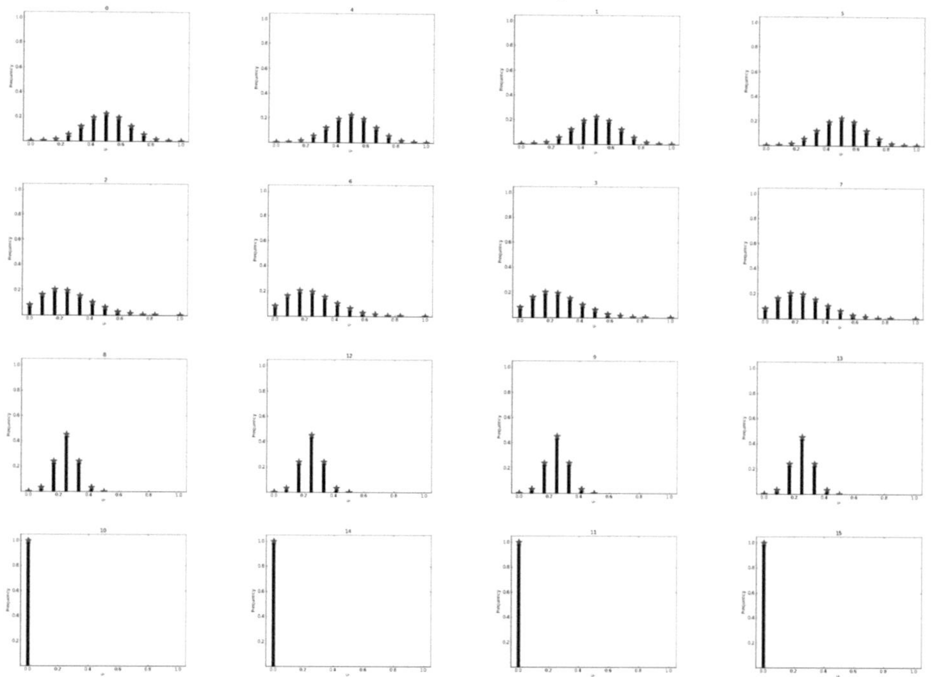

(M26) u_- C group

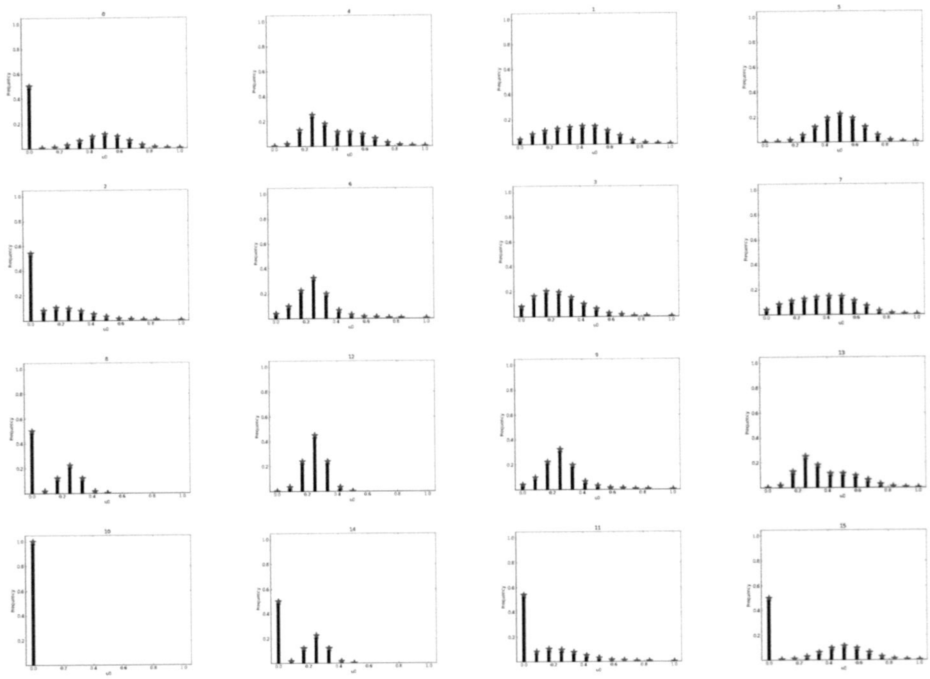

(M27) u_0 C group

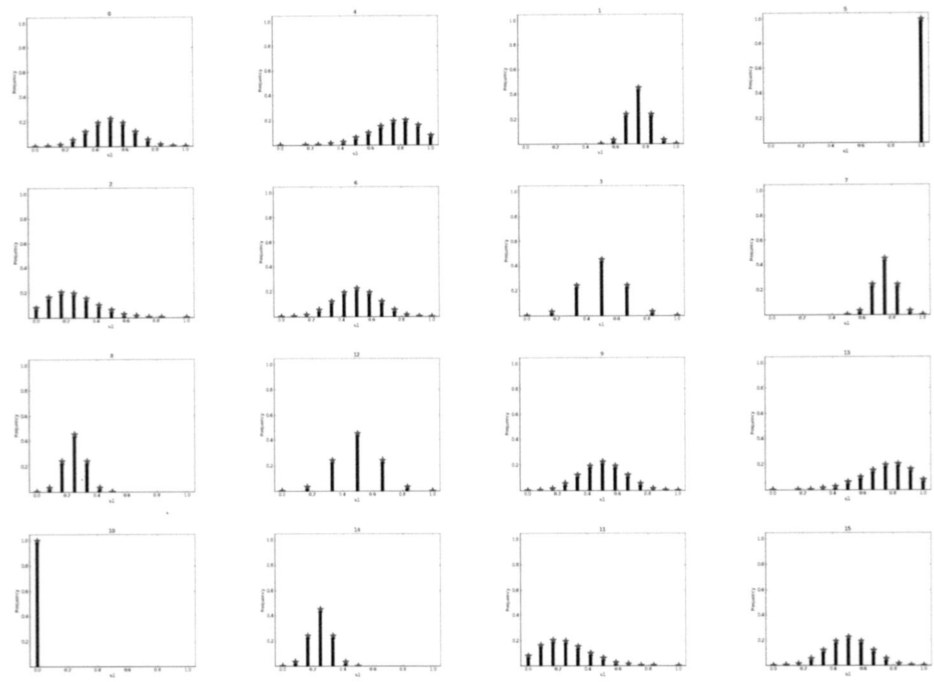

(M28) u_1 C group

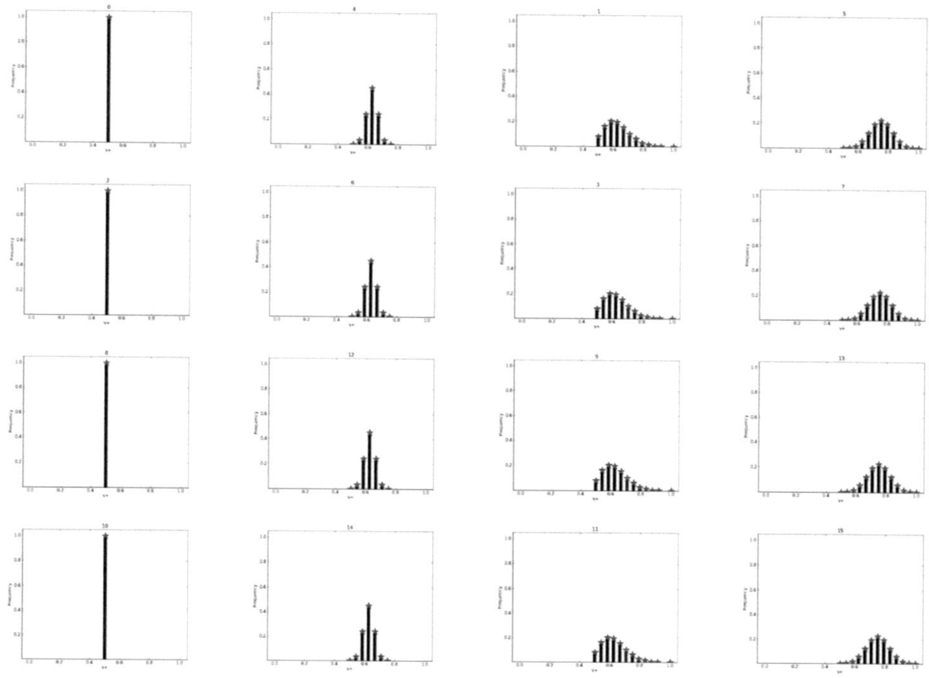

(M29) v_+ C group

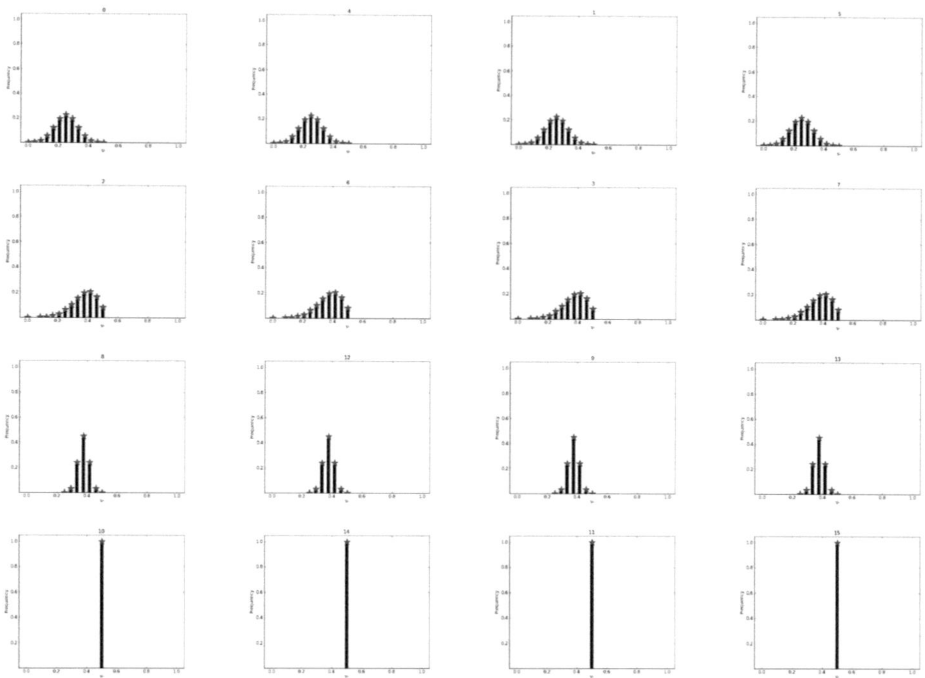

(M30) v_- C group

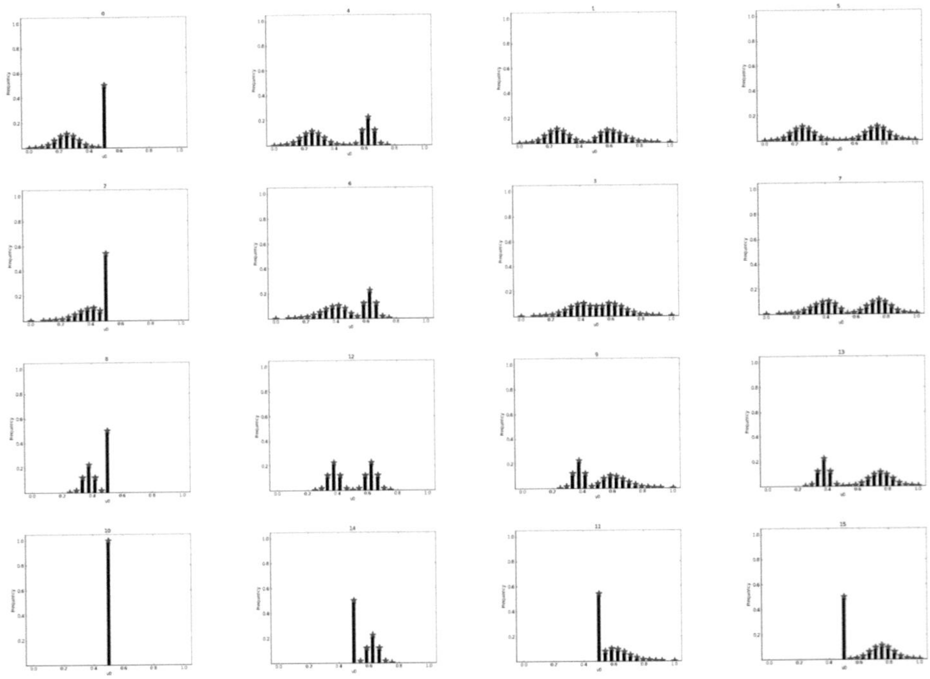

(M31) v_0 C group

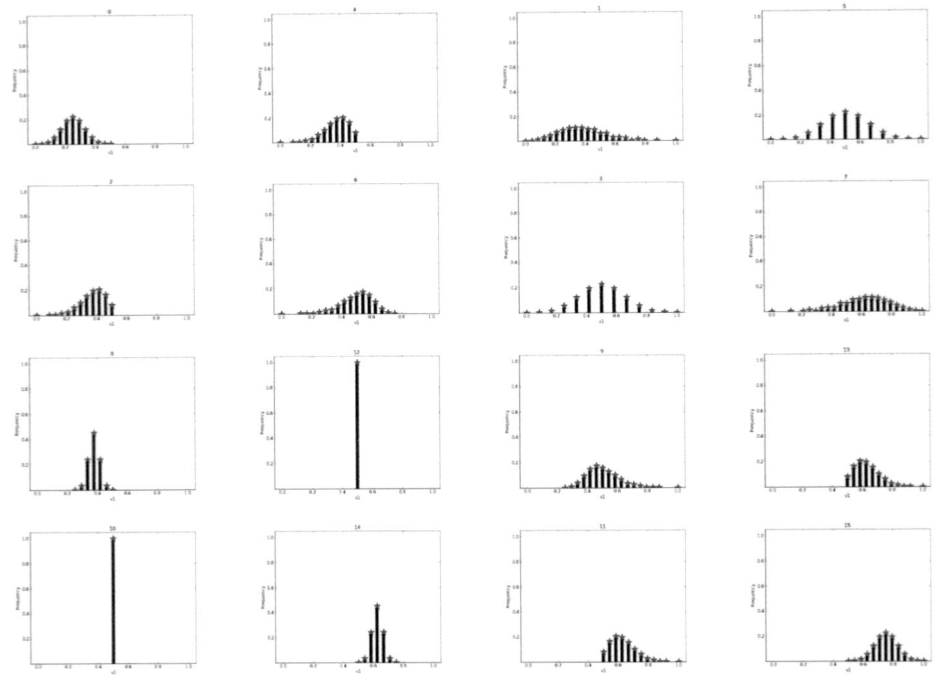

(M32) v_1 C group

Figure 9. (M1-M32) IMM for MPS; (M1-M8) SL group; (M9-M16) W group; (M17-M24) F group; (M25-M-32) C group.

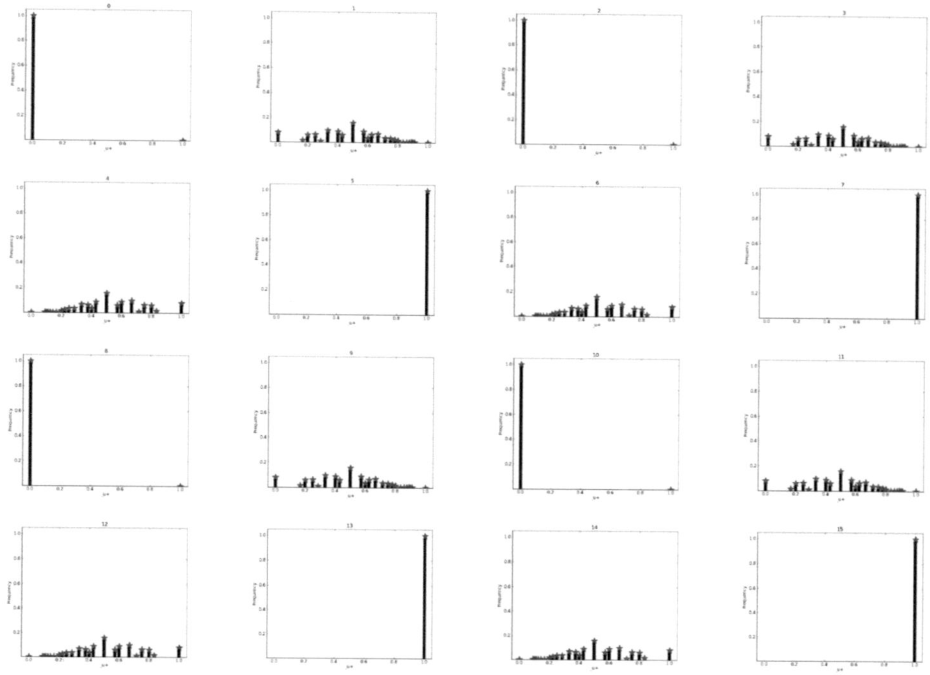

(C1) $\tilde{u}_+$ SL group

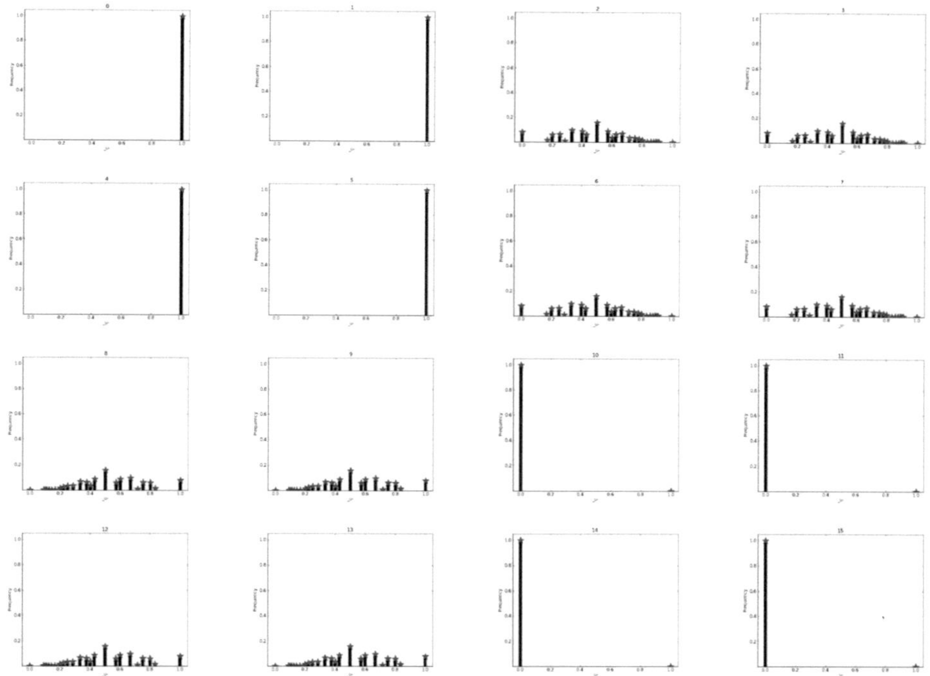

(C2) $\tilde{u}_-$ SL group

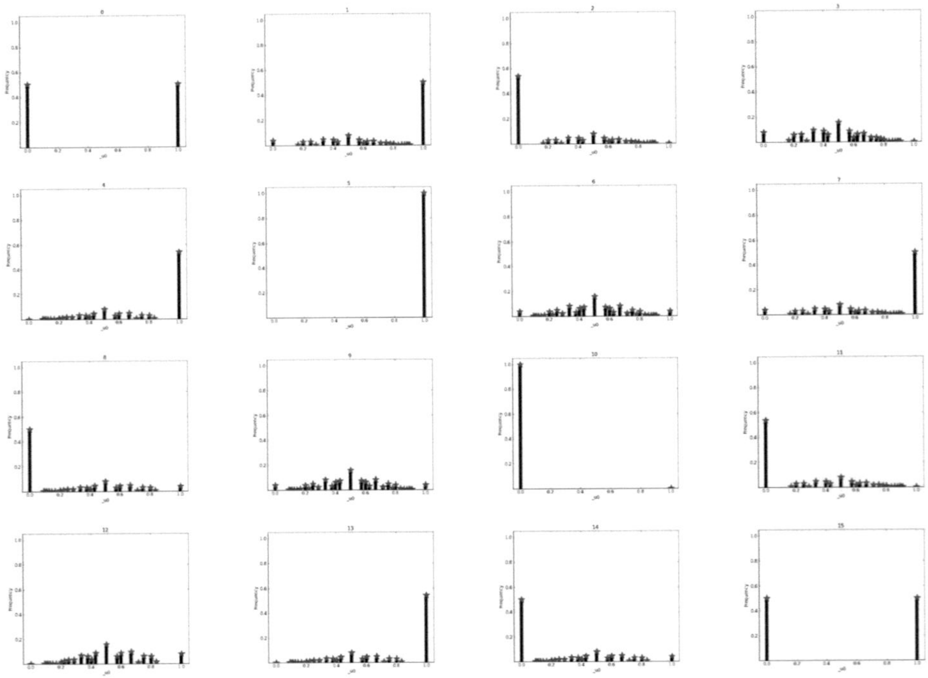

(C3) $\tilde{u}_0$ SL group

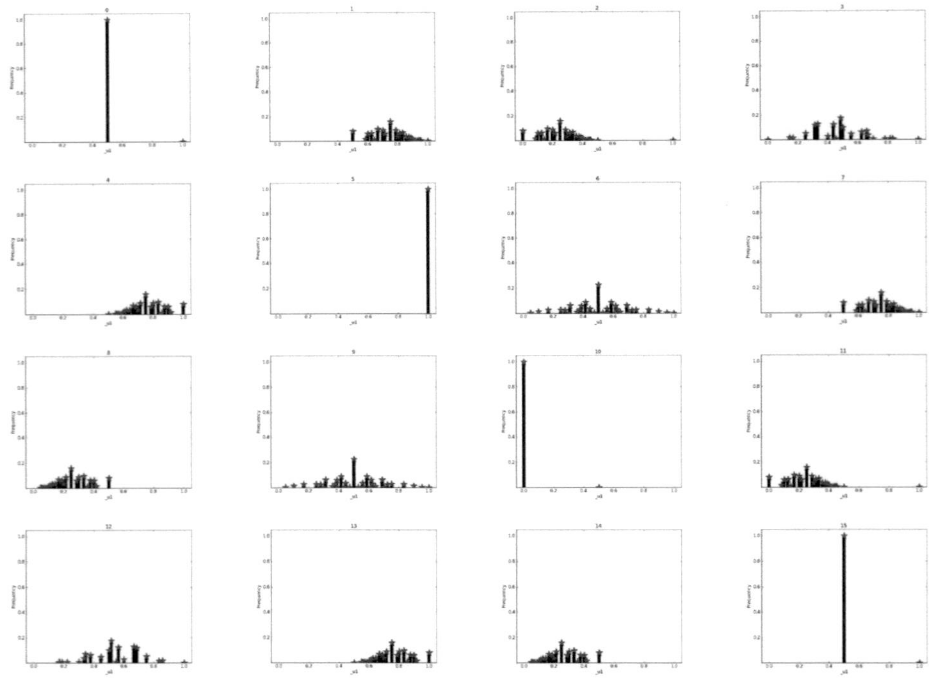

(C4) $\tilde{u}_1$ SL group

http://dx.doi.org/10.5772/51635

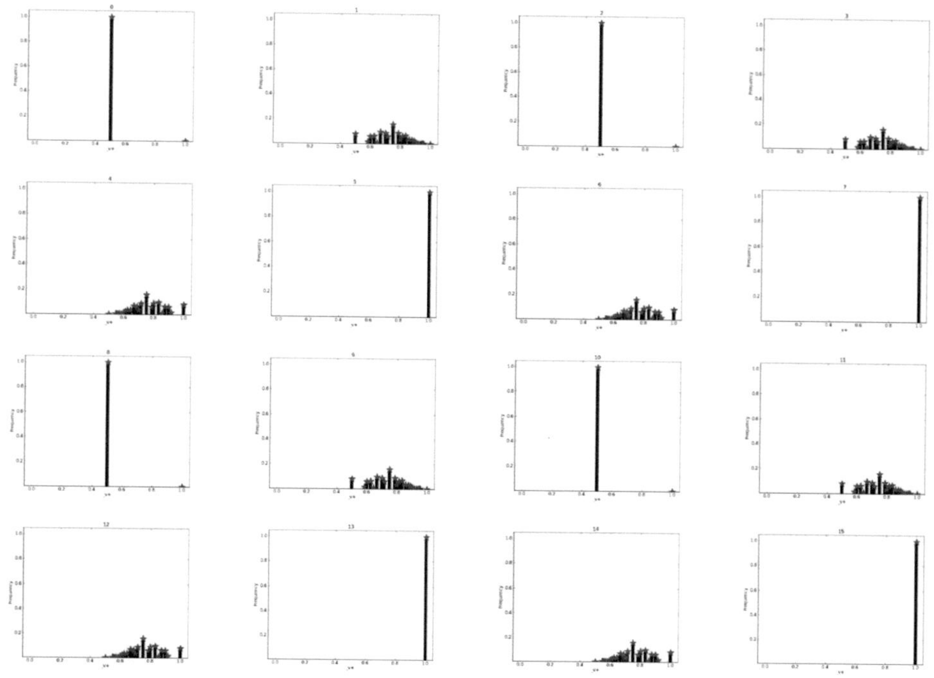

(C5) $\tilde{v}_+$ SL group

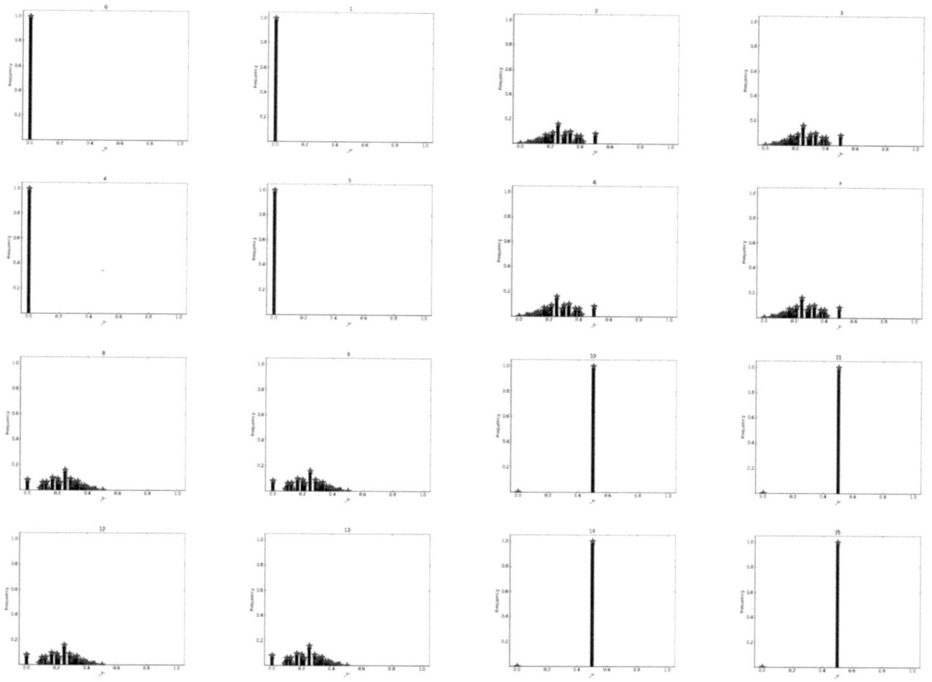

(C6) $\tilde{v}_-$ SL group

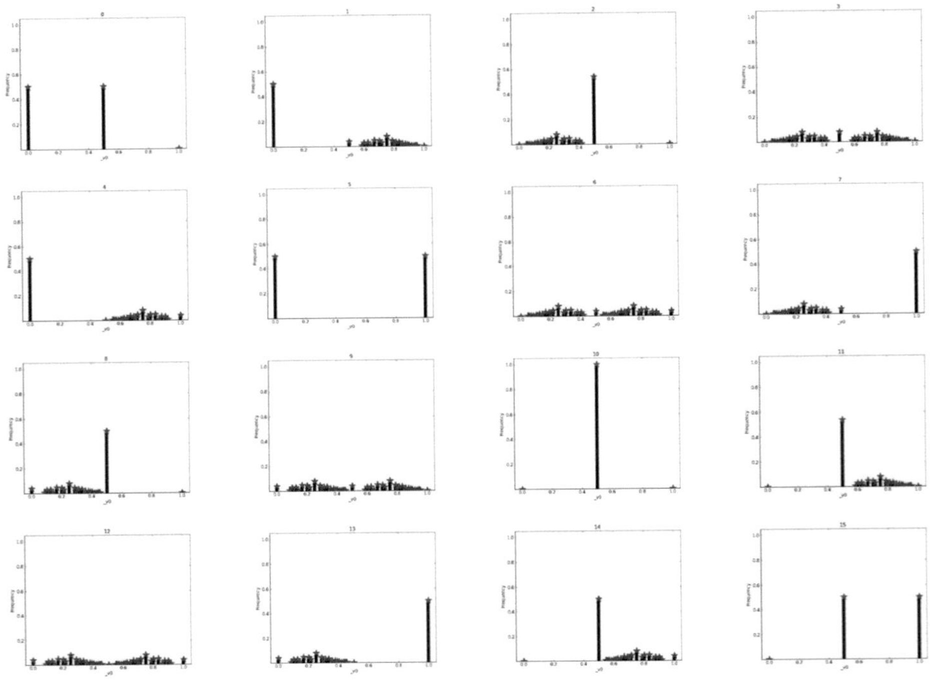

(C7) $\tilde{v}_0$ SL group

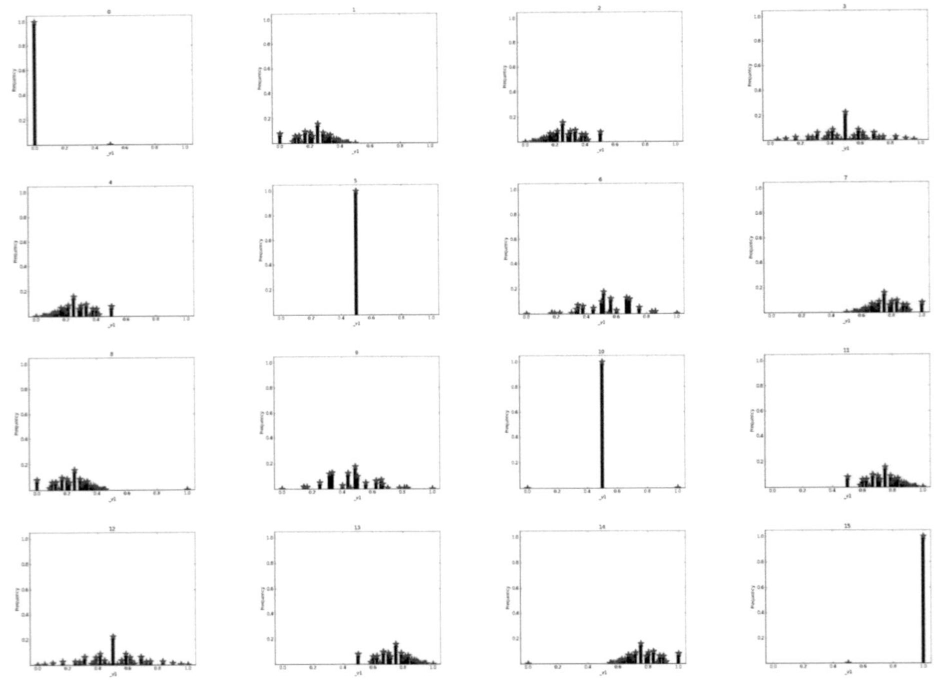

(C8) $\tilde{v}_1$ SL group

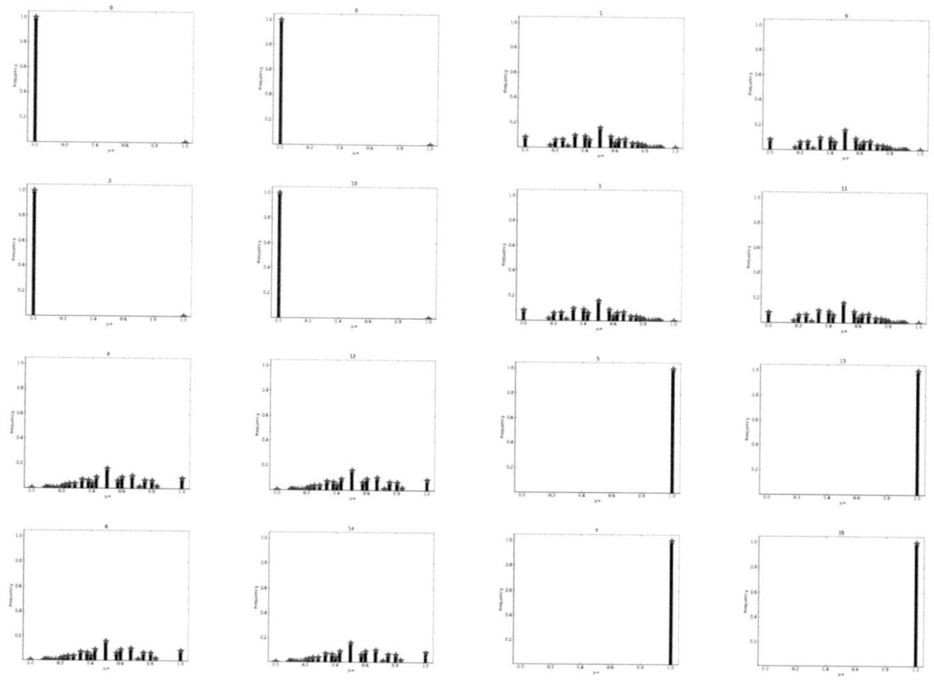

(C9) $\tilde{u}_+$ W group

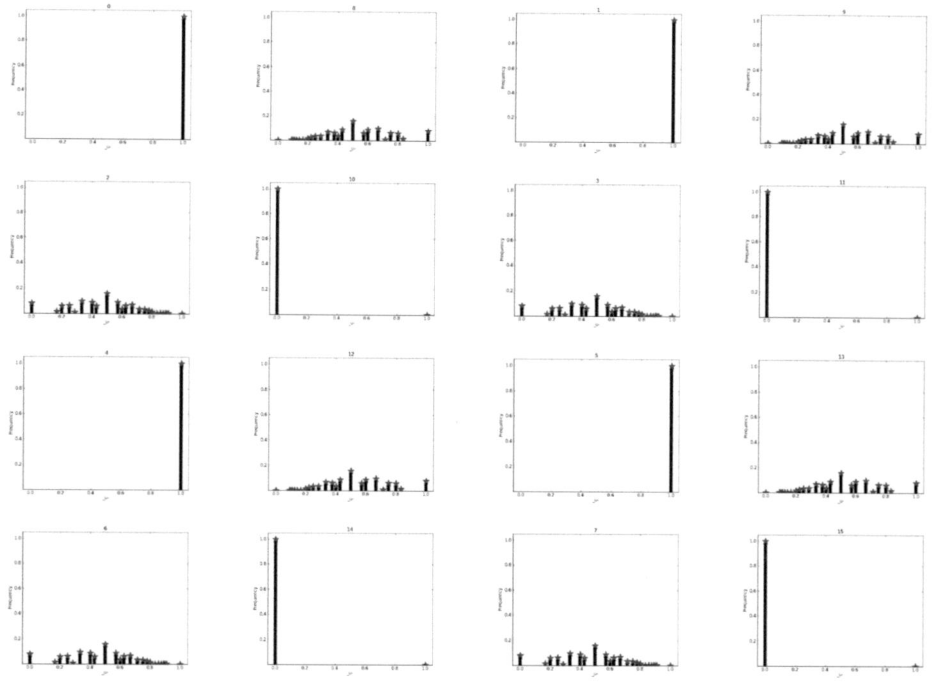

(C10) $\tilde{u}_-$ W group

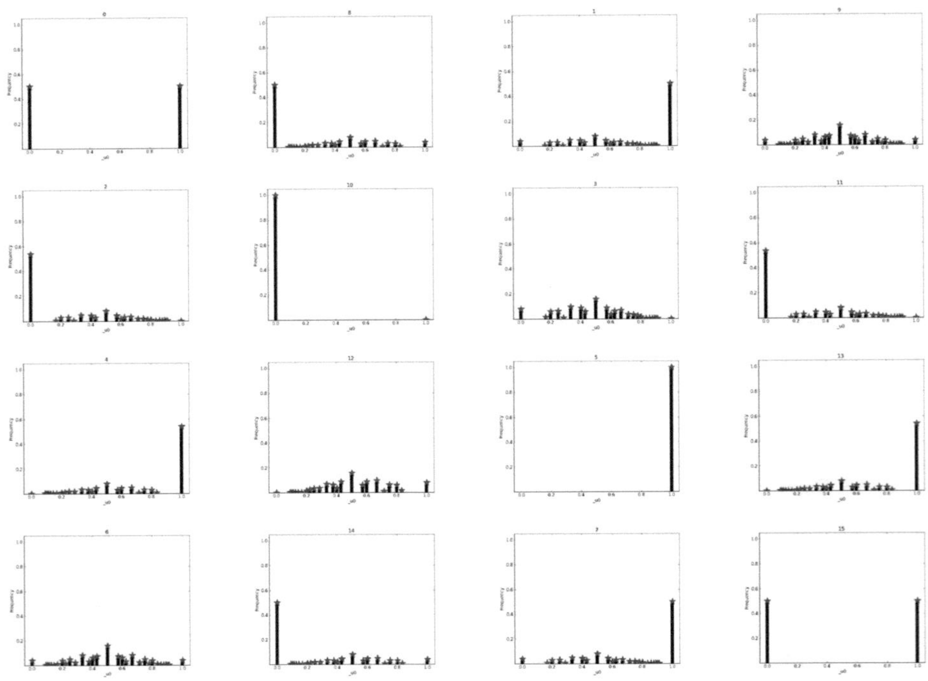

(C11) $\tilde{u}_0$ W group

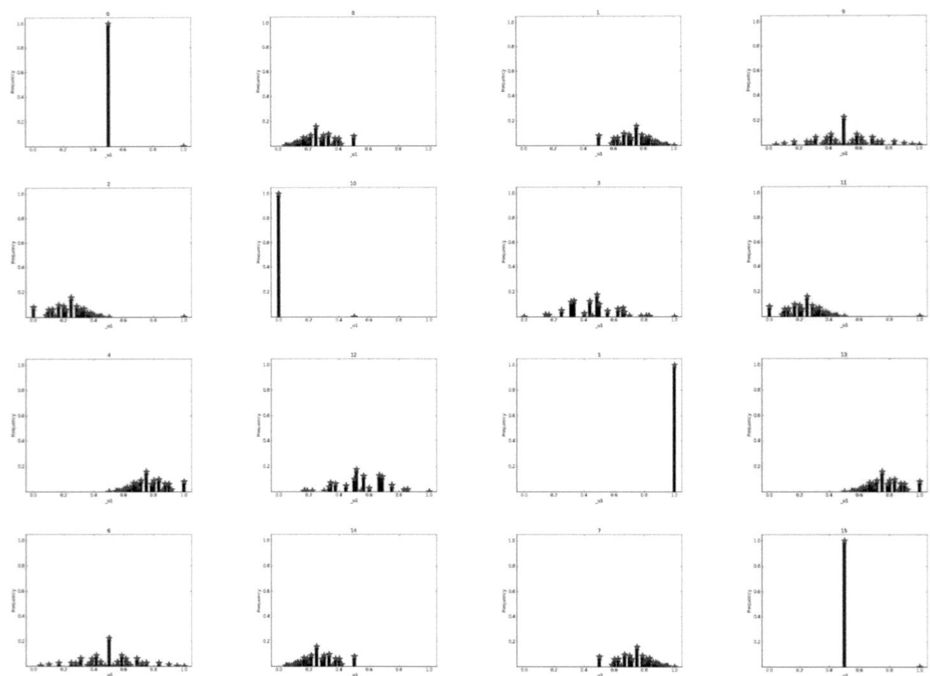

(C12) $\tilde{u}_1$ W group

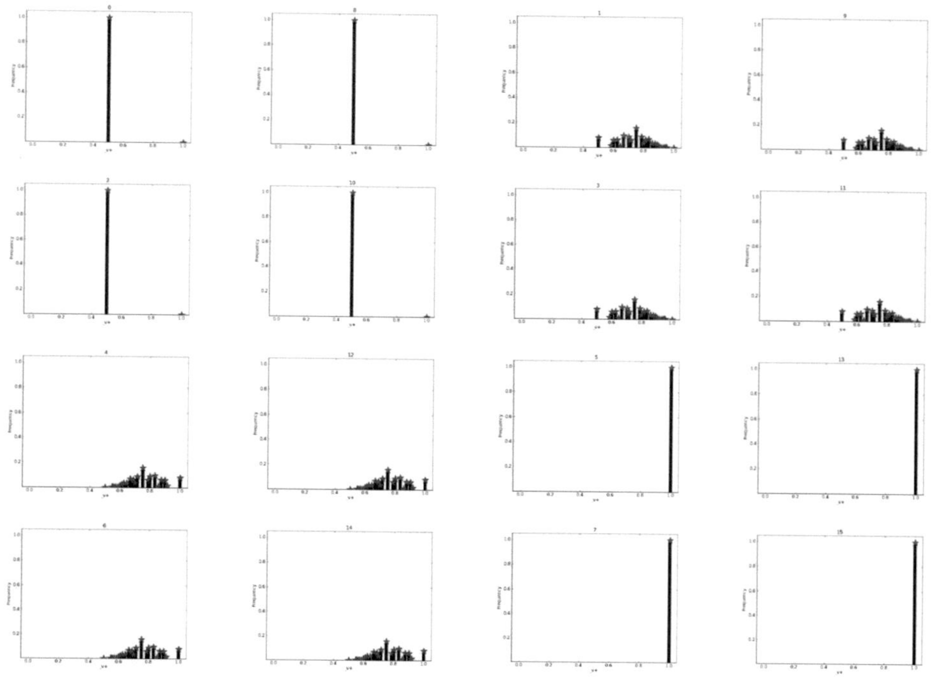

(C13) $\tilde{v}_{+}$ W group

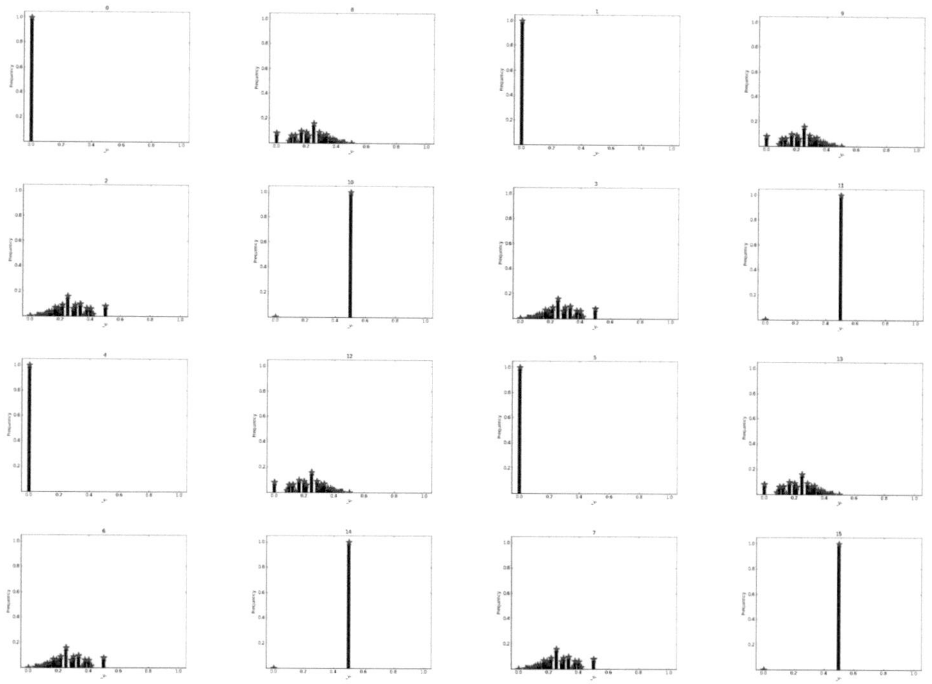

(C14) $\tilde{v}_{-}$ W group

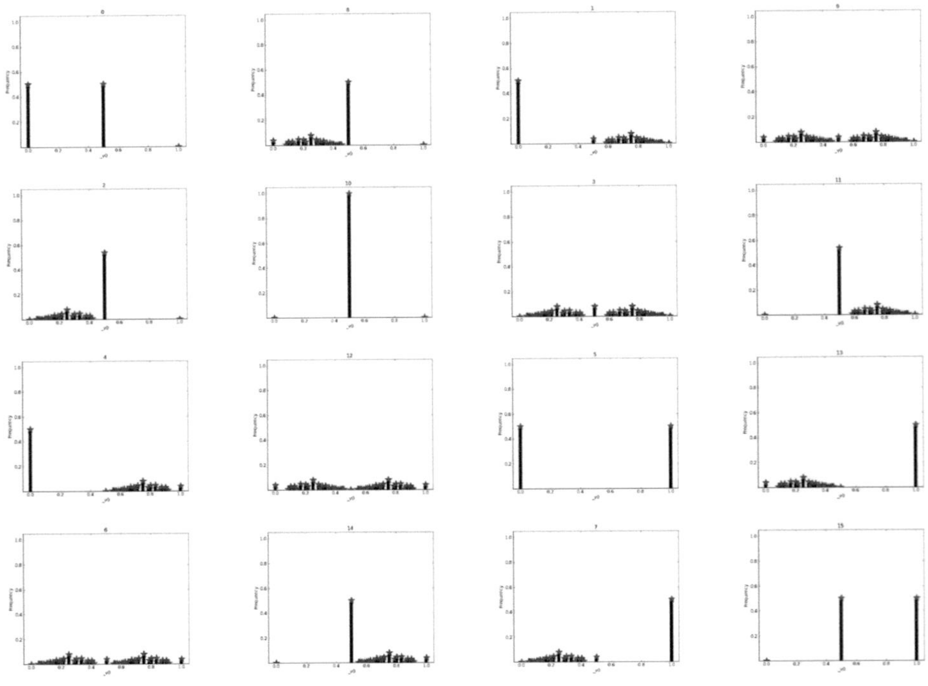

(C15) $\tilde{v}_0$ W group

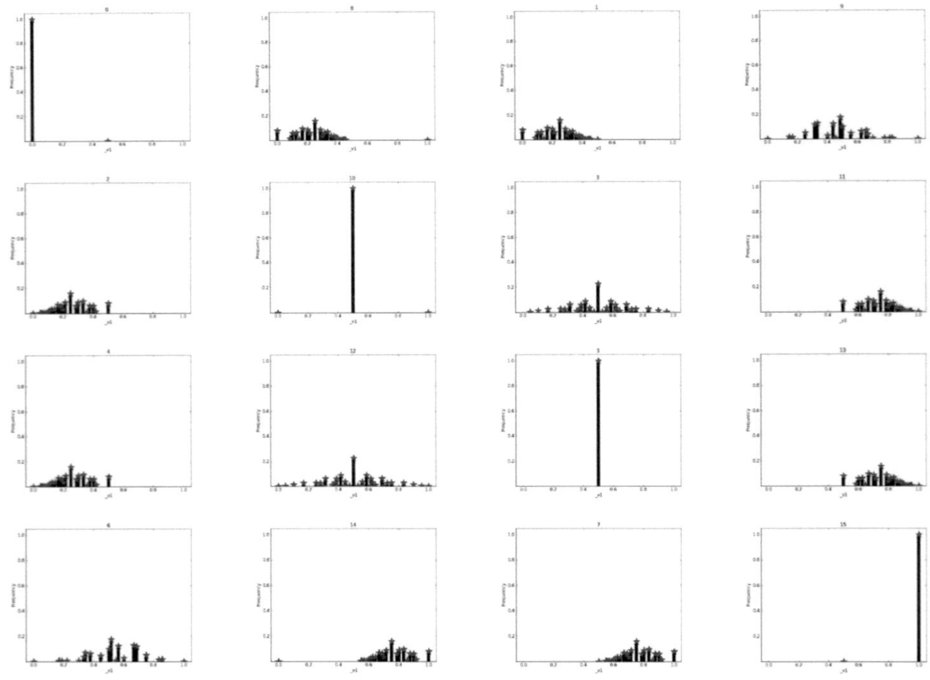

(C16) $\tilde{v}_1$ W group

http://dx.doi.org/10.5772/51635

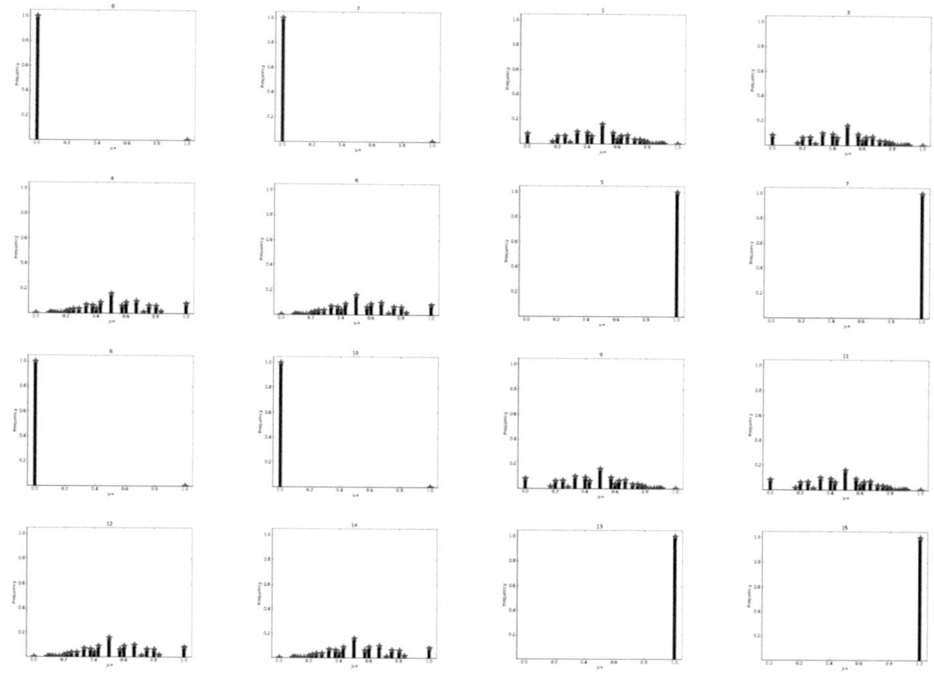

(C17) $\tilde{u}_+$ F group

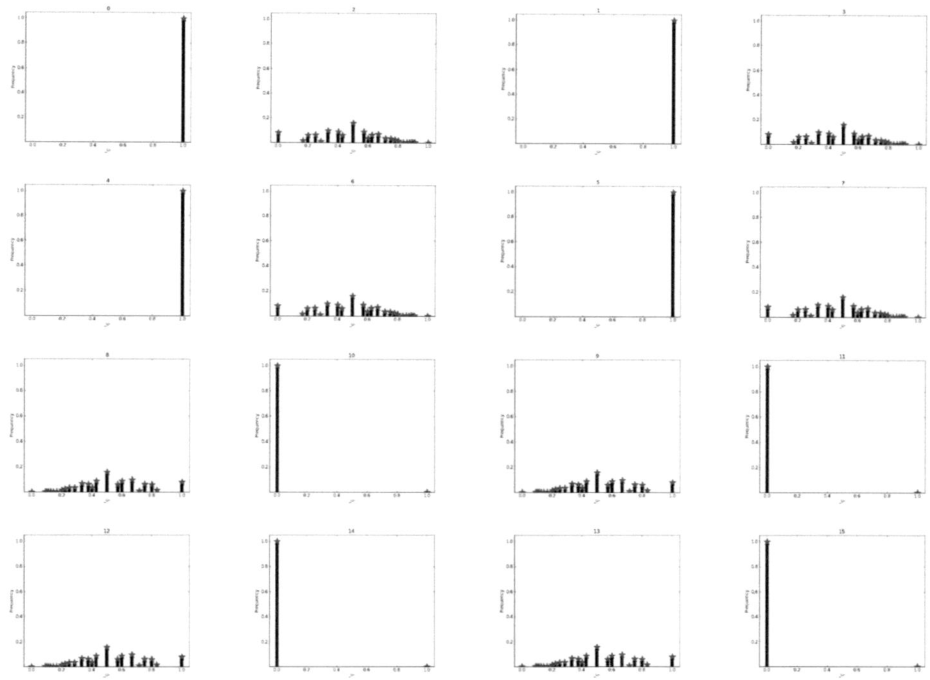

(C18) $\tilde{u}_-$ F group

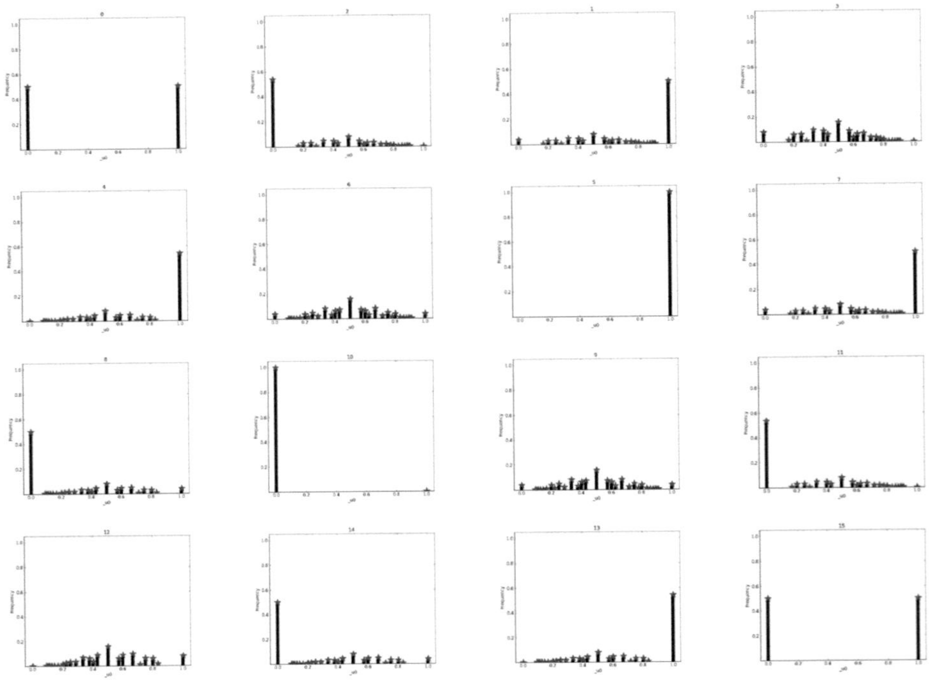

(C19) $\tilde{u}_0$ F group

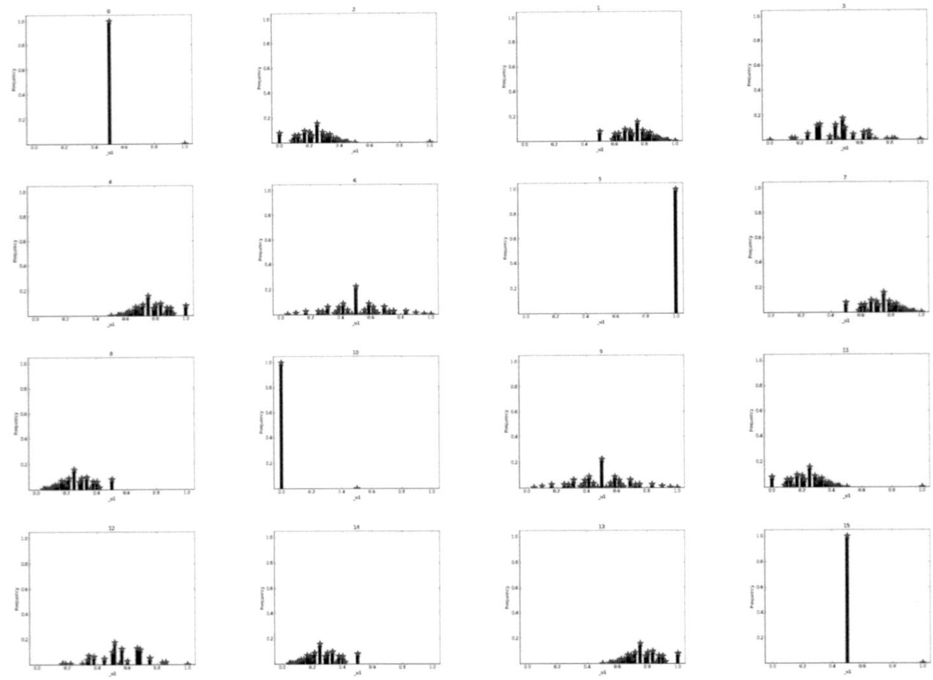

(C20) $\tilde{u}_1$ F group

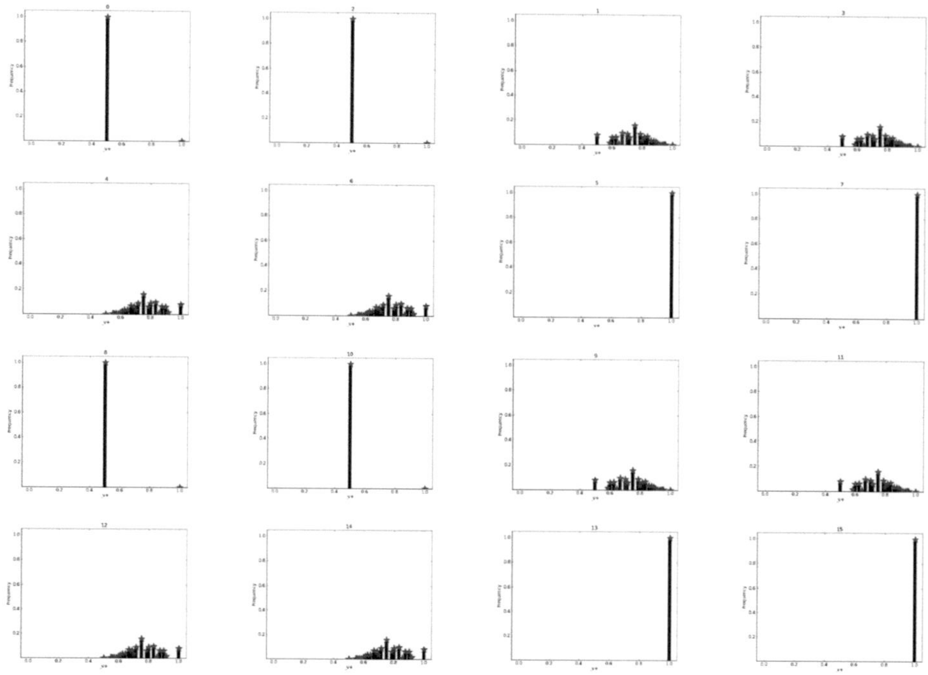

(C21) $\tilde{v}_+$ F group

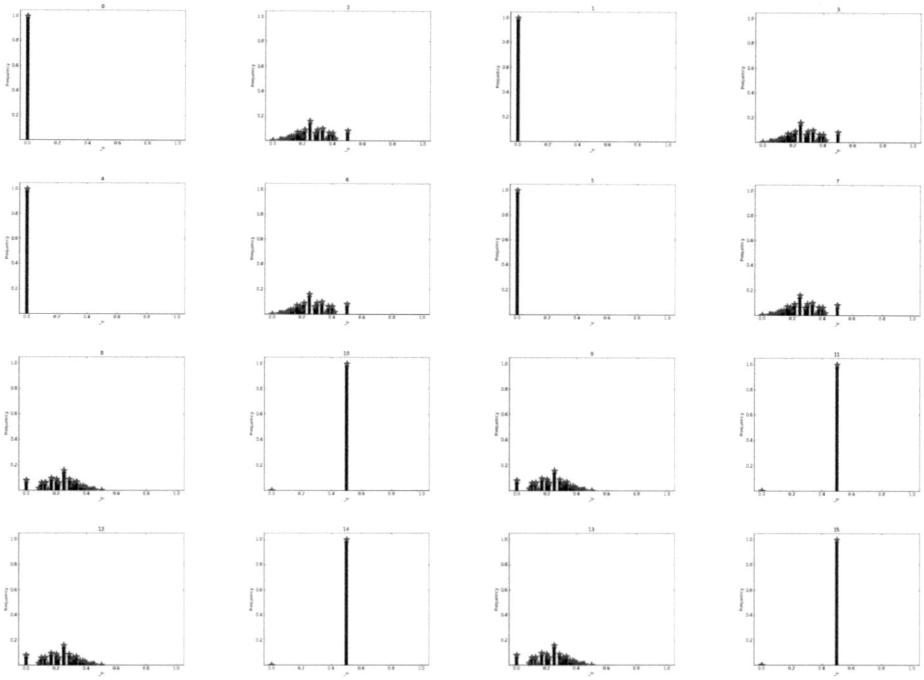

(C22) $\tilde{v}_-$ F group

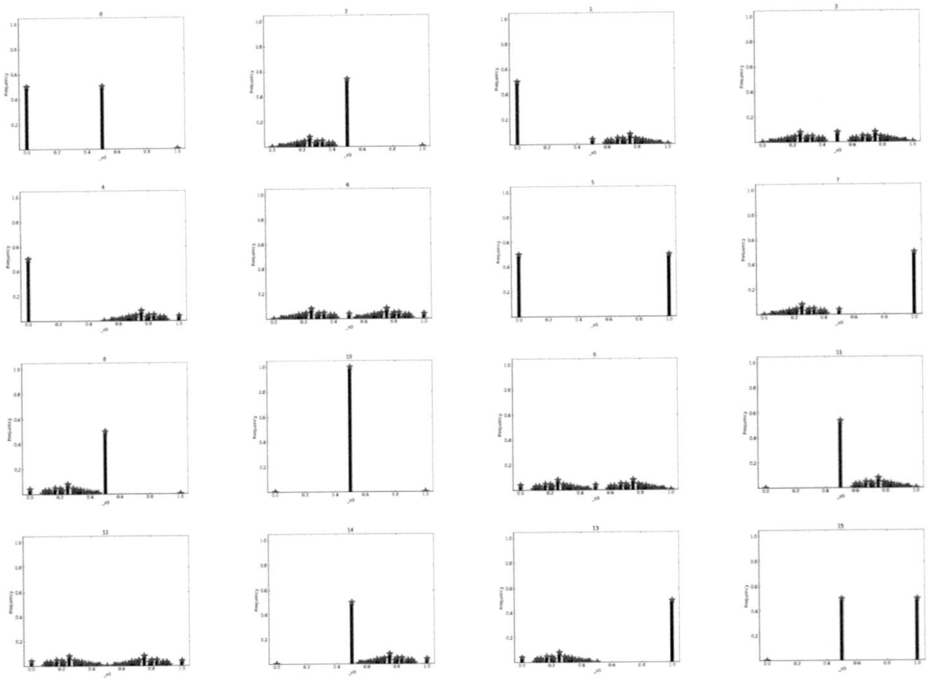

(C23) $\tilde{v}_0$ F group

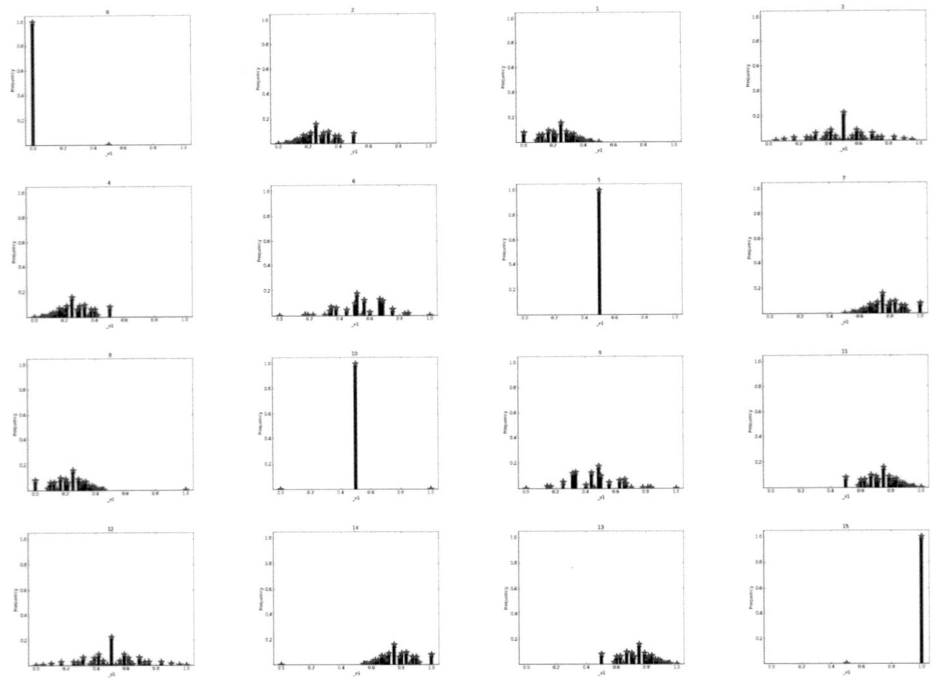

(C24) $\tilde{v}_1$ F group

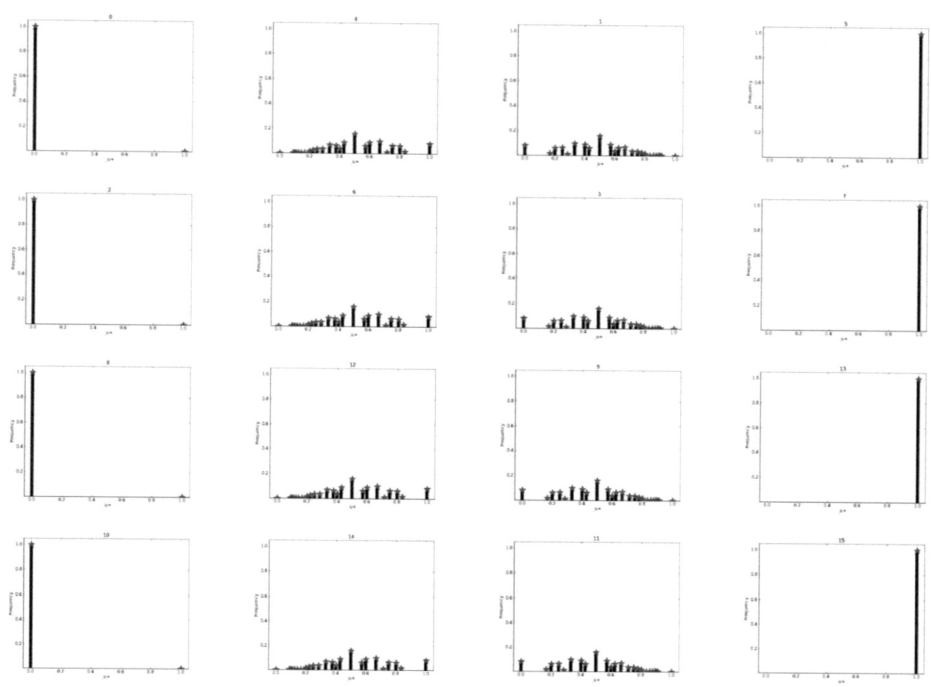

(C25) $\tilde{u}_+$ C group

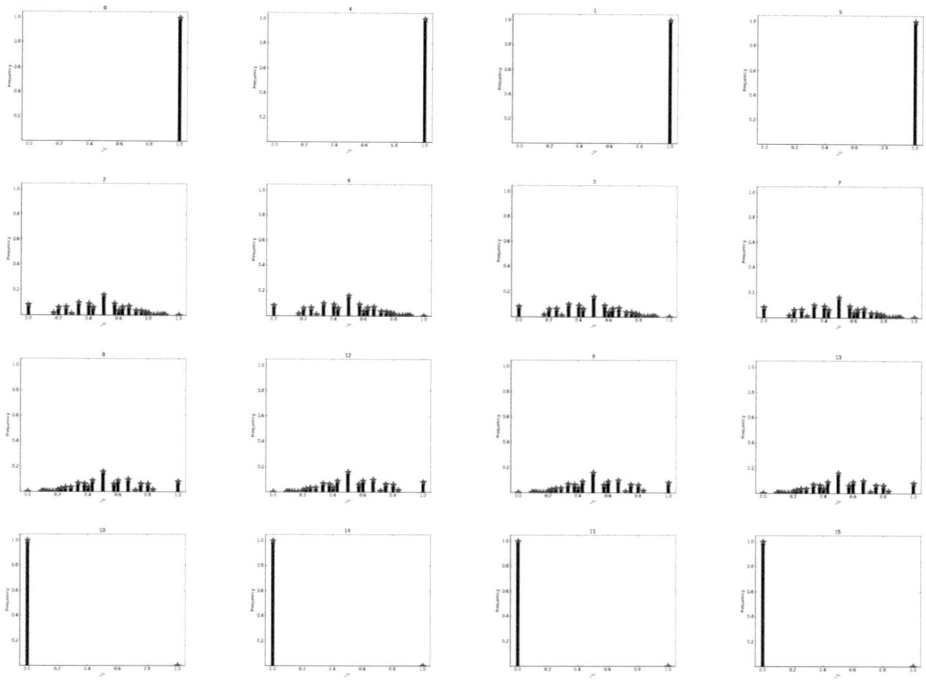

(C26) $\tilde{u}_-$ C group

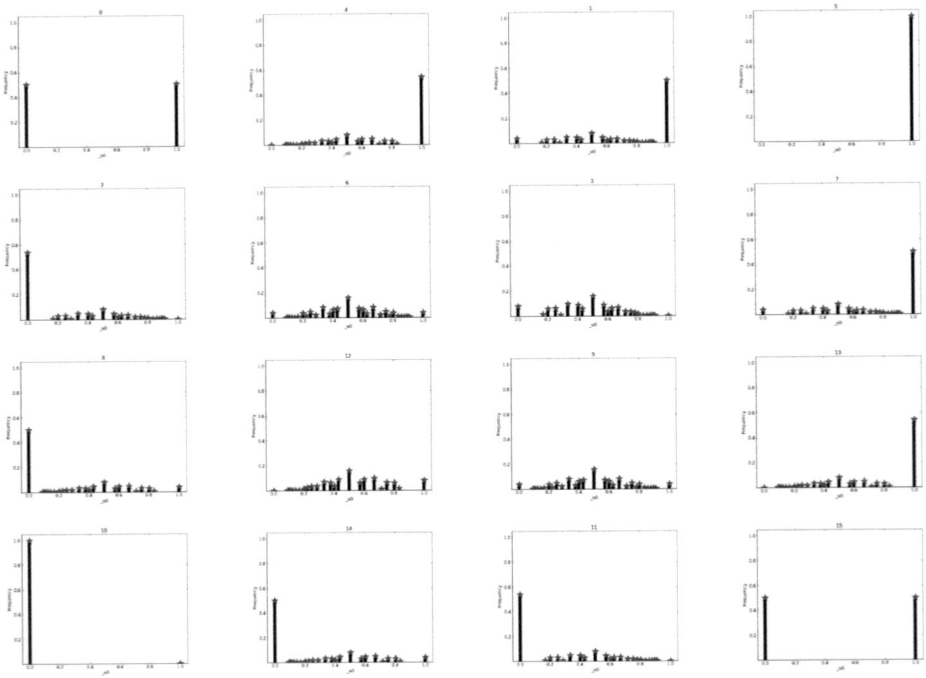

(C27) $\tilde{u}_0$ C group

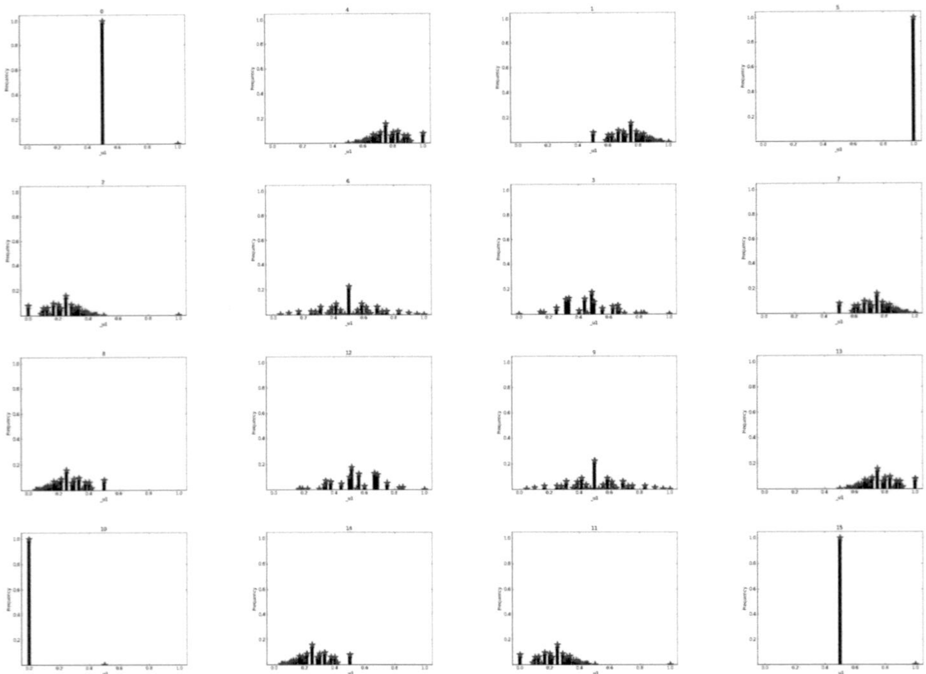

(C28) $\tilde{u}_1$ C group

http://dx.doi.org/10.5772/51635

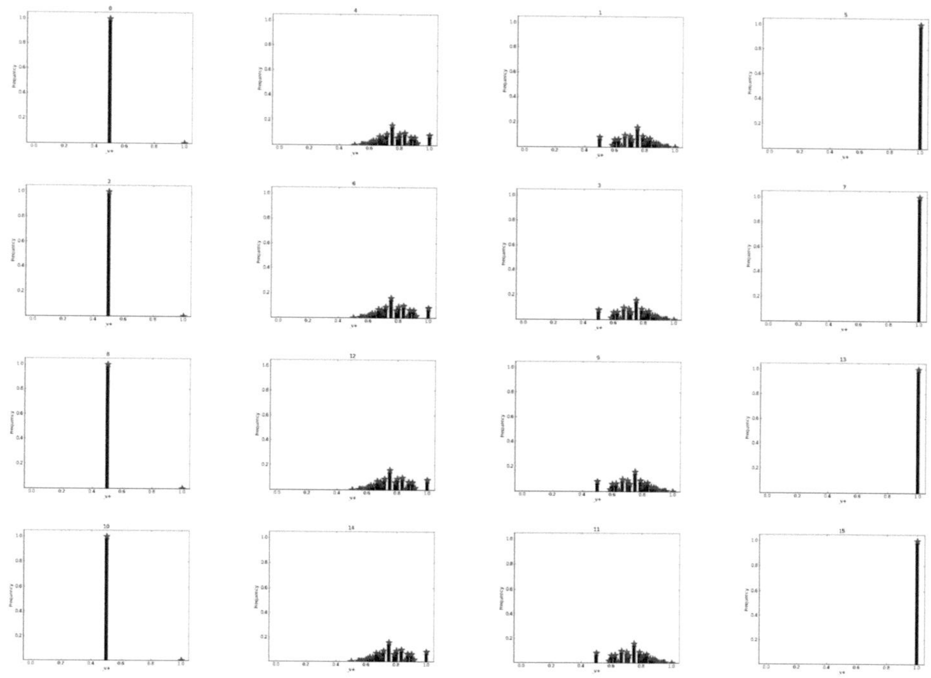

(C29) $\tilde{v}_+$ C group

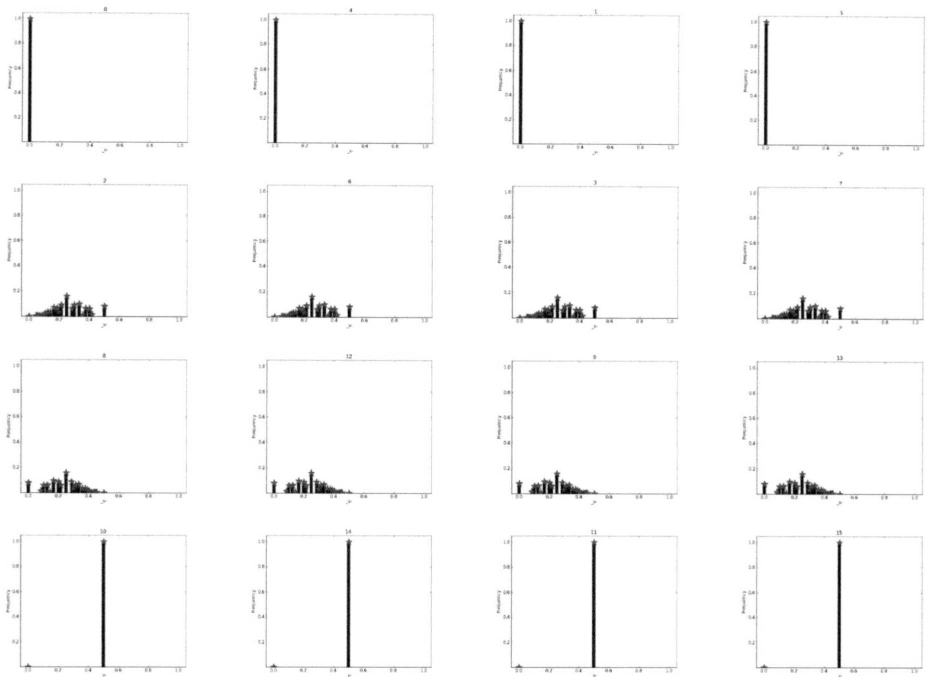

(C30) $\tilde{v}_-$ C group

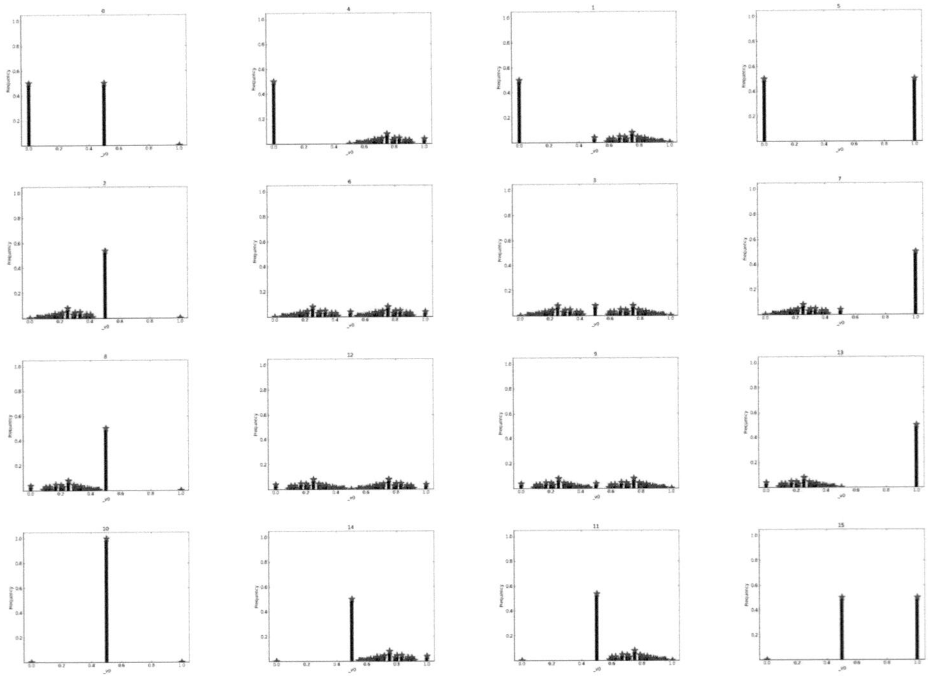

(C31) $\tilde{v}_0$ C group

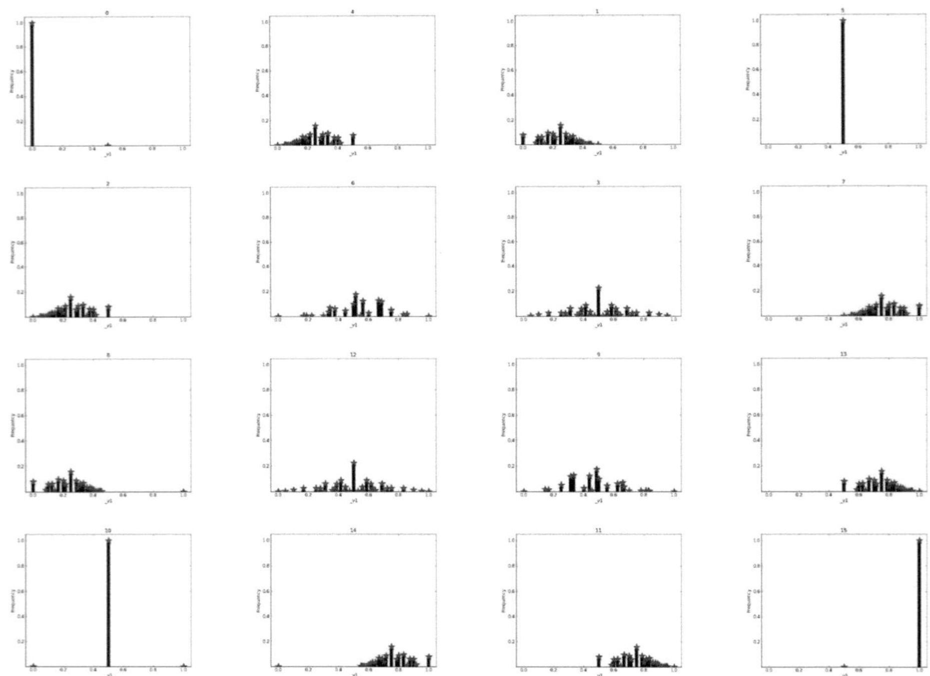

(C32) $\tilde{v}_1$ C group

Figure 10. (C1-C32) IMM for CPS; (C1-C8) SL group; (C9-C16) W group; (C17-C24) F group; (C25-C32) C group.

12. Conclusion

This chapter provides a brief investigation into Variant Phase Space (VPS) construction. Using an n variable 0-1 function and an N bit vector, a VPS hierarchy can be progressively established via variant measures, multiple or conditional probability measurements, and selected pair of measurements to determine a Micro Ensemble (ME) and its eight interactive projections. Collecting all possible 2^N pairs of probability measurements, a Canonical Ensemble (CE) and its eight Interactive Maps (IMs) are generated following a bottom-up approach.

Applying a Maxwell demon mechanism, all possible 2^{2^n} functions can be calculated to create a result comprising a {CE} and eight sets of {IM}. Using either a CE or an IM as an element, it is possible to use a variant logic configuration to organize each set of distributions to be a $2^{2^{n-1}} \times 2^{2^{n-1}}$ matrix as a CE Matrix (CEM) or IM Matrix (IMM), respectively. Following a top-down approach, a CEM or IMM can be decomposed into two polarized matrices with each matrix having periodic properties that meet the requirements of a Fourier-like transformation.

The main results are presented as ten propositions and four predictions to provide a foundation for further exploration of quantum interpretations, statistical mechanics, complex dynamic systems, and cellular automata.

The chapter does not explore global properties in detail, and further detailed investigations and expansions are necessary.

Anticipating that the principles put forward in this chapter will prove to be well founded, we look forward to exploring advanced scientific and technological applications in the near future.

Acknowledgements

Thanks to Professor Hui C. Shen of USTC for the selected works of de Broglie, and a historical review of statistical interpretation and modern development of statistical mechanics, to Colin W. Campbell for help with the English edition, to Jie Wan for MPS and CPS figures, to The School of Software Engineering, Yunnan University, The Key Laboratory of Software Engineering of Yunnan Province, and The Yunnan Advanced Overseas Scholar Project (W8110305) for financial support to the Information Security research projects (2010EI02, 2010KS06).

Author details

Jeffrey Zheng[1], Christian Zheng[2] and Tosiyasu Kunii[3]

1 Yunnan University, Key Lab of Yunnan Software Engineering, P.R. China
2 University of Melbourne, Australia
3 University of Tokyo, Japan

References

[1] Ash, R. B. & Doléans-Dade, C. A. [2000]. *Probability & Measure Theory*, Elsevier.

[2] Barrow, J. D., Davies, P. C. W. & Charles L. Harper, J. E. [2004]. *SCIENCE AND ULTIMATE REALITY: Quantum Theory, Cosmology and Complexity*, Cambridge University Press.

[3] Belevitch V. [1962]. Summary of the history of circuit theory, *Proceedings of the IRE*, Vol 50, Iss 5, 848-855.

[4] Bender E.A. [2000]. *An Introduction to Mathematical Modeling*, Dover, New York.

[5] Birkhoff G.D. [1927]. *Dynamic Systems*, American Mathematical Society, New York.

[6] Blokhintsev D.I. [1964]. *Quantum Mechanics*, Dordrecht-Holland.

[7] Bohr, N. [1935]. Can quantum-mechanical description of physical reality be considered complete?, *Physical Review* 48. 696-702.

[8] Bohr, N. [1949]. *Discussion with Einstein on Epistemological Problems in Atomic Physics*, Evanston. 200-241.

[9] de Broglie, L.; Translated by Shen H.C. [2012]. Selected Works of de Broglie. in Chinese, Peijing University Press.

[10] Einstein, A., Podolsky, B. & Rosen, N. [1935]. Can quantum-mechanical description of physical reality be considered complete?, *Physical Review* 47. 770-780.

[11] Feynman, R. [1965]. *The Character of Physical Law*, MIT Press.

[12] Feynman, R., Leighton, R. & Sands, M. [1965,1989]. *The Feynman Lectures on Physics*, Vol. 3, Addison-Wesley, Reading, Mass.

[13] Gershenfeld N. [1998]. *The Nature of Mathematical Modeling*, Cambridge Uni. Press.

[14] Gibbs J.W. [1902]. *Elementary Principles in Statistical Mechanics*, Yale Uni. Press, New Haven.

[15] Goodwin G.C. and Payne R.L. [1977]. *Dynamic System Identification:Experiment Design and Data Analysis*, Academic Press.

[16] Healey, R., Hellman, G. & Edited. [1998]. *Quantum Measurement: Beyond Paradox*, Uni. Minnesota Press.

[17] Hume J.N.P. [1974]. *Physics in two volums, Vol. 2 Relativity, Electromagnetism and Quantum Physics*, The Ronald Press Company, New York.

[18] Ivey D.G. [1974]. *Physics in two volums, Vol. 1 Classical Mechanics and Introductory Statistical Mechanics*, The Ronald Press Company, New York.

[19] Jammer, M. [1974]. *The Philosophy of Quantum Mechanics*, Wiley-Interscience Publication.

[20] Khinchin A.J. [1949]. *Mathematical Foundations of Statistical Mechanics*, Dover, New York.

[21] Kurth R. [1960]. *Axiomatics of Classical Statistical Mechanics*, Pergamon Press, Oxford.

[22] Kuzemsky A.L. [2008]. Works by D.I. Blokhintsev and the Development of Quantum Physics, *Physics of Partcles and Nuclei*, Vol 39, No.2 137-172. DOI:10.1134/S1063779608020019

[23] Landau L.D. and Lifshitz E.M. [1996]. *Statistical Physics*, 3rd Edition Part 1, Butterworth-Heinemann, Oxford.

[24] Lee Tsung-Dao [2006]. *Statistical Mechanics*, in Chinese, Shanghai Science and Technology Press.

[25] Nelles O. [2001]. *Nonlinear System Identification*, Springer.

[26] Nolte D.D. [2010]. The tangled tale of phase space. Physics Today, April 2010. 33-39. http://www.physicstoday.org

[27] Penrose, R. [2004]. *The Road to Reality*, Vintage Books, London.

[28] Pintelon P. and Schoukens J. [2001]. *System Identification: A frequency domain approach*, IEEE Press, New York.

[29] Pring M.J. [2002]. *Breaking the Black Box*, McGraw-Hill.

[30] Reif F. [1967]. *Statistical Physics, Berkley Physics Course - Vol. 5*, McGraw-Hill.

[31] Shen Hui-Chuan [2011]. *Statistical Mechanics*, in Chinese, University of Science and Technology of China Press.

[32] von Neumann, J. [1932,1996]. *Mathematical Foundations of Quantum Mechanics*, Princeton Univ. Press.

[33] Wu, Ta-You [2010]. *Thermodynamics, Gas-dynamics and Statistical Mechanics* , in Chinese, Scientific Press, Beijing.

[34] Zeh, H. D. [1970]. On the interpretation of measurement in quantum theory, *Foundation of Physics* 1. 69-76.

[35] Zheng, J., Zheng, C. & Kunii T. [2012]. From Local Interactive Measurements to Global Matrix Representations on Variant Construction ÂÍC A Particle Model of Quantum Interactions for Double Path Experiments, *Advanced Topics in Measurements, edited by: Z. Haq* 371-400.
URL: *http://www.intechopen.com/books/advanced-topics-in-measurements*

[36] Zheng, J., Zheng, C. & Kunii T. [2012]. From Conditional Probability Measurements to Global Matrix Representations on Variant Construction ÂÍC A Particle Model of Intrinsic Quantum Waves for Double Path Experiments, *Advanced Topics in Measurements, edited by: Z. Haq* 337-370.
URL: *http://www.intechopen.com/books/advanced-topics-in-measurements*

[37] Zheng, J. [2012]. Multiple and Conditional Probabilities and Their Statistical Distributions for Variant Measures, *Laser & Optoelectronics Progress* 49(4): 042701. URL: *http://www.opticsjournal.net/abstract.htm?aid=OJ120119000021MjPlSo*

[38] Zheng, J. [2011]. Synchronous properties in quantum interferences, *Journal of Computations & Modelling, International Scientific Press* 1(1). 73-90. URL: *http://www.scienpress.com/upload/JCM/Vol%201_1_6.pdf*

[39] Zheng, J. & Zheng, C. [2011]. Variant measures and visualized statistical distributions, *Acta Photonica Sinica, Science Press* 40(9). 1397-1404. URL: *http://www.photon.ac.cn/CN /article/downloadArticleFile.do?attachType=PDF&id=15668*

[40] Zheng, J., Zheng, C. & Kunii, T. [2011]. A framework of variant-logic construction for cellular automata, *Cellular Automata - Innovative Modelling for Science and Engineering edited Dr. A. Salcido, InTech Press.* 325-352. URL: *http://www.intechopen.com/articles/show/title/a-framework-of-variant-logic-construction-for-cellular-automata*

[41] Zheng, J. [2011]. Conditional Probability Statistical Distributions in Variant Measurement Simulations, *Acta Photonica Sinica, Science Press* 40(11): 1662-1666. URL: *http://www.opticsjournal.net/viewFull.htm?aid=OJ1112120000332y5B8D*

[42] Zheng, J. & Zheng, C. [2011]. Variant simulation system using quaternion structures, *Journal of Modern Optics, Taylor & Francis Group* 59(5): 484-492. URL: *http://www.tandfonline.com/doi/abs/10.1080/09500340.2011.636152*

[43] Zheng, J. [2011]. Two Dimensional Symmetry Properties of GlobalCoding Family on Configuration Function Spacesof Variant Logic , *Journal of Chengdu University of Information Technology* Dec. 2011. URL: *http://www.cnki.net/kcms/detail/51.1625.TN.20111227.1043.001.html*

[44] Zheng, J. & Zheng, C. [2010]. A framework to express variant and invariant functional spaces for binary logic, *Frontiers of Electrical and Electronic Engineering in China, Higher Education Press and Springer* 5(2): 163–172. URL: *http://www.springerlink.com/content/91474403127n446u/*